A SLAYER WAITS

The true story of a
Michigan double murder

For my wife

Acknowledgements

First and foremost, this book would not have been possible without the cooperation of several people. I would like to thank Mike Woodworth, who shared his recollections of the case with me and spurred my interest in writing my second book. Beyond that, Perry Johnson, former Director of the Michigan Department of Corrections, was gracious enough to share his experiences with the killer over a thirty-year period that extended from his first days as a counselor at Jackson Prison to his last days as the Director.

Thank you to Eric Eggan, the former Assistant Attorney General who fought to keep the killer behind bars. He was a valuable asset as he shared his memories of the case from his early days as a young attorney.

I'd also like to thank Frank Eaman, who was a young defense attorney when he accepted an appointment to represent the killer as he filed numerous appeals that ultimately led to the United States Supreme Court. Frank still had his entire file, and while he wasn't able to share all of it with me, he did share all of the public pleadings and appeals he filed, many of which contained crucial information about the case.

The are several other people who either had information to share, or knew someone else who did. Beyond that, they may have helped in some other way, so to these people I say thank you: Rosie Merriman, Jon Foreman, Jodi Gebolys, Jeff Weiss, Gene Wriggelsworth, Tom Reich, Evan Benehoff, Phil Maiville, Gina Woodworth, George Sinas, Les Turner, John Prescott, Mona Makel, Mike Stevens, Don Stevens, Lisa Sherman, Dick Sherman, Vince Green, Chuck Kennedy, Rod Clark, Jeff Hull, Scott Wriggelsworth, Harvey Clark, and Diane Bartig.

Finally, I'd like to thank my sister Lisa Wheatcraft, and my friend Deb Ackley, who devoted numerous hours to copy editing for me.

Other books by Rod Sadler

To Hell I Must Go: The True Story of
Michigan's Own Lizzie Borden

Contents

Preface

I've often thought it's amazing what a person can remember from their past. Simple, minute details that mean nothing. As a child in the '60s, I remember historical events; the assassination of Dr. Martin Luther King, the assassination of Bobby Kennedy, and Neil Armstrong's first words as he stepped onto the moon. I even remember stepping in front of a wooden swing when I was three and breaking my nose. Beyond the historical and the traumatic, I can still remember riding in a car with my parents in the 1960s and hearing them talk about a farm we had just passed as the car travelled along M-52 (formerly M-92) in Ingham County. They spoke about the horrific murder of two people. I thought the case had gone unsolved. It wasn't long and the mind of a young seven or eight-year-old switched to something else that was no doubt very mundane, and the murder was forgotten.

After publishing my first book, I had already decided to follow-up with a second. I loved the idea of more research. To me, it was the most interesting part of writing a book about true-crime. I had so many ideas, yet no specifics about any particular case.

Mike Woodworth, a seasoned attorney in the Lansing area, had become a good friend over the years. While still working at the sheriff's office, I had testified on his client's behalf in a civil trial after a fatal crash. After my departure from law enforcement, I began working as a consultant in traffic crash reconstruction and was retained by Mike's office. It was a complicated case, and Mike and I spent numerous hours in discussion about it. During a moment of Mike reminiscing about his early years as an assistant prosecuting attorney in Ingham County, he mentioned a case he had become involved in. He had been assigned to handle court appeals in his office. He described the brutal murder of two people near Stockbridge in 1955. There was instant recognition. I knew the case he was talking about. My mind raced back to the car ride in the 1960s. Mike obviously had some information, and it would surely be an interesting story.

In subsequent visits to his office, Mike added small bits of information that he could recall. I mentioned that I had done some quick research and come up with the name of another attorney who had handled the killer's appeal after it had passed to the attorney general's office. Odd, at least to me, Mike knew him and was willing to set up a dinner meeting with him.

We met with Eric Eggan for dinner. Eric had been a young attorney in the early 1980s and was working for Michigan's Attorney General. The murder appeal had been handed to him. As we spoke over dinner, Eric mentioned another colleague who had retired as Director of the Michigan Department of Corrections and had published a book about Jackson Prison. His book included a short chapter describing his contact with the killer.

There was no doubt now. My second book would be about the 1955 murder near Stockbridge, Michigan. I had already started to build my resources.

I met with Perry Johnson at the Kellogg Center on the Michigan State University campus. Perry had begun his career in the prison system in 1955 as a counselor. He continued to build his resume by making his way through the ranks, and eventually he became not only the warden to Jackson Prison, and was also selected as the Director of the Michigan Department of Corrections overseenig the entire prison system for the State of Michigan. When he finally retired, he wrote his book titled *Jackson: The Rise and Fall of the World's Largest Walled Prison*. The book included a complete history of what was once known as the State Prison of Southern Michigan. Perry's compassion for documenting the history of the fortress where he had spent the majority of his career was a testament to his dedication during his tenure. Having become acquainted with the killer would clearly help my research.

At my first chance, I would have to start the research. While the murders had occurred over sixty years prior, there would be a lot more information available than what I had researched for my first book.

The research would involve endless hours at the library looking at microfilmed newspapers and later trying to read my own handwritten notes. It would include trips to the Archives of Michigan, a virtual treasure trove of original historical documents. I would begin to do interviews with other lawyers, prison officials, former cops, family members, and anyone else I could think of who might be able to contribute. Beyond that, I would need photos of the crime scene, and I would definitely need to find additional books for reference.

After my first book, *To Hell I Must Go*, I was invited to speak in several different venues about what was involved in piecing together a 118-year-old murder. While audiences enjoyed hearing about the murder and the research put into the book, they enjoyed hearing about small coincidences and odd things that happened after it was published even more. I started to think that maybe it was more than coincidence that Mike Woodworth had actually handled the appeals in Ingham County.

At an afternoon meeting, I mentioned my proposed book to my friend Jeff Weiss of the Ingham County Sheriff's Office. Jeff thought the murder weapon might still exist and invited me to go through their old murder case files to try and find any record of it. No luck. He also invited me to search through two large storage containers of old photos from the sheriff's office. Maybe I could find some crime scene photos. I opened the large container and there had to be over 1000 photos, both color and black and white inside. I thought this would probably take some time. I reached in and grabbed a stack of black and white pictures. I started to thumb through them when I quickly realized they weren't some random pictures taken inside a barn. The photos I held in my hand were the original crime scene photos taken on the night of the crime. It was certainly a little odd that I found those photos so quickly without ever having to really look for them.

It wasn't long afterward that I really started noticing odd things about my proposed masterpiece.

My wife decided that she wanted a flagpole in our yard, and she decided on an area in the backyard

A SLAYER WAITS

where it would be visible from both the road and the deck. She chose one small spot on our vast nine-acre piece of property, and that's where I began to dig. As it turned out, the posthole digger was the perfect implement to break through the grass and rupture the LP gas line running to the house. With the sudden hiss of escaping gas, and the unmistakable odor of propane rising from the small hole, I realized I was in trouble. The tank had been filled the previous week, and I quickly turned it off to save my winter's investment. A call to my propane dealer and I was set; the repairman would arrive in the morning.

I watched with great interest as Mike Stevens, the repairman, dug down gently with his shovel and started clearing dirt from around the perfectly re-molded piece of copper tubing. I had expected a much more difficult repair job involving a large backhoe, and an even larger bill. I began a trivial conversation about a former teacher from high school who had lost his life when his house exploded after a gas leak in his basement. The repairman remembered hearing about it. I asked where he was from. He told me he was from Stockbridge. Having no thought about any coincidence at this point, I mentioned I was writing a book about a double murder in 1955 near the small Ingham County town. Mike stopped what he was doing and squinted through the morning sunshine as he looked up at me. "Escaped convict," he asked. I nodded. As it turned out, Mike's uncle lived across the road from where the murders had occurred, and had later bought the house. The repairman had been in and out of that house a hundred times, and had often played in the barn as a kid. He told me I should talk with his 88-year-old mother. She would remember everything.

I had to pause. What were the odds that my wife

would pick one small spot on nine acres in Olivet for a flagpole, I would puncture the gas line in that tiny spot, a repairman would be sent from Marshall, and his uncle owned the grocery store across from the murder scene in Stockbridge in 1955? I could only shake my head, and whenever I would tell friends about that day, my first words were always, "You're not going to believe this."

That wasn't the end. I knew as part of my research that I would have to visit the gravesite of the victims. Mr. and Mrs. Herrick were buried in Dansville, a small hamlet between Mason and Stockbridge. Using Google maps, I quickly found the location of the cemetery. On a warm summer day, I headed out to find out where they were buried.

It didn't take long to realize the mistake I had made. As I drove into the first drive, there were endless marble and sandstone monuments. They seemed to stretch on forever, and I quickly realized without some direction, there was no way I would locate the graves. I drove slowly toward the back expecting I would make a quick pass through and my quest would be over. I noticed a truck parked in the back portion of the cemetery and decided to stop. I walked up to the man working near a headstone and asked if he worked in the cemetery. He didn't. He worked for a monument company and was only there to put an armed services plaque on an existing headstone. I explained to him that I was searching for the graves of an elderly couple who had been viciously murdered in 1955. He asked their name. "Herrick," I replied. He looked down at the plaque he held in his hand and slowly looked back up at me. "I'm putting this on a Herrick grave," he said. My eyes widened. I looked at the plaque. It belonged to their son. He slowly raised his hand, pointing to another headstone and said, "They're buried right there." I had parked in front of their headstone, but hadn't seen the name because of overgrown foliage.

Surely, these were just coincidences. Coincidence or not, I was convinced I had to write the story of Howard and Myra Herrick's brutal 1955 murder and the man who killed them.

What began simply as a story about the murder has turned into much more. Read on.

CHAPTER 1

The Escape

The small headline, barely noticeable at the bottom of the page in the Detroit Free Press Saturday Edition read 'Detroit Trusty [sic] Flees Prison.' The three-sentence feature continued, "Nealy Buchanon, Detroit trustee serving one to 15 years for breaking and entering, escaped from Jackson Prison Friday. Buchanon was driver of a dump truck that picked up rubbish around prison. The truck was found at noon at Stockbridge."

The retired chicken farmer and his wife never saw the article. It was September 3, 1955.

He glanced briefly at the old woman's body, her face covered in blood. She was lying near the stairway leading to a lower level in the hot, dimly lit barn. Reaching down, he grabbed her frail arms, dragging her limp body toward the large stacks of baled hay along the side of the large outbuilding. She lay on her back in her floral print dress, trimmed with a white collar, and the country apron tied around her waist. It was spattered with her own blood. As he dragged her between two hay bales and released his grip, her right arm folded as it fell, with her hand now resting near her throat. He never noticed her shallow, labored breaths as she unconsciously struggled for air.

Nealy Buchanon turned and walked quickly back toward the 1952 green Desoto parked just inside the barn door. Panic began to set in. The sudden sound of a bird taking flight from a barn beam startled him as he quickly glanced around. He pulled the heavy barn door shut, being careful to stay out of sight. With the large door closed, the only available light streamed through cracks in the weathered barn siding, offering little illumination. He looked at the farmer's bloodied body lying face down next to the car. Crouching over him, he quickly surveyed the barn floor for keys to the car. Nothing.

Wiping the sweat from his hands by rubbing them on his own pants, he grabbed the old man by his wrists and dragged him to the rear of the barn. The man's body was much heavier than the woman's. Buchanon's hands were still sweaty, making it even harder to pull the dead weight of the farmer. Blood poured from the man's crushed head, smearing along the barn floor, leaving a crimson trail. He dragged the body to the same place he had left the woman. Leaving the man at the foot of his wife, his body lay perpendicular to her in an awkward, half-fetal position. Much like the woman's dress and apron, the man's light gray shirt, suspenders, and pants slowly became soaked in his own blood. He made a quick check of the dead man's pockets. No keys, but there was $45 in his wallet, a book of checks, and a bankbook. Buchanon quickly grabbed the money, the man's social security card, and the other items, stuffing them into his own back pocket. He found a cigarette lighter in the man's front pocket, taking it along with the man's wristwatch. As he put the wristwatch on his own arm, he glanced at it, then grabbed nearby bales of hay, laying them on top of the elderly farm couple in a haphazard way, trying to conceal their lifeless bodies.

Grabbing the bloodied hammer from the floor near where he had just bludgeoned the farm couple, he set it on a small stack of bales near the bodies.

Walking quickly back to the car, he noticed the hand grinder lying on the floor near the car door. He picked it up and tossed it into the hay near where his victims lay, then climbed into the front seat. His eyes, with broken blood vessels, were a strange maroon color, and they darted back and forth, scanning the dash, front seat, and floorboards. No keys. He stepped from the car, scanning the floor again. Still no keys. He walked to a work bench along a wall in the barn, grabbing a screwdriver and pliers. Sitting back in the driver's seat, he reached under the dash panel and pulled the plastic downward while prying the heater controls from the bottom of the control panel with the pliers. Having never hot-wired a car before, he had to make it work if he wanted to escape. With sweat now streaming down his face, he was desperately hoping his feeble attempt would spark the ignition. Without success, he glanced around the interior again for the keys. A black lunchbox and a set of neatly-folded clothes lay on the passenger seat. Dropping the screwdriver next to him, he reached for the clothes. It was some sort of work uniform and included both shirt and pants. Still dressed in denim prison garb, he knew he would have to change clothes.

Still cautious, he quickly walked toward the side of the barn to his hiding place; a carefully constructed semi-circle wall of hay bales stacked six high. He had used it to conceal himself. Even knowing there was no one else at the farm, he still stood behind it, peeling off his own blood-spattered denim prison shirt and pants, while carefully listening for anyone approaching from outside. Tossing them aside, he slid on the gray pants and the shirt he had taken from the car. They were snug, but they would have to do. He paused. In his own mind, his attempt to disguise himself was still too obvious. He needed more. The clothes were such a close fit, and there was probably something else in the house he could wear. Walking back toward the Desoto, he picked up the ball cap lying next to the driver's door, put it on, and peered from the shadows of the barn into the bright sunlight. He saw the small general store across the road, but didn't see anyone outside and quickly walked to the back door of the farmhouse. Once inside, he quietly looked around, knowing from his own surveillance throughout the day that no one else was in the house.

His growling stomach had become a constant reminder that he hadn't eaten in over a day. Opening the icebox, he searched for something to settle his hunger. Grabbing a hard-boiled egg and tomato, he was ravenous as he devoured both. After quickly washing it down with a bottle of beer and pausing for only a moment, the killer continued his search of the house. A woman's pocketbook lay on the table. He made a quick check, but there was no cash, only change. He walked to a bedroom, found a light green, whipcord jacket, and slipped it on over the gray uniform shirt, knowing it would have to work. Anything might help conceal his identity.

In the back of his mind, he still knew the keys to the Desoto had to be in the barn. After all, he had seen the farmer drive the car inside.

Still careful not to be detected, he slipped back outside to the barn, sliding the large door open just far enough to squeeze through. It was only then, with a beam of sunlight streaming through the small opening and onto the floor, he noticed the trail of blood leading from the car to where the bodies were hidden beneath the hay. Grabbing handfuls of loose hay from the floor of the barn, he quickly covered the trail of death.

Moving back to the driver's side of the car, he searched one more time and still couldn't find the keys. Without success, he would have to continue his escape on foot.

While surveying the yard between the barn and the house, he could hear the soft cluck of several chickens from the lower floor. Still no one in sight. He paused, almost statuesque, unknowingly holding his breath while listening intently for anything. A single bead of sweat ran slowly down the side of his face. It was hot inside the barn. Stifling hot. With the temperature nearing 80 degrees outside, it seemed like an oven inside the wooden structure. As he slowly let out his breath, he heard an approaching car. The soft hum of the tires on the blacktop road grew louder. He nervously waited, hoping it would pass. Hunching over slightly to peer outside, he watched as the car slowly made its way south along Stockbridge Road, the quiet engine and the sound of the rolling tires gradually diminishing as it disappeared along the horizon. Now there was only silence, save for the occasional caw of a crow in the distance.

The Herrick farm.
Photo courtesy of the Ingham County Sheriff's Office.

Hesitation. Ever so slowly, he stepped from the outbuilding. The cool, late afternoon breeze hit him like a rush of fresh water, temporarily drying the beads of sweat on his face.

Almost fearful he might wake the victims of his vicious attack, he slowly slid the large door along its track, back into place, then walked quickly toward the field of corn behind the house. As he made his way, he listened intently for approaching traffic. Nothing. Reaching the field, he stepped just inside the tasseled stalks, pausing for a brief moment while inhaling deeply. The fresh air was intense. He had longed for it. It was only then he noticed the sweet smell of the freshly-cut hay wafting in the warm, late summer breeze; the same hay he had concealed the elderly couple's bodies in only a few minutes before. To Nealy Buchanon, the

A SLAYER WAITS

31-year-old escapee from the State Prison of Southern Michigan, it was the smell of freedom.

A wide expanse of farm field lay before him. Glancing back toward the old farmhouse and barn, he turned his attention back to the vast field of crops and quickly picked the direction of his escape route, knowing the field would provide perfect cover. His breath was short as he nervously contemplated his next move, feeling the pounding in his chest. He was certain someone would hear it. He paused, listening again. Nothing. His decision made, he began walking just inside the concealment of the corn rows. He headed north, away from the horror he had just wrought, quickly glancing back one more time at the barn and two-story farm house. Beyond the farm, on the opposite side, he could see the small general store. The sign over the entrance read Oakwood. There was still no one visible and he refocused his attention.

It had been a banner season for crops in mid-Michigan, and the tassels on the corn peaked above Nealy Buchanon's 6-foot 1-inch, 190-pound frame. Three rows in, he knew he wouldn't be seen. After a few hundred feet, he reached into his back pocket, removing the checkbook and bankbook, throwing them on the ground.

Reaching the end of the cornfield, he tenaciously planned his next move. Hitchhiking would be risky, and for just a moment, his mind flashed back to the Desoto, wishing he'd have been able to hot-wire it. Now watching in both directions along the roadway to ensure no one would see him leave the cornfield, he walked to the side of the road and nonchalantly extended his thumb in the air as if he had been hitchhiking all along. He watched as the next car approached. As he nervously walked backward with his thumb raised, he could see the farm at 2532 Stockbridge Road only a few hundred yards from where he stood, and the small store. Uncertainty overtook him and streams of sweat reappeared on his forehead.

Harry Doesburg's store Oakwood at the intersection of M-36 and M-92. The Herrick home appears just beyond the large tree in the center of the photo.
Photo courtesy of the Ingham County Sheriff's Office.

In the distance, the northbound car slowed before getting to him, turning into Oakwood. With his thumb in the air, he watched as Harry Doesburg, the store's proprietor, walked outside and greeted his customer.

As Doesburg started pumping gas, he glanced up briefly and noticed the man with a baseball cap hitch-hiking northbound. He thought it was unusual to see a black man. The best Harry could recall, there were on-ly two black men in the entire area, living on a farm as

A SLAYER WAITS

hired hands east of town, and Harry knew both of them. He didn't recognize the man with his thumb in the air. As the conversation continued with his customer, his attention turned back to watching the gas pump, and he thought nothing more of it. Hitchhikers weren't uncommon.

Elmer Rowe, a local farmer driving north on Stockbridge Road, passed Oakwood and saw the same hitchhiker Doesburg had noticed. Depressing the clutch in his truck, then touching the brake, he shifted the old pickup into neutral, slowly came to a stop alongside the man and offered him a ride. The passenger asked Rowe where he might catch a bus. Rowe thought he might be able to find one in Millville and drove the mile and a half north to the small village, dropping his passenger at Wayne Baker's store, another small country store similar to Oakwood.

In front of the Millville store, the Sinclair gas pumps stood like silent sentinels casting long shadows across the drive in the early evening twilight as the evening fall temperature had started to dip. Like endless other small communities scattered around the 1955 Michigan countryside, Millville was nothing more than a dot on a roadmap; a few houses scattered about, a church on the west side of the road, with Baker's store on the east side, and a one-room school. Besides Sinclair gas, Baker sold everything from groceries, to clothing, to shoes, and like his competitor Harry Doesburg, who owned Oakwood to the south, he even offered ice cream to his customers. The biggest difference between the two businessmen was simple; Harry offered credit to his customers, keeping the debt slips in a cigar box, while Baker made his sales based strictly on cash only.

It was getting late. The paltry egg and tomato taken from the farmhouse kitchen where he had just fled, along with the beer he had used to wash it down, hadn't eased the growing hunger in his stomach. Buchanon calmly walked inside the store, casually surveying the merchandise while trying to look at ease. Nervous, his heart still pounding, he was short of breath. He knew it was unlikely anyone could have possibly discovered the bodies yet. He desperately hoped no one recognized him as the escaped convict from the prison.

Wayne Baker glanced up at his customer. Much like Doesburg, Baker knew there weren't many black men in the area, but thought nothing more of it.

As Buchanon's eyes scanned the store, he saw products stacked to the ceiling. Baker, using some sort of hooked pole, was grabbing something from a top shelf. There seemed to be a little bit of everything in the small building. Nealy eyed a cherry pie on the counter. Paying ten cents, he hurriedly ate it while he kept nervously glancing outside. Looking back at Baker, he told him he had car trouble and needed a ride. He asked about bus schedules and Baker, shaking his head, suggested he hitchhike.

Discouraged, Buchanon walked out of the store. He desperately needed transportation. The clock was ticking. Sooner or later, someone would make the discovery, and he wanted to be long gone before it ever happened.

George Ousley, inside Baker's store at the same time Buchanon had been asking questions, came out with his purchase, and Buchanon asked him for a ride. Suspicious of the man, Ousley turned him down.

As Buchanon stood at the edge of M-97, he looked to the north and south, impatiently waiting for another car to come along.

Having just left the Nottingham farm northeast of

Millville, Jarvis Wireman, known as Jarvie to his friends, and Patrick McCoy had just finished their long day. Now heading home, the two farmhands neared Millville and saw Buchanon standing near the edge of road waving both arms. Wireman eased his truck to the shoulder of the state highway, slowing it until he came to a stop. The five dollars Buchanon offered Wireman for a ride to Mason was enticing. The local hired hand had no way of knowing the money had been taken from the man Buchanon had just murdered. Wireman took the wadded-up dollar bills, and the three men headed south but only for a short distance. McCoy was dropped off at Cooper Road, south of Millville, and Jarvie continued on to Mason with his fare.

On their short ride, Wireman noticed his passenger's baseball cap with the large letter C, and when he mentioned it, Buchanon commented he had played baseball for Chicago, but offered nothing more, still being cautious. Curious, Wireman asked why he was hitchhiking. Staring out the passenger window at the endless farms along the country road, the escaped convict offered a canned response; his car had broken down. He hoped Wireman wouldn't ask where the car was, or worse yet, offer to help fix the imaginary vehicle.

Winding westward along M-36 through the small village of Dansville, the ride lasted a short fifteen minutes or so and ended in Mason, the seat of government for Ingham County.

As Wireman and Nealy Buchanon came into town from the east, Jarvie maneuvered his pickup slowly along Ash Street, passing the grandiose Ingham County Courthouse, then turned right onto South Jefferson. The large, four-story structure stood in the center of the town square surrounded by green grass and trees that would soon change to a kaleidoscope of fall colors. Huge pillars extending three stories stood on both sides of the entrance, and a large, white cupola towered over the center of the building, with clocks on all four sides.

On Maple Street, along the north side of the elegant courthouse, sat a small, brown brick, three-story building with steel bars covering the windows. Buchanon never noticed.

Wireman dropped his passenger at the Mason bus stop and headed back toward his original destination. When the farmhand reached M-92, he stopped at Oakwood. Paying for a small purchase, he took the five, crumpled, one-dollar bills from his pocket and laid three of them on the counter. Harry Doesburg joked with Wireman about winning a small amount of money in a dice game, basing his assumption on the condition of the bills. Wireman chuckled, telling Harry of the passenger he had ferried to Mason, and Doesburg figured it was the same hitchhiker he had seen around 5:00 pm. They both chuckled about the crumpled bills and nothing more was said.

It was now 7:00 pm, and in Mason, there were no buses running. Desperate, Buchanon needed a way out. He had made it this far and was determined to complete his escape.

On Ingham Court, a small side street along the west side of the town square, Buchanon saw two Our Cab taxis parked along the side of the street. One of the cabbies, Paul Willett, had just finished for the day, while another driver, Percy Ruffett, was just starting the evening shift. Knowing this might be his last chance to get away without having to steal a car, and likely draw attention to himself, Nealy Buchanon approached the men, told them he wanted to be taken to the Lansing bus station, and asked how much it would cost for the trip. It would be $3.75. He climbed into Ruffett's cab for the 20-minute ride. Paul Willett looked suspiciously at the backseat passenger in his friend's cab. Although he was now off duty, he left his own cab, climbing into the passenger seat of his friend's. As the evening sun began to settle into dusk, the three pulled away from the curb, drove east through the shaded streets of Mason, and then headed north on Cedar Street toward Michigan's Capital City, Lansing.

Along the way, the conversation was filled with disinformation. There was no way Buchanon was going to offer too much. When asked where he was heading, he told the two cabbies he was due in Chicago, as he was going to be married tomorrow. He was lying, yet he needed them to believe him. He briefly joked with them about the impending nuptials. In between the jokes about married life, he casually asked about busses to Chicago. Willett and Ruffett were sure he'd be able to catch one.

As the Our Cab taxi pulled up to the bus station on Washington Avenue in Lansing twenty minutes later, Buchanon pulled a twenty-dollar bill from his pocket and handed it to Willett. The cabbie began to count out change, while Buchanon insisted Willett keep the quarter from the $20 as a tip. Buchanon pocketed the other $16. With their fare delivered, the two cab drivers headed back toward Mason, never realizing the man they had just delivered was a desperate escapee from the world's largest walled prison who had just killed an elderly farmer and his wife.

Buchanon walked cautiously through the doors to the bus station into the open lobby, and layers of cigarette smoke hung like a low fog in the large, dimly lit room. Large ceiling fans rotated in slow motion, and several people were seated among the rows of chairs, their baggage placed strategically next to them as they waited for their coach. The overwhelming smell of sweat, stale cigarettes, and urine was almost unbearable. Buchanon looked at the board, quickly checking for a bus headed to Chicago. It had been his plan from the beginning, figuring he would mix in with everyone else there. In a big city like Chicago, he was certain he could evade arrest, and he would simply blend in. Walking cautiously up to the counter and asking for a ticket to Chicago, he paused, almost in a panic when he was told the Chicago bus wouldn't be leaving until much later. Looking up at the schedule posted behind the ticket agent, he saw New York. Yes...New York was the better choice, further away, and he wouldn't have to wait around for the bus to get there. If the cops ended up talking to the cabbies, they would surely start their search in Chicago. By that time, he would be eight hundred miles away in the opposite direction.

The escaped convict used the change from his cab ride, quietly purchasing his ticket, then took a seat among the waiting passengers, purposely avoiding conversation with anyone. When the New York bound coach arrived, he unassumingly stepped aboard the bus with his ticket in hand. Pulling away from the station, the large bus turned slowly onto South Washington Avenue, heading south toward the interstate. As the carrier merged into eastbound traffic, it disappeared into the now cool, fall evening with Howard and Myra Herrick's killer on board. Whatever trail Nealy Buchanon left had now turned cold.

Coming from a family of seven children, a southern

A SLAYER WAITS

laborer named Porter Buchanon moved to Michigan in 1926 with his wife, Gladys, and his young family. After marrying Gladys Floyd on November 4, 1923 in Elmore County, Alabama, it was March 31 of the following year when their first child, Nealy, arrived. Another son, Willie, would follow two years later, and then a sister.

By the time Nealy turned six, the family had made their move to Michigan and were renting a home at 1079 Stewart Street in Flint, while his dad worked as a chipper in an auto factory.

Labeled as incorrigible by the age of fifteen, he had already served time in juvenile detention for assaulting his dad. Later stealing a bicycle, Nealy Joseph Buchanon was confined to the Boys' Vocational School at 400 N. Pennsylvania Street in Lansing's Seventh Ward. The campus stretched between Michigan Avenue and Saginaw Street with a small separated portion located south of Michigan Avenue, stretching to the Red Cedar River. In total, there were almost 500 acres of land at the complex.

Buchanon's temporary residence was the result of his troubled childhood. Other simple offenses, like driving without a license and window peeping, eventually grew into more serious offenses like theft.

It hadn't always been that way. As a youth, he was well liked in the neighborhood where he lived. His neighbors had even hoped he would continue his education beyond high school and get a scholarship for college, thinking he might study law. Their hopes were dashed when Nealy's schooling was interrupted by his repeated arrests. It had become clear to everyone, prior to his reaching an age of higher education, that he would be jailed for a long time.

In 1855, one hundred years before Howard and Myra Herrick were viciously murdered in their barn, with Michigan having been a state for only eighteen years, the Legislature approved funding for a House of Correction for Juvenile Offenders. The appropriation totaled $25,000 and even at its opening, overcrowding had already become a problem. Of the first 96 new residents, there were beds for only 74, so 22 residents had to sleep in halls.

Originally, the large complex housed both male and female youthful offenders, but in 1861, a new law was drafted ordering only male offenders to be housed there. By the end of 1898, there were over 600 boys, and the campus had grown to a total of twenty-eight buildings. It was renamed the Industrial School for Boys in 1900.

To the average citizen, at first glance, the area resembled a private school. Facing Pennsylvania Avenue toward the west, the red brick three-story Administration Building, with its bell tower standing over the center of the structure, was built in 1881 and was surrounded by large, older shade trees. A long, concrete sidewalk led to the front of the building, while smaller structures surrounded the main building on three sides.

On the north side, fifteen smaller flat-roofed buildings called cottages served as housing units for the residents. Each building was divided in half, and each half was identical to the other holding about 100 residents.

The first floor of each cottage consisted of a living and dining area with plain wooden tables and chairs, while the second floor served as a dorm where bunk beds were used to consolidate space. Each cottage had a basement with a locker room, bathing facilities, toilets, and a recreation area. The small basement windows peaked above ground level.

By the time Nealy Buchanon arrived in 1940, there were two counselors assigned to the staff, in addition to a chaplain and a supervisor serving as a counselor. There were also two psychologists on staff and four trainers.

Upon each boy's arrival at their new home, the Juvenile Institute Commission had the Hospital Commission test each boy's intelligence level using the Binet-Simon Scale. The average IQ for the population was 82.1.

While Nealy's life at the school was regimented, the ultimate goal was to help him return to a normal life when he was released to his family and to society in general.

Each cottage was supervised by a married couple working from 6:30 am to 8:30 pm six days per week. All of the meals, while served in the cottages, were prepared in the main kitchen on the grounds and then taken to each cottage on carts. The meals were made from scratch, all the produce was grown on the grounds, and the entire facility was considered self-sufficient.

Each day, Nealy Buchanon's routine was repetitive. Beginning at 5:45 am, the day began for boys who were assigned to the kitchen, which was considered a prized job. The 'night-watch' picked them up for their daily assignment, and at 6:00 am, the others, including Buchanon, were awakened with a bell and required to wash. Calisthenics started at 6:30 am, lasting ten minutes, and the boys were then required to brush their teeth. Breakfast was served at 6:45 am and lasted for a short fifteen minutes. For the next 45 minutes, general housekeeping duties were the norm.

Nealy's work detail began at 8:15 am and continued until 11:30 am. At 11:30, after a five-minute walk to the cottages, he was required to wash for the meal. There were ten extra minutes allowed for dinner, and after the dinner, there was time allowed for cleaning up the cottages. At 12:45 pm, a thirty-minute military drill was part of the everyday routine, and at 1:15 pm, it was back to his detail.

Every evening at 5:00 pm, fifteen minutes were allowed for supper, and then it was time to clean the cottages. Recreation time was at 6 pm, lasting for two hours, and at 8 pm, Buchanon was required to prepare for bed and say prayers. At 8:30, lights were extinguished.

Four times each day, Nealy would march in military formations on the center walkway of the grounds with the rest of the boys from his cottage.

In addition to the schooling he received, the facility had several different work details he could choose to be involved in.

If a resident had to be disciplined, it began with removal from his group to either cottage 4 or to detention, simply known as 'Number Five.' If a resident was assigned to Number Five for disciplinary reasons, aggression was often acted out by setting mattresses on fire, flooding the room, or yelling obscenities at staff.

Originally, the Corrections Commission oversaw operations at the Vocational School, but in 1939, the Juvenile Institute had become the governing body. It didn't take long for rumors and criticism to begin circulating about how the entire operation was managed, and during the years Nealy resided there, Michigan Governor Murray Van Wagoner ordered a study of the institution.

In part, criticism of life inside the cottages and the discipline used on the residents was documented:

> *"The repression and regimentation, the lack of wholesale recreation, the enforcement of silence rules and other rules that not only lack constructive value but are definitely harmful to the growing boys, the failure to give training in normal, natural, well-ordered life with others, the use of such outmoded punishment as 'stand on the line,' the segregations of runaways with punishment conditions for months on end, and the use of physical force in disciplining boys. These should all be done away with at once."[1]*

After the release of the report, the nineteen-year veteran superintendent of what had now become known as the Boys' Vocational School tendered his resignation. Soon after, Nealy Buchanon was also released from the school.

In 1942, shortly after Nealy's return to society, he was charged with grand larceny, and with his pending military draft into World War II, the charge was dismissed.

After three years of military service in Europe driving an ammunition truck, and with an honorable discharge, Buchanon floated around for another year working odd jobs, but in December of 1947, he was arrested for window peeping and was convicted. A suspended sentence was given with his rejoining the military, and he served two additional years. It was 1946, just prior to his reentering the military when he met his future wife, Jeanette, and in 1949, before his discharge, she travelled to Fort Dix, New Jersey, where the two were married.

The Boys' Vocational School in Lansing, which had been a large part of Nealy's teenage years, would soon seem insignificant compared to his final destination.

The adult criminal justice system welcomed Nealy J. Buchanon on September 17, 1952 after he was sentenced by Wayne County Circuit Court Judge I. W. Jayne for an October 1951 armed robbery in Inkster. Known as an indeterminate sentence, Judge Jayne's January 4 sentencing specified Buchanon would serve a term of not less than two years, but was not to exceed four. His conviction was the result of robbing twelve dollars from a cab driver at gunpoint. A few weeks before the robbery, Buchanon had been laid off from his factory job.

At the age of 28, the 212-pound Detroit auto mechanic, described literally as having maroon-colored eyes and now known as prisoner 79322-JM, began serving his sentence at the State Prison of Southern Michigan, and his wife, Jeanette, refused to speak to him from that point on.

Fear and apprehension swept through Buchanon as the squad car he was in made its way across I-92 toward Jackson. He had read the headlines and watched the news reports of prison riots in Jackson only a few months before.

The riots had started on an early Sunday evening in April when Ray Young, an inmate at the State Prison of Southern Michigan, asked a guard to take a box he had in his cell and give it to another inmate. The rookie guard, Thomas Elliot, opened Young's cell, and he was confronted by the armed inmate who had hidden a butcher knife in the cell. The guard, now forced to give up his keys, was quickly locked in Young's cell. Young didn't delay in releasing two more inmates, Earl Ward and "Crazy" Jack Hyatt. The three inmates became the ringleaders of the insurrection, and they were able to take several other guards hostage before taking over Cell Block 15. After securing their hostages in cells, they released 185 more inmates, and Cell Block 15 erupted into pandemonium.

While there was chaos resulting from the takeover, it only involved a small portion of the entire inmate population. The Michigan State Police, though they had been notified on Sunday evening, were not asked for assistance until Tuesday, when a squad of 200 state troopers finally entered the prison to quell the resistance.

The troopers started with Cell Block 6, where inmates began cursing and throwing bottles from the galleries in the block. As they moved through, the troopers had to extinguish small fires set by the rioters, and the inmates were shoved into their cells as the troopers advanced. The squad of officers then moved to the north side where they came face-to-face with the main troublemakers, who moved slowly on orders from the troopers, often stopping to argue. Three inmates were wounded when the troopers began firing after the inmates sat down, refusing to enter their cells. Several sweeps of the cell block had to be made in order to keep the rioters confined.

As a result of the riot, there were eleven demands made by the hostage takers, including remodeling of Cell Block 15 to improve lighting and provide treatment facilities, allowing access to the disciplinary cells by counselors in the block, revision of segregation policies, in addition to the Segregation Board having a treatment person as a member. Additional demands included the elimination of weapons and cruel restraint equipment by prison staff, selection of guards who would be humane to the prisoners, trained personnel to provide for psychiatric cases, and revision of parole procedures so all prisoners received equal treatment. Finally, the inmates demanded post-operative care given under the supervision of a medical director, dental treatment for everyone, with no buying of privileges, the establishment of an inmate council to confer with prison officials, and no reprisals against anyone involved in the revolt.[2]

After a threat by Hyatt to kill all the hostages in Cell Block 15, a document was quickly drafted by prison officials accepting the inmates' demands. It was given to the media, and upon the surrender of the inmates involved, they filed into the mess hall and were fed steaks and ice cream.

Deputy Warden Fox, in his statement to the inmates, said in part:

> *"Earl Ward is the head leader, he and the other boys are to be congratulated on the ability with which they have bargained, their word has been good. My word has been good. This may project a new era of good, sound interrelationship between inmates, and administration, in American prisons. They have done a service, congratulations to you, men in 15-block."*[3]

After the 1952 riot, smaller uprisings continued throughout the prison, but not at the level of the April riot. The following month, an inmate was shot and killed by state troopers who were frequently called in to quell the disturbances. Another small riot broke out on July 6, and as a result, the prison warden was fired.

Most of the uprisings and disturbances managed to avoid the press. Thus, the public wasn't aware of what went on behind the confines of the prison system; but Nealy Buchanon knew. He also knew if he kept to himself he would be eligible for parole even before serving his first year.

Parole, long sought after by the majority of inmates in Michigan's prison system, was finally granted to Buchanon on July 15, 1953. Moving back to the Detroit area, he found a job working intermittently as a window washer earning $50 a week, but he quickly returned to his life of crime.

It was a cold night on October 26, 1954. Funston Chevrolet, at 13105 Gratiot in Detroit, was an enticing target to Buchanon, and while his motives were unclear, Nealy seized the opportunity and attempted to break into the car dealership. Yet another appearance in Wayne County Circuit Court after his capture would not bode well for the recent parolee.

His sentence was swift and hard. On November 9, Judge George Murphy sentenced Buchanon to one to fifteen years for the attempted break-in. In addition, Judge Murphy added he should serve the balance of his robbery conviction for the parole violation.

By this time, Nealy Buchanon knew the game. He kept to himself. He would be the model prisoner. He would do his time. He would tell the parole board exactly what he thought they wanted to hear, and in a very short time, he was certain he would be back on the streets.

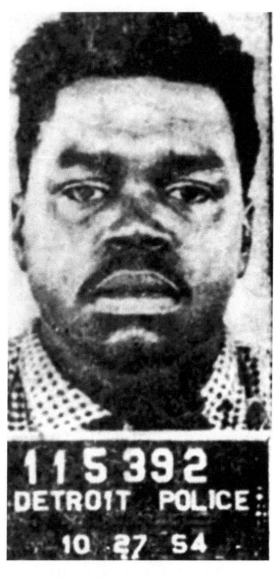

Nealy Buchanon's mug shot taken ten months before the murder of Howard and Myra Herrick.

While serving his sentence, Buchanon was well liked by the other inmates and became the model prisoner he told himself he would be. To prison officials, he seemed harmless, and it wasn't long into his sentence when he was selected as a trustee.

It was the last day of August in 1955 when Nealy Buchanon would finally have his chance at parole again, and it would be his first hearing since the sentence was imposed ten months earlier. With his quick selection as a trustee in March, he was certain it would work in his favor. His spotless record made him eligible for the earliest possible parole, and because he was considered a 'trusted' inmate, he had already been moved from inside the walled prison structure to a building outside the prison walls six months earlier.

He longed to see his wife, he longed to see his children, and he desperately wanted freedom.

Loosely based on the French word 'parole d'honneur,' or word of honor, a prisoner like Nealy Buchanon, eligible for parole, would be considered reformed based on his model behavior while incarcerated, and considered safe to be discharged back into society.

Some of the earliest ideas of parole in Michigan originated in the mid-1800s, when in 1869, the Superintendent for the Detroit House of Corrections had an act passed in the legislature titled the Three Years Law, generally thought of as the first legislative action dealing with an indeterminate sentence, but it only applied to prostitutes.

Another bill introduced in 1871, but failing to pass in the legislature, still offered provisions used in later parole statutes:

"When it appears to said board that there is a strong or reasonable probability that any ward possess a serious purpose to become a good citizen and the requisite moral power, and self-control to live at liberty without violating the law and that such ward will become a fair member of society, then they shall issue to such ward an absolute release."[4]

In finally adopting parole, it was said:

"Criminals can be reformed; that reformation is the right of [convicts] and the duty of the state; that every prisoner must be individualized and given special treatment adapted to develop him to the point in which he is weak—physical, intellectual, or moral culture, in combination, but in varying proportions, according to the diagnosis of each case; that time must be given for the reformatory process to take effect, before allowing him to be sent away, uncured; that his cure is always facilitated by his cooperation, and often impossible without it."[5]

Buchanon, like so many others, took his first opportunity under his current sentence. Mirroring his first appearance before a parole board for his previous conviction, he hoped this second board would allow him an early, conditional release. He would live as a law-abiding citizen once more.

By the time he had been sentenced for the attempted break-in, each state had parole systems in place.

It was President Franklin Roosevelt who had said, "Parole, when it is honestly and expertly managed, provides better protection for society than does any other method of release from prison." Many believed the simple idea of parole as a reward was far more effective than the punishment of a prison sentence.

In spite of already having a parole hearing under his belt, Buchanon still had no idea the entire system was fraught with subjectivity and lacked any legislative guidance to grant or deny a prisoner parole. Decisions of the board were seldom questioned because they lacked judicial oversight to review them.

Nealy went into his hearing never knowing what the parole board would be looking for. He assumed it would be the same as his first hearing a few years before. Inside the prison, word was passed to the potential parolee through the inmates that remorse was mandatory. Knowing that's what the potential parolee was told by other inmates, the Parole Board always doubted any sincerity the prisoner expressed.

Nealy was not allowed any counsel at his hearing, because the Board wanted to compare his sincerity with independent information they had learned about him. They would be searching for signs of his rehabilitation and his accepting responsibility for the attempted break-in. While it was true they would be looking for his repentance, they would also be looking for much more; his chance of recidivism, his physical and mental health, his behavior before he was sentenced, his level of intelligence, the possibility of his future employment somewhere, and his history of any alcohol or drug use. In addition to all of those, they would be looking at the history of his criminal behavior and the safety of the public, if he were ultimately released.

At Nealy's parole hearing, there was no way the

board could foresee the murders of Howard and Myra Herrick. Buchanon had clearly been given a chance once before, and he had failed by violating the conditions of his previous release by attempting the break-in at Funston Chevrolet. Now before the Board again, having only served ten months of his indeterminate sentence, the Board felt it was too soon, and his request for parole was denied. He wouldn't be allowed to re-apply for two years.

On its face, it appeared he took their decision well, but in reality, those two years seemed an eternity away.

Since the State Prison of Southern Michigan had opened in 1928, there had been fourteen successful escapes from the institution and forty-seven attempts. Inmates had used every means imaginable to free themselves, including climbing over cell blocks, crawling through sewer tunnels, and even hiding in large boxes.

The only escape ever to involve a fatality occurred on November 5, 1939, when six inmates armed with knives grabbed a guard on his way to the tower on top of the prison rotunda and tied him up. They gained access to the tower, because the guard on post believed it was his relief knocking on the windowless door. They overpowered the second guard, stole a shotgun, then threw a rope down the 40-foot prison wall to begin their descent.

As the inmates were scaling down the wall, Warden Harry Jackson was in the prison barber shop for a shave, and he caught a glimpse of a shadow coming down the wall of 5 block. He quickly sounded the

A SLAYER WAITS

alarm in the main lobby, which was filled with visitors, as he grabbed a gun from the front desk.

Two of the men quickly surrendered when Inspector Fred Boucher, who had run past the Warden with Deputy Warden Carpenter, ordered the inmates to the ground. Three others had managed to steal a truck in the parking lot, and they were trying to flee. As Boucher turned toward the fleeing truck, a shotgun was fired from inside, striking Boucher in his left side. A visitor in the lobby of the jail was also struck in the face by stray pellets when they penetrated a window, and Inspector Boucher died from his gunshot wound.

Carpenter, who had run out with Boucher, pursued the escapees north on Cooper Street, managing to shoot out the tire of the pickup truck, and they crashed into a tree. The inmates fled on foot, but were quickly captured. The last of the six inmates was located on the roof of the prison, and they were taken into custody. All of the inmates were charged with the murder of Inspector Fred Boucher.

In another escape not quite as dramatic, thirteen inmates climbed through the sewer in December of 1953. After their escape, the thirteen broke into a home near the prison, stole clothing and food, and they tied up the residents. In Jackson, the group decided to split up, and six were caught a short time later in a stolen car from the home they had just fled from. Two more were caught in Jackson the following day. The remaining five escapees kidnapped two women, stole another car, and drove to Detroit, letting their unharmed hostages free a few hours later. They were captured a short time later. It was the largest number of escapees at one time in the prison's history.

In yet another escape, two men hid in boxes of shell casings, and they were carried out of the prison on a truck, while in another escape, shortly before Buchanon's, an inmate hid in an onion crate loaded onto a truck with several other empty crates, without anyone knowing he was inside.

Nealy Buchanon had already made his plan, and it wouldn't be nearly as creative as the other escapes, simply because he was already outside of the walled institution as a trustee.

It was Friday, September 2. Like every other day, trustee Nealy Buchanon began his work detail at 4:00 am. The long-sleeved denim prison shirt and pants offered only moderate warmth from the cool 44-degree morning temperature. It seemed he had something on his mind, as he slowly inserted the key into the ignition and started the prison dump truck. As it quietly idled, he could smell the exhaust fumes hanging in the moist air, then quickly dissipating. He never looked at the gas gauge. His assignment was to go to area farms and pick up the garbage. On a normal day, he would bring it back to the prison, and it would be fed to the hogs raised by the inmates at Michigan's largest walled prison.

Buchanon left the prison, heading east on M-106. Still hedging on his plan, he made his first stop in Munith, a small town between Jackson and Stockbridge. After his first stop, he continued following M-106 into Stockbridge. It wasn't long before he noticed the gas gauge. He knew he was about to run out, and he made the decision to park the truck away from the main street running through Stockbridge. He chose a field near the high school a few blocks west of the main street.

He had already made his decision to continue on and he never looked back. He would have nothing to do with the parole board's decision.

A SLAYER WAITS

At 8:15 am, an abandoned prison dump truck be-longing to the State Prison of Southern Michigan was found at the local baseball field behind the school. A quick call to the prison was made by the investigating deputies, and it didn't take long to determine who the driver had been.

Nealy Buchanon was no longer considered a prison trustee. He was now a prison escapee.

CHAPTER **2**

Howard and Myra

Organized in 1836, Stockbridge Township was the first township in Ingham County. By 1884, the first railroad had come through the southeastern portion of the county, and by 1889, the township began to prosper. Sixty-six years later, Stockbridge Township was made up mostly of small family farms. The majority of those were dairy farms and muck farmers in the area, while several country stores dotted the quiet, rural countryside. It was a time when business was often done with a simple handshake.

In the rural mid-Michigan farming community, Sunday afternoon family gatherings had become a tradition at Howard and Myra Herrick's small farm. Everyone, including all of their grandkids, gathered for the occasional Sunday dinners, oftentimes having venison and always chicken. As a former chicken farmer, Howard would select one of his brood and slaughter it using an axe and a large stump of wood as a chopping block. While the grandkids played on a rope swing in the barn after the afternoon feast, the adults would sit on the front porch swapping stories.

Photo courtesy of the Ingham County Sheriff's Office.

Beyond the family dinners, the grandkids were treated to much more over the summer months. It was the occasional week-long visit from one of the ten that both Howard and Myra enjoyed so much. Having four adult children of their own, they would allow one of the grandkids to stay at their farm for a week or so, while they were out of school for the summer, and like any other kid who ever had the chance to stay with their grandparents, they loved it. For the Herrick grandchildren, a highlight of their stay was always a visit to Harry Doesburg's store to get candy or pop. But this week-long stay was different.

It was early in the week when Myra opened her pocketbook and discovered a dollar missing. She always knew the exact amount of money she had in her small purse, and she quickly determined the dollar had been taken by her fifteen-year-old grandson. It was the start of his week-long visit, and he had gone to Harry Doesburg's store, spending his ill-gotten gain on candy.

It was the last week of August and fall was fast approaching, as was Labor Day. School would be starting soon, and Myra knew her grandkids savored those last days of summer, but she also knew there should be consequences for the theft. As punishment, he would not be allowed to stay through the Labor Day weekend, and he was sent home early. While Myra was a very happy woman and she adored her grandchildren, it pained her to send him home with the holiday weekend quickly approaching, but she would not tolerate theft.

By late in the week, the weather had started to turn. The days were shorter, temperatures had dropped slightly and there was a slight hint of fall colors starting to appear in the trees.

It was a beautiful Friday morning as Howard kissed his wife goodbye. He had taken a part-time job at Wyeth Industries in Mason, a plant specializing in the production of baby formula. He was due there by 8 a.m. By the age of 63, the tall, former chicken farmer, who was blind in his left eye with the lid drooping to a point where it appeared closed, wore horn-rimmed glasses every day. He picked up his black lunchbox from the kitchen counter as he walked toward the door. His uniform of matching shirt and pants with suspenders was clean and crisp, as he walked outside and toward the barn. Inside the barn sat Howard's workbench where he kept his tools, and it was where he parked his car. The 1952 Desoto was three years old, and having lived through the depression, he wanted it to last. There was no garage, so the barn served the same purpose.

Just a year younger than her tall husband and much shorter at the age of 62, Myra helped Howard tend to the 55 chickens they still kept in the lower level of the barn. She had been born in the house and lived there with her parents until she married Howard. Her mother had passed in 1917, and it had only been after her father's death in 1941 when she and Howard moved back into the house. In three months, they would celebrate their 42nd wedding anniversary.

As Howard walked out the back door, Myra grabbed a small container of birdseed and carefully opened the bird cage in their living room, slowly filling the small dish inside. It was an everyday joy for Myra to feed their parakeet, and she loved listening to the small, colorful bird chirp and whistle throughout the day while she cleaned, cooked, and tended to other household tasks. A friend and co-member of the Women's Club in Stockbridge had raised the small birds, selling them for $5 each to some of the other members of the club. After talking briefly to the colorful bird, Myra continued on with her morning routine.

While Howard and Myra owned 80 acres, there was only a two-story farm house sitting just 20 yards or so from the edge of M-92. A large barn sat a short distance to the south of the house and was built slightly to the rear, while most of their acreage was leased out to another farmer. Behind the house was a small pump house. A large shade tree cast long, cool shadows on the southeast corner of their home in the summer sun. The barn, sitting perpendicular to the road, had two large doors hanging on the north side. In addition to the barn being used as a garage, there was baled hay stored inside, and Howard kept his chickens on the lower level.

Howard served as sexton at the local cemetery, and he and his wife were well known in and around Stockbridge. The community as a whole was very tight-knit and everyone seemed to know everyone else, while community picnics, where entire families would gather to share home-cooked meals, play games, and trade stories were commonplace.

As a member of the Ladies Club, Myra would occasionally host a meeting at their home, and the women would sew, garden, or do some canning as part of their gatherings.

The main road connecting Mason to the small town of Dansville was known as M-36, continuing east from Dansville until it stopped at M-92. Reconnecting a few miles to the south, it continued east from M-92 to the small village of Gregory in Livingston County. It was at the southern intersection of the two state roads where the Herricks' home and Harry Doesburg's store sat.

It was between 3 pm and 4 pm on Friday, September 2 when Howard left Wyeth Industries and drove east along M-36 from Mason over to M-92, and then south to his farm. It was the holiday weekend, and he still had to be back at the plant on Saturday morning, but he had only one more day to work before he could enjoy a relaxing Sunday.

As the Desoto slowed and Howard turned into the driveway on the north side of the house, he drove up a slight incline, as the drive circled around to the back of the house and then toward the barn. Howard eased the sturdy vehicle inside the large structure and slowly positioned the car just inside the large barn doors, as he did every day. He removed the keys from the ignition and took his lunchbox from the front seat, shutting the car door as he left the barn and walked toward the house. The thud from the door slamming startled some small birds nesting on the beams and they took flight. Howard never noticed the man hiding in the hay loft above him, poised to drop a large chopping block on the unsuspecting farmer. The retired chicken farmer never knew it, but he had received a stay of execution for one more day.

That night, as the Herricks slept, a slayer waited in their barn for his next chance.

The temperature had reached the high 70s on Saturday, September 3. Howard readied himself for the day at Wyeth Industries in his uniform, which was nothing more than a plain gray matching shirt and pants. He could easily have been mistaken for a milk man. Grabbing his lunchbox, he gave Myra a kiss and walked out the back door and toward the barn. The creaking screen door slammed behind him as he made his way across the yard. They were planning a trip north to visit a cousin on Sunday, and he was looking forward to it.

As the lazy Saturday morning passed to afternoon, everything seemed very quiet. At the farm, birds could be heard in the distance, and the gentle breeze was barely noticeable as an occasional car would pass.

It was 3:00 pm when Howard punched out of work in Mason, making the daily trek back to Stockbridge, and like every other Saturday, he stopped at Oakwood before pulling into his own drive. It had become a sort of ritual for Howard. Harry Doesburg was dressed in his white shirt and casual pants. He came outside, and without any request from Howard, started filling the 52 Desoto with gas. It was a routine for both of them. They visited for a short time as the gas tank filled and then Howard noticed Margaret, Harry's wife, inside the store. He stepped inside to visit with her for a minute and glanced at some cold cuts in the glass case along the side wall. Just before he left, Margaret asked if he had any plans for Labor Day, and he mentioned the trip north for the rest of the holiday weekend to visit a cousin.

Howard walked back outside to speak with Harry for a moment. He slipped back into the driver's seat after paying Doesburg, started the car, and carefully drove out of the store driveway, as he waved to his neighbor. He carefully crossed the road and turned into his own drive, circling around to the back of house and parking just inside the barn, like he had done so many other times.

Harry walked back into his store and busied himself stocking some shelves. Doesburg's wife always enjoyed chatting with Howard, and she busied herself inside the store after her neighbor had left. The scream she suddenly heard cut through the autumn air and sounded as if it had come from the direction of the Herricks'. Howard had only left a few minutes before, and she knew both of her neighbors had some difficulty hearing, so she was certain they must have turned up the volume on their television. The screams must have been from a television show, and she thought nothing more of it.

As the fall afternoon slowly settled into quiet darkness, Margaret, still tending to duties around the store casually noted her neighbor's house was completely dark. Puzzled for only a moment, she quickly recalled

Howard telling her they were heading north, so in her mind, there was no cause for alarm.

It was early on Sunday morning when Lester Herrick, Howard and Myra's son, woke to a beam of sunlight cutting through a small separation in the bedroom curtains. His wife was ready to fix Sunday breakfast, and she noticed they were low on eggs. She asked her husband if he could run over to his parents and pick up a dozen. She joined him for the short ride.

As Lester and his wife arrived, they found the back door to the house unlocked, which wasn't unusual. It was never locked when they were home. They walked in expecting the smell of country ham frying on the stove, with fresh biscuits baking in the oven and a warm greeting from Myra. Instead, they found the house silent. It seemed odd because on Sunday, his mom was always in the kitchen cooking. Lester walked from room to room. The house was empty, and he assumed they had left to visit with some friends or to run an errand. While his wife stayed in the house, Lester walked to the barn to see if their car was inside. First noticing the large sliding barn doors were closed, he slid one of them open, and he saw the Desoto parked inside. He paused, thinking it was unusual, but figured his parents must have been called away suddenly for some reason; they must have ridden with someone else. He thought nothing more of it except to briefly wonder where they had gone. Lester gathered a dozen eggs from the hens in the lower level of the barn. Walking back up the stairs to the main floor, he slid the large barn door closed and left with his wife. He would let them know he had stopped by later.

By Monday, September 5, Lester decided to drive back over to his parents' house to see where they had been the day before. His attempts to reach them by phone had gone unanswered. As he pulled into the drive, he noticed the barn door was still closed. As he reached the back door to the house, he noticed it was still unlocked, and there were still no signs of his mom or dad anywhere. Lester walked back outside and paused, wondering where they could be. Unknowingly scratching his head out of curiosity, he strolled toward the barn and slid the large door open again. The Desoto hadn't been moved. Walking up to the passenger window in the dim light of the barn interior, he saw his dad's lunchbox sitting on the passenger seat. That wasn't normal, so Lester became even more concerned. He walked past the car and down to the lower level of the barn. He looked quickly to see if the 55 chickens had been fed. They hadn't. Walking back up the stairs to the main level, he walked outside and stopped, glancing back at the car parked inside. After a moment, he slid the barn door shut and headed back toward the house. After another check, he stopped at the bird cage in the living room to peer in at the small bird. The parakeet hadn't been fed. That was strange, knowing his mom would never leave without feeding their bird.

If his parents had been called away for some sort of emergency, surely their friends in Dansville would know where they were. Lester made a call to Olin West, but neither he nor his wife had seen or heard from Howard and Myra for the entire weekend.

Now more concerned than ever, Lester called his brother, Harold, wondering if his younger brother had heard from them. His brother's response was not what he wanted to hear. "Something is wrong. Mother wouldn't let the parakeet go hungry," Lester said, and Harold agreed. Harold told his older brother he would meet him at the farm. Collectively, they decided not to call their sisters, Monnie and Lucille, yet.

Harold and his wife, who lived across the county near the small village of Onondaga, started for Stockbridge, but they decided to drive toward Mason first. Harold knew something was very wrong, and it was a feeling he couldn't put to rest. He was going to stop at the Ingham County Sheriff's Department.

Captain Versile Babcock was on duty at the front desk, along with Special Deputy E. W. Gannaway. After a quick introduction, Harold shared the information he had been told by his brother; his parents were missing. Their dad's car was parked inside the barn with his lunchbox still on the front seat. The parakeet had not been fed. Their small brood of chickens hadn't been fed. Their closest friends had not seen or heard from them. Something was wrong.

Babcock suddenly realized who Harold was talking about. He had met both Howard and Myra the year before.

Babcock and Gannaway agreed it certainly seemed odd, but assured Harold there was likely a perfectly good explanation for their absence. Since Captain Babcock knew the Herricks personally, he agreed to follow Harold to Stockbridge. The late afternoon sun had already dipped below the horizon and the evening was fast approaching.

Babcock and Gannaway had the same information the law enforcement community had. They knew about the abandoned prison dump truck found in Stockbridge and knew the driver, prison trustee Nealy Buchanon, had not been found. Babcock didn't know if Harold had heard of the escape and didn't want to panic him, so he decided not to mention it. But Babcock, like Harold, had a troublesome feeling he couldn't explain.

Versile Babcock started his career with the Ingham County Sheriff's Department only eight years earlier. Now at the age of 35, he was the department's photographer, and he was often called to photograph crime scenes when the need arose. As the department's photographer, he was one of three local law enforcement officers who had attended the first Eastman-Kodak Crime Photography School in Rochester, New York, where he learned special techniques in crime scene photography.

Before joining the sheriff's department, he had served in the Marines during World War II as a Staff Sergeant. After being sworn in as a deputy in 1947, he quickly climbed the promotion ladder, and in 1951, he was promoted to Lieutenant of Investigations. Four years later, he was promoted to Captain of Detectives.

His knowledge and expertise when it came to fingerprints, and his understanding of the value they offered, came to light when a story about one of his cases was featured in a fingerprint magazine. The article highlighted a case in Ingham County's Vevay Township detailing a sexual assault where the victim thought she recognized her assailant. The youthful suspect was picked up as a result of her suspicions, and he was charged with the assault. Still doubting they had the right man in custody, Captain Babcock returned to the crime scene, and he took a glass the assailant had used to drink water from. The fingerprint found on the glass didn't match the young man who had been picked up. Babcock, remembering another man just released from prison for the same type of offense, contacted the State Police and asked to have the fingerprint from the glass compared with the other man's prints; a match was made. The youth was released, and the charges were dropped against him, while the other former inmate was arrested and charged with the crime.

Known as 'Babs' among his co-workers, Versile Babcock had a slight build, but was considered the consummate police professional. Wearing a hat and tie every day to work, he was admired by everyone. He ensured that all deputies within the Ingham County Sheriff's Department were trained in the basics of photography, and many of those deputies considered him a mentor.

A necessity for anyone in law enforcement was a sense of humor, and Babcock was no exception. A few years earlier, someone had found an old sheriff's badge from the early 1900s in the Mason city dump on Barnes Street. It was turned over to Mason Police Chief Ralph Hall. Eventually, Hall gave it to Babcock, and for the rest of his career, Captain Babcock carried both the old badge and the badge he had been issued. He was often asked why he carried two badges, and his response was always the same, "Just to make it official."

While Babcock was known as a family man with a wife and three kids, it was said he never discussed his work at home.

Babcock and Gannaway followed Harold and his wife from Mason across M-36 to M-92. They drove the short distance south to the next intersection with M-36, and turned slowly into Howard and Myra's drive. Lester and his wife were there waiting.

Harold introduced the officers to his brother, and the suspicious circumstances were discussed again. By that time, everyone suspected something was amiss, but no one wanted to admit it. Babcock's suspicions were tenfold compared to the Herrick boys, as he knew of the prison escape just three days before and the vehicle having been found only four miles from the Herrick farm.

Captain Babcock knew if there were any sort of crime involved, the house would be considered a crime scene, but at that point, he still had nothing to confirm it. Lester had already been through the house a couple of times and agreed to go through it again with Babcock to search for anything suggesting Howard and Myra had just gone away for the weekend. The Captain of Detectives suggested Gannaway stay outside with Harold and his wife, knowing the fewer number of people inside, the better.

Nightfall had come. It was nearly 11:00 pm. The experienced command officer walked slowly and methodically through the country farm house, pausing in each room before moving on, as he slowly looked around. Babcock took note of the doors being unlocked and the open windows. There were two long guns in the house, and according to Lester, neither had been touched. Mrs. Herrick's pocketbook lay on the kitchen table. Everything seemed to be in order, other than the parakeet hadn't been fed.

While Lester helped search the house, Harold waited impatiently outside with Deputy Gannaway, feeling as if their hands were tied. Harold needed to be doing something. His parents had been missing for at least two days and not knowing where they were was the worst.

As Babcock and the Herricks' oldest son came out the back door, the detective suggested they look through the barn again, even though he knew Lester had already been through the entire structure. Harold pushed the large barn door open so they could enter, and Babcock saw the Desoto parked just inside.

They paused, peering inside, waiting for their eyes to adjust to the darkness. The two law enforcement officers with their flashlights in hand walked slowly past the threshold. Captain Babcock, with several years of experience as a detective, quickly took note of the unusual odor. His suspicions immediately began to mount because he had smelled the odor many times before.

The beams from both flashlights slashed back and forth through the barn interior like Hollywood searchlights at a movie premier. A short wall, three and half feet high, ran across the east side of the barn separating the center portion from neatly stacked bales of freshly cut hay. Lester, who had brought a flashlight from the house, shined the beam of light on his dad's lunchbox. He had only glanced at it in the dim light on Sunday, but now as he moved the beam of light around the interior, he noticed something he had overlooked the day before; there was a small screwdriver lying on the driver's seat and pliers were lying on the driver's floorboard. Lester's breathing suddenly became rapid and heavy, as he saw the heater controls pulled down from the bottom of the dash, hanging by the wires, and the bottom of the dash pried outward. His suspicions were confirmed. He knew his parents hadn't gone to visit friends, and even more, having noticed the peculiar odor, he suspected they might be somewhere in the barn. A sinking feeling of apprehension and fear began to set in.

Lester directed his flashlight around the interior of the barn, looking for his brother. He hadn't realized Harold had gone to the lower level with Babcock and Gannaway.

At the same time Lester was looking for him, the three other men were sweeping their flashlights back and forth across the lower level in search of anything suspicious. Unaware of his brother's find in the car, Harold moved the beam of his flashlight across the caged chickens when something caught his eye. In the gray, dusty lower level of the barn, he caught a glimpse of color. It was very dark, almost black, and it looked as if something had spilled on top of the cages. Keeping his light beam on it, he moved closer. Deep, dark red. He paused, slowly raising the flashlight beam to illuminate the ceiling of the lower level. He knew what it was. It had dripped through the cracks in the floor from above. Without saying a word, Babcock looked at the same dried, crimson colored drops of blood.

Lester was still on the main floor in search of his brother and the officers, when he headed toward the stairs leading to the lower level. He paused when he heard quick footsteps coming up the stairs. Both men stopped and looked at each other. Both had crucial information to share with the other, but weren't quite sure what to say. Lester quickly mentioned the damaged dashboard in the car. Harold paused, as both he and Lester watched Babcock and Gannaway.

The two officers walked on the main floor of the barn to the area where the chickens would be located below, slowly sweeping their flashlights back and forth. They could only see the stacked hay bales. Knowing blood had dripped through the cracks in the barn floor, Babcock knew whatever had caused it had to be right in the area where they were standing. The strong odor had become even more pungent. As he angled his flashlight downward and at a slight angle in front of him, the knee and arm protruding from beneath a bale of hay were unmistakable.

Standing slightly behind Babcock, Harold saw the same thing. He suddenly felt sick to his stomach. He quietly called for Lester. Lester turned and walked back toward his brother. The four men stared at the macabre scene. Lester turned away in disgust, tears filling his eyes. Slowly backing away while trying to grasp the reality of their grisly discovery, he moved toward the door. As they left the barn, the looks on their faces told their story. Without being told, their wives instinctively knew Howard and Myra were dead.

The law enforcement officials accompanied the brothers outside, and Babcock asked that they not go back into the house or the barn. Although he didn't know for sure, he suspected Myra's body was hidden nearby. The two officers made their way back toward the barn while drawing their service revolvers, not knowing if a suspect might still be hiding somewhere inside. While Gannaway watched the area around the Desoto, Babcock looked through the window on the passenger side confirming what Lester had seen. There wasn't any doubt; someone had tried to hot-wire the ignition. He slowly swept his flashlight around the barn's interior, as did Gannaway... watching... searching, but there was no movement. They moved their flashlights across opposite sides of the barn as they made their way toward the area where they had made the grim discovery, their flashlights cutting through the dust in the air like headlights through dense fog. Still watching the area around them, Gannaway panned the beam of his flashlight around as Captain Babcock shined his downward.

The bloodied body of a man long since dead lay at their feet. Howard Herrick's body was on his right side with only his left arm and leg visible. Babcock peered under the bale of hay with his flashlight, being careful not to move anything. It was obvious Howard had been dead for some time, and the putrid odor of decaying flesh wasn't anything new to the officers. Howard Herrick was unrecognizable, his face bloated and black, with his tongue swollen and protruding from his slightly open mouth.

A thousand thoughts began racing through Babcock's mind. Most importantly; where was Mrs. Herrick? Was she dead and her body hidden beneath the hay? Had she been kidnapped? Did the prison escapee do this? Was a suspect still hiding in the barn somewhere?

The officers left the body undisturbed under the hay bale, and after a search of the rest of the barn for a suspect, they left, closing the sliding barn doors behind them to secure the building while still unsure of where Myra was. A radio call was placed from the squad car for assistance. A double murder would be big news, and Babcock, in addition to asking for additional help from the sheriff's department, also requested the help of the Michigan State Police Crime Laboratory.

In the back of Babcock's mind, it was more than just coincidence that a prison escapee had abandoned a vehicle in Stockbridge on Friday, and within two days, only four miles away, a farm couple was brutally murdered. Babcock knew in his own mind who was responsible, but he would need more than suspicion.

While police units from all over Ingham County raced toward the Herrick farm, over 650 miles away, the killer, later described by the media as 'a powerful-ly-built Detroiter,' had already begun his new life in New York City using the name of Howard Herrick.

CHAPTER **3**

Ignored Screams

*"Emotions remained tuned to a feverish pitch here
Wednesday as this rural community took on the atmosphere of an army camp."*[6]

The search was underway. While there was no solid information, there was a strong suspicion that Nealy J.
Buchanon was the likely suspect in the double murder.
As investigators began arriving at the elderly couple's
farm, plans were already being put into place to do a
more thorough search for the escapee as soon as daylight broke. It was well past midnight as more help began to arrive, but because it was so late, the best the
officers could do was to simply drive the back roads in
search of the killer.

Ingham County Sheriff Willard Barnes was sound asleep when his phone rang shortly after midnight. His home was designated as the Sheriff's residence and it sat next to the jail in Mason. He quickly dressed, sliding his belt through the leather holster and along his left side, then headed for Stockbridge.

Now at the age of 43, with his short wavy hair and stocky build, Ingham County Sheriff Willard Barnes, a democrat, had been elected in 1950 and was known for the pearl grips on his two-inch revolver. The right-handed law enforcement official wore it on his left side with the butt of the gun facing forward in a cross-draw fashion. He had won the election campaigning against John Lechler, a former Texas Ranger and former mayor of Williamston. Lechler had won eight consecutive elections as Williamston's leader and had joined the Ingham County Sheriff's Department as a deputy in 1935. He had served sixteen years, with the last eight years as undersheriff to Allan MacDonald. When Barnes won the election, Lechler decided to leave the department.

Before being elected as the county's sheriff, Barnes had served as a weighmaster and sealer of weights and measures for the city of Lansing. In his campaign ads, he advertised having been a deputy for five years, in addition to having attended both Michigan State University and Albion College.

As the new sheriff, Barnes had nineteen full-time deputies to patrol the county roads, and he inherited a $90,000 yearly budget. After only three years in office, he formed the Ingham County Sheriff's Posse. The mounted posse consisted of deputies and volunteers on horseback, and they were used in public relations and other special events. Barnes was also responsible for the county providing police vehicles to the deputies.

Before he was elected, deputies used their own vehicles and were given money by the county for insurance, maintenance, and other expenses. In addition to purchasing police vehicles, Barnes put police radios in the cars and added lights and sirens.

The Ingham County Sheriff's Office, circa 1956. Sheriff Banes is wearing a dark suit in the center of the main doorway, while Captain Babcock stands in the front row wearing a bow tie and hat. Photo courtesy of the Ingham County Sheriff's Office.

By some accounts, the sheriff was known as a heavy drinker, and while there were those who considered him an alcoholic, he was still respected by his subordinates.

Captain Babcock briefed the sheriff as soon as he

arrived, as well as all the other officers. Each officer was assigned a specific duty to help in processing the crime scene. Still, no one knew the whereabouts of Myra. A deputy was also assigned to accompany the Herrick boys and their wives back to Lester's house in Gregory.

Knowing of Nealy Buchanon's escape, the sheriff wanted him brought in for questioning about the murder if he was captured. Barnes ordered a broadcast by radio to let every police agency in the county know Buchanon was a likely suspect in the homicide. He had no physical evidence to back up his suspicions yet, but he also knew it would only be a matter of time before he had it.

Babcock was leading the investigation and was going to photograph the scene, but before any photos were taken, another slow and methodical search of the barn had to be done, in hopes of locating the body of Myra.

Beginning their investigation, detectives noted what had been initially observed by Lester...the lunchbox and screwdriver on the front seat of the car, in addition to the pliers lying on the floor on the driver's side. The obvious attempt to hot-wire the Desoto was documented by Babcock in his photographs. Deputies used their heavy six-cell flashlights to illuminate the car as Babcock adjusted the shutter on his camera. They could see blood spattered across the driver-side mirror as they examined the car even closer.

After documenting the car, they began to slowly move through the barn. They discovered a wall of carefully stacked hay bales along the east side that was several feet high. It looked out of place. It looked as if the bales were set up intentionally to conceal something or maybe someone. As they circled around it, the first piece of hard evidence linking the escaped prison inmate to the crime scene was found. There was a denim shirt and pants lying in the hay, and they appeared to be the same clothing worn by trustees at the state prison. After photographing the prison clothing, the investigators looked closer at it. Both the pants and the shirt were covered in blood spatter. There was no name on the clothing, but they all knew who it belonged to, and it confirmed their suspicions about who had committed the brutal murders. It also became clear the killer had changed clothes before he fled the scene.

As they began to build their case by documenting and collecting the evidence, the call had already gone out to all police agencies in the area; Nealy J. Buchanon, the escapee from the State Prison of Southern Michigan was wanted for questioning in the homicides.

The investigators continued moving through the barn, inch by inch, being careful not to disturb anything until every angle was photographed and the entire scene was documented.

As they reached Howard Herrick's body, Babcock snapped photos of him in his awkward position with his left arm and leg protruding from under the bale of hay. Even though he knew the Herricks, as difficult as it was, Versile still knew he had a job to do. After photographs from several different angles, Babcock gave the okay, and a deputy grabbed two pieces of twine holding the hay bale together, lifting it from atop Howard Herrick. The deputy winced at the sight of the farmer's bloated body and quickly raised his arm across his nose to mask the odor of decomposition. The deputy's $3,750 yearly salary hardly seemed worth it at that moment.

Dried blood was caked on Herrick's face and on

the surrounding hay beneath his head. The gross deformation and discoloration made it clear he had been dead for some time.

More photographs were taken of the body. It was difficult to work in the dark and fearing they might miss something, the investigators took extreme care to move slowly.

As the officers turned their flashlights on the body of Howard Herrick for more illumination, they quickly noticed the obvious; a woman's shoe was protruding from under another hay bale behind Howard's body. They silently glanced at each other knowing they had found Myra.

More photos were taken before anything else was moved. The second bale of straw was then slowly lifted to reveal Mrs. Herrick's badly beaten and decomposing body, clad in her blood-stained country dress and farm apron. Tight-lipped, there was a noticeable hesitation among the men before anyone proceeded. More pictures. The positioning of the farmer and his wife and their close proximity to each other was documented.

As the police continued to search for clues in the barn, it had become obvious the Herricks were not killed in the same place where their bodies were found. With blood spattered on the driver's mirror of the car, investigators suspected at least one of them had been killed near there. There should have been much more blood around the bodies, and they began to check the floor of the barn for trace evidence. They found the smeared trail of dried blood hidden under loose hay leading from the driver's side of the car to where the bodies had been hidden. There was no doubt now; at least one body had been dragged from there. Whoever had killed the Herricks had taken the time to conceal the trail of death.

A large are of blood on the barn floor where Howard Herrick was
bludgeoned to death.
Photo courtesy of the Ingham County Sheriff's Office.

Babcock leaned over Howard's body looking for
any evidence of a murder weapon. He slowly moved to
Howard's wife. They had both suffered massive head
trauma. Babcock surmised they had been struck multiple times. There was no question they had been bludgeoned to death, but with what?

The search continued slowly and methodically,
inch by inch, almost at a snail's pace. As flashlight
beams continued to sweep through the barn, police
found an axe propped against the wall just a few feet
from the bodies. It was difficult to see, but using their
flashlights to illuminate the double-bladed implement,
it looked as if there might be blood on the blade. There
were some boards nailed across the wall near the axe,

and a pitchfork stood behind them. Looking closer at the bodies in their original positions, the officers searched for any evidence of puncture wounds caused by the pitchfork, but couldn't find any. All options were still open as to how the elderly couple might have been murdered.

As the search intensified deeper into the barn, the crime scene investigators began to check stacks of hay bales around where the bodies had been found. As one of the officers shined his flashlight across the top of some bales, something caught his eye. Looking closer, he discovered a ball-peen hammer. As the deputy looked at the tool in the low light, another officer glanced down at the base of the stacked hay bales, seeing a hand grinder which was normally attached to a workbench. Captain Babcock took photos of both, and before moving them, he looked closely at the grinder, much like he had with the ball-peen hammer. Like the hammer and the axe, there was blood on the grinder, too.

Questions and theories began to abound among the law enforcement professionals at the scene. Were the Herricks surprised in the barn somehow? There was no question they had been killed inside the barn. Where were the keys to the car? How long had they been in the barn? Had the killer secreted himself and lain in wait? Why had the killer chosen the Herricks' barn? They were all good questions and no one had the answers.

While Versile Babcock was spearheading the investigation, he knew numerous things had to be done, and he was a firm believer that the first step in every investigation was to canvass the neighborhood. Maybe someone had seen something. The decision was made to not wait until daybreak. Sheriff Barnes was thinking the same thing and directed his men to begin checking with neighbors. It didn't matter to him or any of the officers what time of the night it was. There was a killer on the loose.

The murder weapons.
Photo courtesy of the Ingham County Sheriff's Office.

Every inch of the barn had been checked, and all the photos had been taken. Babcock, working with other investigators now assigned to the case, began adding to his notes so a crime scene diagram could be done. Measuring tapes were used to document the physical layout of the barn, the location of the Herricks' bodies, where the tools and implements were found in relation to Howard and Myra's bodies, the prison clothing, and the location of the car.

The Herrick's Desoto parked just inside the barn door.
Photo courtesy of the Ingham County Sheriff's Office.

Before police moved the car, detectives began to process the Desoto, checking to see if there were any fingerprints left by whoever had attempted to hot-wire it. Using a small brush and special fingerprint powder, it was slowly spread across any of the smooth areas that might have been touched by the killer. Invisible impressions caused by friction ridges on the suspect's fingers would be damning evidence.

Mr. Herrick's lunchbox was dusted first, but there didn't appear to be any prints on it that would be useful to identify someone. State Police fingerprint expert Lawrence Stackable swirled his fingerprint brush in the dark powder, then slowly began to apply it to the smooth areas around the heater controls pulled from the dash, and then the dashboard itself. Small, careful circular motions produced the best results. As he swirled the brush handle, an impression began to slowly appear. Stackable was careful not to apply too much powder for fear of destroying the print. As he continued his painstaking efforts, the print became more distinct, and at last, it became clearly visible.

The detective used a roll of specially made clear adhesive fingerprint tape to lift the fingerprint from the surface. He slowly placed the tape over the print and then pressed across the entire print with an even pressure, moving his finger across the tape from one side toward the other. The powder, which adhered to the print and made it visible, was now stuck to the tape. He slowly and very carefully pulled the tape from the dash in a single, smooth motion and then pressed it onto a clear piece of thin plastic. He had preserved the fingerprint perfectly.

Buchanon's efforts to hot-wire the car.
Photo courtesy of the Ingham County Sheriff's Office.

A SLAYER WAITS

Most importantly, investigators needed to confirm whether the fingerprint in the Herricks' car belonged to prison escapee, Nealy Buchanon. As soon as daybreak hit, the print was rushed to the State Police Headquarters in East Lansing, along with the suspected murder weapons, scrapings of dried blood, pieces of hair, and the prison clothing. The fingerprint would be the first item to be examined to see if a match could be made with Nealy Buchanon's prints. Because Buchanon had been in prison, his fingerprints were already kept on file with the state's largest police force.

As the investigation continued at the Herricks' farm early into the morning of September 6, deputies began canvassing door-to-door in an effort to see if anyone had seen or heard anything. Their first stop was Harry Doesburg's store. Harry lived in a house next to the store, and when he was awakened by the police at 2:00 am, he was initially confused. Still trying to make sense of it all, he was stunned when he was told of his neighbors' murders. The police, without releasing any details to Doesburg, asked if he had seen anything unusual or suspicious over the previous few days. They knew the abandoned prison truck had been found on Friday, September 2, so they were able to narrow the time frame to between Friday and Monday. Their hope was Doesburg could help narrow it even more.

Harry was still in shock as he struggled to think. His mind raced. He asked if the officer knew when the killing had occurred, and he was told it was probably within the last two or three days.

Beginning to describe the last time he had seen his

neighbor, Doesburg told the officer he and his wife had both seen Howard on Saturday. He thought for a minute. It must have been around 3 or 4 pm. Howard was on his way home and always stopped on Saturdays to fill his gas tank. Harry included the fact that every weekend, there was always a clean uniform from Wyeth. It was always on the front seat, along with his lunchbox. As Harry tried to remember everything about Saturday afternoon, his wife, Margaret, still half asleep, walked into the room while tying her robe at the waist. She had heard the pounding on the door, and then she heard conversation in their living room. The deputy, apologizing for the intrusion, was interrupted when Harry began to explain to his wife why the deputy was there. Margaret's hand quickly covered her mouth as tears welled in her eyes. She asked when, and Harry told her it was sometime after Howard had stopped at the store on Saturday afternoon. Margaret gasped! The deputy told her they likely never left. Margaret's tears were streaming down her cheeks. She wiped them from her eyes as she told the deputy, "We visited a minute. He told me he was going north to visit a cousin. Then he drove across the street into his barn. Five minutes later, I heard loud screams. But I didn't pay much attention because I thought they had turned their television up loud. They were both hard of hearing."[7] Harry hugged his wife as she began to sob. Nothing more had to be said. The ignored screams of Myra Herrick had delayed the discovery of the murders and the search for the Herricks' killer.

As Harry was trying to comfort his wife, his mind was racing, trying to remember anything he could about Saturday afternoon. He thought for a moment. It wasn't too long after that, maybe an hour or two, when he had seen a hitchhiker. It was sometime around 5 pm. *Wait! Wireman had given a ride to the guy.* Harry remembered bantering with Jarvis Wireman about the crumpled dollar bills. Doesburg told the deputy of Wireman's encounter with the hitchhiker and the ride to Mason. He remembered Pat McCoy had been with Wireman when they picked him up near Millville. The deputy eagerly scribbled notes as Doesburg described the hitchhiker. He was black, wearing a gray shirt and pants, a green jacket, and baseball cap, but he was too far away to be able to see his face. Now the deputy needed to know where both Wireman and McCoy lived.

As the officers left, Doesburg quickly locked the front door and peered out the window at the surreal sight across from their house. It was only now that Margaret fully realized the screams she had heard on Saturday were from her neighbor, Myra, as she was being beaten to death. As Harry's hug tightened around her, she sobbed uncontrollably.

Investigators already had a picture of Nealy Buchanon. The picture had been provided by the prison, and it was circulated when the dump truck was found in town. With the photo in hand, they headed to Wireman's house.

Jarvis Wireman was sound asleep at 3:00 am, but the banging on his front door quickly brought him to reality. He was surprised to find a police officer standing there. Once again, the deputy explained his reason for the intrusion, and Wireman's eyes widened when he learned of the elderly couple's murder. The deputy explained his interview with Harry Doesburg and repeated the information he had received about Wireman having given a ride to a black man hitchhiking. He was shown the picture of Buchanon. He paused while scratching his head. He couldn't help but wonder if he was dreaming while he stared at the picture. *The Herricks are dead? The police are at my front door? What time is it again?* He studied Buchanon's face and then told the deputies he couldn't be sure. He said the man he had given the ride to had been wearing a baseball cap with the letter C on it and had said he used to play baseball for Chicago. Wireman described his rider wearing a clean, cotton uniform of some sort. Still, he just couldn't be positive. He told the deputy he had driven the man to Mason, dropped him off at the bus stop, and mentioned that the hitchhiker hadn't said much during the ride. Wireman confirmed Pat McCoy was with him when he picked up the hitchhiker, and it was possible that McCoy might be able to identify their rider.

From Wireman's house, the investigation moved to Patrick McCoy's house. With daylight still a few hours away, McCoy was awakened to the sound of pounding on his front door, and he too was stunned to learn of the Herrick murders. He had thought nothing more of the rider Wireman had picked up, but now struggled to remember his face. The deputy handed a photo to McCoy. McCoy paused, but only for a moment. Yes, McCoy was positive. He studied the picture of Nealy Buchanon, and he was certain it was the man Wireman had picked up. The deputy quickly wrote down more notes. McCoy told him they had picked up the hitchhiker near Baker's store in Millville. Maybe Wayne Baker could help in the identification, too.

It was now nearly 4 am when the deputy knocked on Wayne Baker's door. Another explanation for the early morning visit, and the deputy shared with Baker the news of the Herrick murders. He detailed the abandoned truck from the prison and the escapee, then told him of Wireman and McCoy giving a ride to a black man who was hitchhiking. Baker quickly recalled the encounter in his store. The deputy showed him Buchanon's picture. Yes, he was certain it was the same man who had come into his store on Saturday afternoon and purchased a small pie, then asked about bus schedules. The police now had positive proof that Buchanon had been in the Herricks' barn where the bodies had been found, and eyewitnesses had identified him from photos. Now they had more leads to follow, knowing Buchanon had been taken to Mason.

Even though the Mason Police were already aware of the escapee, and now the murder, they were quickly put on alert about the killer being dropped off in their small community. The suspect, Nealy Buchanon, now confirmed by two eyewitnesses, had been dropped off in the small hamlet on Saturday night. While the police knew he was looking to catch a bus, there was still a possibility he could be anywhere in the area. The tension, suspicion, and fear in Ingham County was only beginning.

By daylight, the State Police had sent more crime laboratory specialists to assist the sheriff's department in their investigation, while deputies used pitchforks to sift through loose hay in the barn hoping to find more evidence. It was only after the Herricks' Desoto was removed and taken back to the sheriff's department when another discovery was made in the barn. Beneath some chaff under the car, deputies discovered the keys to Howard's car. It was likely they were dropped as he was struck by the killer. Lying near the keys were his glasses. As daylight offered more light inside the barn, detectives also noticed a large stump placed on a barn beam over the area where the Desoto had been parked. It was documented with some photos while investigators wondered why it had been put there.

After the early morning witness interviews, the deputy raced back to the farm and relayed his findings to the investigators still there. When told of Doesburg's encounter on Saturday afternoon and what was normally in the front seat of the car, the investigators paused. There were no clothes found in the Herricks' car; only the lunchbox. It was already clear that Buchanon had changed into different clothing at some point, and now they knew where he had gotten them and what he might be wearing.

As the crime scene investigation began to wind down, Dorwin Hoffmeyer, the Ingham County Coroner, had arrived, and after an inspection of the murder scene, he ordered autopsies to be done on both Howard and Myra. His initial impression was Howard had been struck with two blows to the back of the head, and he had died instantly. As Howard's body was moved, another piece of evidence was found; a half-empty pack of cigarettes was located under his head, likely dropped by the killer as he struggled to drag the farmer into the hay.

Howard and Myra Herrick's bodies were removed from the barn and were taken to Lansing's Sparrow Hospital, where Dr. Charles Black would perform autopsies on the husband and wife later that morning.

Babcock was still at the scene and was taking any extra pictures needed. He decided to go one step further, checking around the house and the barn to see if anything had been missed under the cloak of darkness. While the house had been processed as a crime scene, there hadn't been a real thorough search outside. Versile Babcock wasn't going to leave any stone unturned. He walked around the barn, his eyes scanning the ground around him as he slowly moved toward the rear. He circled around to the edge of the field and then moved south along the field's edge. As he neared the cornfield behind the house, he stopped. His eye caught something. It looked like a checkbook. He picked it up and opened it, saw Howard's name, and he immediately knew the direction the killer had fled.

By the time the crime scene had been completely processed, daybreak had long since passed. There was still work to be done, but investigators now knew who they were looking for. The story was quickly provided to the press. Buchanon had to be caught!

Harold and Lester had collectively decided to tell Lucille and Monnie the following morning. Howard and Myra's two daughters had married the brothers, Otto and Bill Foreman, from Williamston, and both couples lived there.

It was early on Tuesday morning when Monnie's phone rang. When her fourteen-year-old daughter Rosie heard her mom scream, she ran into the house to find her mom in tears. Rosie asked her dad what was wrong, and he struggled to tell his daughter that her grandparents were gone. She didn't understand and struggled to process what her dad had just told her. "What do you mean they're gone? Where'd they go?" she asked. Her dad, in shock and stoic, simply said, "They were killed." He paused, choking back his emotions, then said, "I can't talk about it right now. We'll sit you kids down and talk about it later."

CHAPTER 4

A Fog of Fear

"It's going to be dangerous around this area for some time."[8]

-Harold Paul, farmer

It had only been five years since Stockbridge had been stunned by another murder and though it didn't happen in or around the town, the victim, Carolyn Brown, was one of their own. The eighteen-year-old was a student at Western Michigan College in Kalamazoo and she disappeared on a cold November evening. Her body was later discovered in a cornfield in Kalamazoo County. Two men were charged with her killing, convicted, and sentenced to life in prison.

Now, word of the Herrick double murder was spreading like wildfire. It seemed as if every newspaper in the state and beyond had some mention of the elderly mid-Michigan chicken farmer and his wife being found bludgeoned to death in their own barn.

As the first newspapers broke the story, a woman living a few miles from the Herrick farm walked outside her Stockbridge Township home. Like the Herricks, the woman's daughter had a pet parakeet, and on that early Tuesday morning, her daughter had let the small bird outside. The young girl's mom knew she would have to capture the bird and return it to the cage. As she walked outside, she could hear the warning siren in Stockbridge start to sound. Checking with other neighbors about the town siren, she discovered it was a notification to anyone within earshot; a killer was on the loose.

When word of the murders hit the one-room school houses in the area, they were immediately closed.

Quotes from Sheriff Barnes were in every paper, and speculation about the motive behind the killings appeared in every news report, as did the gory details of the murder. In each case mention was made of the man wanted for questioning…Nealy J. Buchanon. That's exactly what Barnes wanted. The public needed to know there was a killer in their midst, and he could be anywhere.

Prior to the 1955 Labor Day weekend, people didn't normally fear for themselves or their neighbors, but it all changed after Howard and Myra's bodies were found. In a town where residents once welcomed strangers, fear passed beyond locked doors and into the heart of the small community.

The reporters quoted both Barnes and Babcock. Captain Babcock told the press that law enforcement was convinced Buchanon had just committed a brutal double murder, yet the killer showed no signs of excitement and said little when he went into the Millville store. He didn't make his movements obvious by trying to steal a car, even though he had just killed an elderly farm couple.

Both men believed Howard Herrick was killed first, and Myra had likely interrupted the killing and then was attacked. They believed the motive behind the murders was Buchanon's need for clothing and an escape vehicle.

Reporting the Herricks were surprised by the killer and brutally murdered, The Detroit Times Night Edition continued, "Both their skulls had been crushed by terrific blows. Sheriff Barnes said possession of Herrick's clothing and robbery were the apparent motives."[9] While giving numerous details of the grisly slaying, Nealy Buchanon's last known address at 1576 Garfield in Detroit was also given in the news report.

Reporters rushed to Stockbridge to get their story, hoping to interview whoever they could, including Harry and Margaret Doesburg. Still others seized on the opportunity to locate someone who might know the suspected killer. While the police already knew the identity of the suspect, they had to quickly set up stakes around his last known address in the hope he might show up there. Racing with the media, law enforcement officers quickly descended upon Buchanon's wife, Jeanette, hoping she might be able to offer something...anything...about her husband's whereabouts. They were disappointed when she told them even though he had been good to her in their marriage, she hadn't spoken to her husband since his 1951 arrest and sentencing for the armed robbery in Inkster. She added, "I just can't believe he could ever do anything as bad as murder. He's never done anything that bad before."[10]

Reporters interviewed friends of Buchanon who described him as being mild-mannered, and added he was never in trouble with anyone, except the police. Like Buchanon's wife, Jeanette, they doubted he was capable of murdering anyone.

With a flood of possible sightings being reported, the community was now more concerned and curious; why hadn't the FBI "officially" joined the manhunt for Nealy Buchanon? While they were poised and ready to assist, the Bureau couldn't help until there was an indication Buchanon had crossed state lines. By September 7, a day after the discovery of the Herricks, a report surfaced about a man matching his description seen boarding a bus heading for Toledo. That was good enough for Barnes to include the FBI in the manhunt, and in addition to southern Michigan being put on alert, northern Ohio quickly became a focal point in hopes the tip could be verified. While some in the small community thought Buchanon could have fled to Ohio, others were certain he was still in Michigan.

That same morning, a prison guard reported to the warden he had seen Buchanon riding in a car on Ganson Street in the city of Jackson. In addition to the Jackson City Police, other law enforcement quickly flooded the city. Officers from the State Police, Ingham County Sheriff's Department, guards from the prison, and FBI agents, although not officially taking part in the investigation in Michigan, searched the city for the killer. At first, the guard's story seemed plausible because he was the last person who saw Buchanon when he unlocked his cell the day of the escape. There were those doubting the guard's story though, believing it was highly unlikely Buchanon would return to Jackson after killing the Herricks. With skepticism about the guard's story growing, he was interrogated by the State Police, and he told them he saw Buchanon at 2 pm. When interviewed by the FBI, he changed his story saying he saw

Buchanon at 4 pm. On the chance there was some credence to his story, deputies in Ingham County staked out both the Herrick house and Harry Doesburg's store. After the interviews and much discussion about the validity of the prison guard's story, it was quickly dismissed.

In neighboring Livingston County, the Sheriff's Department investigated a report of a man resembling Buchanon near the small town of Pinckney. The man was quickly located and turned out not to be the murder suspect.

On Wednesday, Sheriff Barnes announced Buchanon's fingerprints had been found at the scene and six different witnesses had identified him as being near the scene of the murders, while law enforcement had tracked his movements to the Lansing bus station. Beyond that, they had reached a dead end in their search for him.

Some of the Stockbridge residents began to voice concern over the ineffective search for the murderer. They insisted when the prison truck was found in the village, the engine was still warm. The townsfolk didn't feel enough had been done initially and law enforcement should have combed every nook and cranny. The search should not have been so quickly abandoned.

William Bannan, Warden for the State Prison of Southern Michigan, assured the public there was nothing in Nealy Buchanon's past to indicate viciousness, adding he was considered a model prisoner and was given trustee status because he seemed harmless. Ingham County authorities were quick to counter Bannan's statement, saying they had 'ironclad proof' he murdered the Herricks.

When Sheriff Barnes addressed the media, he refused to reveal the details leading him to believe

Buchanon had fled the state, saying, "Disclosure might give Buchanon warning that his trail has not been completely covered."[11] While he also wouldn't say which items at the crime scene had Buchanon's prints on them, he was clear and concise when he said the fingerprints definitely placed Nealy Buchanon at the Herrick farm.

While the FBI concentrated their efforts on trying to confirm reports Buchanon was seen boarding a bus to Toledo, local officers in Detroit, Flint, Grand Rapids, Chicago, Cleveland, and all points in between, including the railroad police, joined the search for the killer. Police were told to use every precaution in taking the killer, thinking by this time he may have armed himself.

In Detroit, a tip was received about Buchanon being on a train at the Union Belt Roundhouse on 21st Street. Twenty officers converged on the scene and a search was made of over 300 train cars in the nine-block-long yard running from Twelfth to Twentieth and Jefferson Street to the river. While they made diligent efforts in their search, they were skeptical of the tip, and they doubted Buchanon would return to Detroit where he was, by now, very well-known because of the media coverage. On Thursday, September 8, Sheriff Barnes headed for Detroit to meet with their homicide squad knowing Buchanon's last address was in their city.

By Friday, September 9, Barnes felt he had enough evidence to present his case to the Ingham County Prosecuting Attorney. The police had confirmed Buchanon was in the barn and had attempted to steal the Herricks' car, while his bloodied prison clothing was found discarded at the murder scene, and eyewitnesses placed him near the Herricks' farm. Sheriff Barnes personally appeared before Ingham County

Prosecutor Charles Chamberlain to seek a complaint and warrant for Nealy J. Buchanon's arrest.

While the legal process had been set into motion charging Buchanon with the Herrick murders, he still hadn't been caught, and law enforcement still had no confirmed sightings of him since the night of the killings.

Each day there was another report of the killer being spotted. With every report, law enforcement quickly and desperately hoped he would be located, but much to their disappointment, every sighting turned out to be a dead-end.

While every detail of the elderly couple's murder was sent to the press, Stockbridge and the nearby communities were on edge. After the initial articles were published, the follow-up stories continued for several weeks and reported on the anxiousness now gripping the entire area and beyond. A fog of fear had ascended over the entire community. It was a fear so convincing, so persuasive and so palpable, it continued for several months afterward. For some, their lives would be changed forever.

With Howard and Myra Herrick's murders fresh in their minds, everyone's normal day-to-day routine changed. Each time someone walked into a barn, there was a nagging feeling they were being watched by the killer. Children began to behave as if they were listening to stories of ghosts, refusing to go to bed, while widowed women refused to stay in their homes, and oftentimes, chose to live with relatives.

On Friday, four days after the discovery of Mr. and Mrs. Herrick, the Bates family, living on Budd Road, reported a man hiding in their potato patch. A quick yet fruitless search was done and the media seized the opportunity to interview Mrs. Bates. A picture in the local paper the following day showed her demonstrating how to load a double-barreled shotgun to her fifteen-year-old daughter, while the young girl's eleven-year-old friend looked on.

In another report, Joe Hudson called the sheriff's office to report someone had attempted to steal his car around 9:30 am. The car stalled and the man fled on foot toward Dansville with Hudson's dog in pursuit, but the man was never located.

Harold Paul, a farmer, was quoted in one report when he said, "It looks to me that something must be wrong at the prison. Our daughter, Kathleen, eleven, who was going to sleep in a tent the night the murders were discovered, won't go upstairs to bed at night."[12]

Jittery residents had taken up night vigils to protect their families and property. The terror always came when darkness descended across central Michigan and locals imagined Buchanon 'slipping through fields, and hiding in shadows,' while residents had changed their lifestyle, moving about cautiously and infrequently outside their homes.

At the southern border of the county, a prowler was spotted by a local farmer. A few miles southwest of Stockbridge, near Baseline and Parman Road, residents were quick to join the sheriff's posse in hopes of finding the lurker, believing it could be the killer. Three sheriff's cars were dispatched to help in a search of the area. The unease in the community was tense and Sheriff Barnes knew it. He ordered Undersheriff Fred Frye to spearhead the search. It had to be the killer. He was certain Nealy Buchanon was cornered.

The posse, along with other volunteers, centered their search in a wooded area near the intersection where the prowler had been spotted. There were at least 125 local residents who joined in the massive manhunt, along with the officers from the Ingham County Sheriff's Department, two sheriff's cars from the Jackson County Sheriff's Department, State Police troopers from the Jackson post, spotters in an airplane, Michigan Conservation Officers, and five guards from the State Prison of Southern Michigan. By late Friday afternoon, there still hadn't been anyone located, and at 5:30 pm, without any indication of a confirmation in what had originally been reported, the search was called off. It had lasted all day and the searchers had thought the killer might be concealed in a blackberry patch near Baseline Road. Discouragement quickly set in when they came up empty-handed, but people who lived close by kept their shotguns and rifles handy and continued to take quick looks before going into their outbuildings. The emotions around Stockbridge had now reached a feverish pitch, and the entire area had taken up arms. The township had been transformed into an arena of rumors, scares, and false alarms, while Barnes and other law enforcement officials were fearful an innocent person might be hurt by accident or because they might be out after nightfall.

Reports of prowlers became commonplace. Because there had been no sign of Buchanon since the murders had been discovered, it was reported, "Farm families…are braced to protect themselves as their ancestors once fought off Indian attacks."[13]

The reports spread far beyond the Stockbridge area, and with each passing day, everyone came to realize the killer could truly be anywhere.

In Lansing, Police Chief Paul Taylor said his department was on a close watch knowing Buchanon was last seen in his city. He agreed the killer could be anywhere.

Ron Lewis, living between Mason and the small town of Leslie, was watching the home of his elderly neighbor. As he walked around the house, he discovered a broken window with the shattered glass neatly placed next to the chimney and the screen on a window missing. Thinking Buchanon might be inside, the sheriff's department was quickly called, and officers sped to the house hoping their suspect might finally be captured, but it was another dead-end.

On Hawley Road, a few miles directly west of the Herrick farm, Robert Powelson's wife returned home after running into town. As she arrived, she thought she saw a man getting into a car in her driveway, describing him to officers as a large man. She knew there weren't any keys in the car, and he wouldn't be able to start it. Then she thought he had moved to a nearby truck, trying to start it instead, but she had lost sight of him. After a quick call to the sheriff's department, the Leslie Village Marshall Don Haynes responded to her call, but before he could arrive, the man disappeared. Mrs. Powelson suspected a passing car might have scared the suspect into the cornfield. Whoever it was couldn't be found.

The hysteria continued to grow when deputies responded to the sighting of a suspicious man who appeared near the burned out farm of Clare Fleming in Ingham County. The man was seen standing behind the burned-out shell of the building. As in every other reported sighting, the man was never located.

> "Loaded shotguns and rifles are typical in almost every farm home, and women who have never before handled a weapon are now prepared to turn their homes into near fortresses."[14]

In the fall of 1955, before the murders, it seemed

every home in the gentle countryside was left unlocked both day and night. With the killer on the run after the Herrick murders and clearly capable of killing anyone, those same farm homes were 'battened down like shops against a stormy sea.' Life had forever changed.

As a rural Ingham County farmer returned to his home late one evening, he was greeted by his own wife holding a loaded shotgun. When asked about it later, he said, "In our neck of the woods, we have buckshot in our shotguns and lights on all night. Even the dogs are restless."[15]

With doors and windows now being locked everywhere and citizens arming themselves as protection against the fugitive, the owners at Lantis Hardware in Stockbridge were exhausting their supply of door locks. During the immediate aftermath of the killings, sales of ammunition had already exceeded their pre-season averages, and Brown's Hardware reported they also had to order additional locks and more ammunition for their store.

With each passing day, the fear seemed to abound. Living alone, an elderly woman in Stockbridge Township nailed her windows shut fearing a visit from the escaped killer. Another placed a revolver in her refrigerator, thinking if the killer came to her home and demanded food, she would reach inside, having her gun at the ready.

While the community's entire day-to-day routine had changed and now revolved around the Herrick murders, there were still others passing through the area completely unaware of what had occurred on September 3. They were surprised when they unexpectedly became the focus of intense interest by law enforcement without ever knowing why. A magazine salesman staying nearby at the Whitmore Lake Hotel had made his way to Stockbridge. He confused police search efforts more than once when he was reported acting suspiciously simply because of his frequent appearances at people's homes. After one of those reports, he disappeared into the brush near a cornfield. A Michigan State Police trooper and a hired hand from the farm found the bewildered salesman. He told the trooper he had stopped at the home to make a potential sale, but the woman living there refused to answer the door when he knocked. Knowing nothing of the killings, and frustrated because he still hadn't made a sale, he decided to take a break nearby where no one would notice him. Unfortunately, someone had taken notice of him as he laid down in the brush for a quick nap.

There were so many reports of Buchanon sightings around Ingham County that a suggestion was made to use bloodhounds in the manhunt. Surely they would be able to track the killer after a sighting. There was quick criticism of the idea when it was suggested, "Sad-eyed dogs trail, but never attack their man."[16] The underlying implication was the residents of Ingham County wanted blood; an eye for an eye in the killing of their friends.

Mrs. Henry Shealthelm, a widow and Myra Herrick's second cousin, lived alone on her 240-acre farm near M-36. Mrs. Shealthelm's children refused to let her stay by herself after the killings. When asked by reporters about her children's feelings and her thoughts about the killings, the brave woman said, "I haven't been really scared myself. It isn't that I'm good with a gun—I'm no good at all, but I'd give up a car or money rather than put up a scrap. After all, your life is what you want." She continued, "This area, armed as it is, stands as a ripe 'plum' to would-be burglars, as frightened farm residents leave the keys, and oftentimes, money in their automobiles just in case a prisoner comes calling." Mrs. Shealthelm was referring to her neighbor who left her car keys, purse, and a twenty-dollar bill on her table, hoping to satisfy the escapee if he chose her property, and then locked herself in her bedroom.[17]

The continued anxiety changed an entire community's way of life after that September day. Men, women, and children payed more attention to 'wanted' cards rather than special bargain sales. It became clear the lock and gun had replaced the friendly handshake and open door in Stockbridge Township.

The reports of possible Buchanon sightings continued late into the month when Will Long reported a prowler walking near his farm, crossing the road, and walking into a cornfield. The sheriff's department was quick to respond, sending three cars to investigate the sighting. Could Nealy Buchanon still be in the area? No one knew. Still another prowler was reported shortly after 10:00 pm the same night near the Glum farm at Wright and Kinneville Road, a half mile east of Leslie.

While everyone was on edge, the State Prison of Southern Michigan at Jackson reported two more trustees had walked away from the Cassidy Lake Prison Camp. This only increased tension in the area.

Harry Doesburg, hearing of the two new escapees, commented to reporters about the continual fear plaguing Stockbridge and the surrounding communities since the grisly discovery:

> "There isn't a home in the community which hasn't become heavily armed. The woman across the road hasn't been in her home since the night when the murders were discovered. People are frightened for their lives—a condition created

by the constant addition of escapers from the prison."[18]

More susceptible to the continued discussion of the murders and the constant fear in the community were the children; children of all ages. Margaret Doesburg's sister, living only a few miles to the north and west of the Herricks' with her husband, had boys attending the one-room school in the area. When word spread of their neighbors' murders, the older boys attending the school took large sticks with them to protect the younger kids as they walked home each day. For some time after the grisly discovery, Mrs. Doesburg's sister refused to go to the barn until someone went out and turned the lights on first.

All the while, replenished ammunition supplies at the local hardware stores continued to dwindle.

While the locals continued to report possible sightings of the killer, sightings were reported all over the mid-Michigan area as well.

A friend of the killer, Glade Miller, who had spent some time with him behind bars, said he saw Buchanon driving a light green, 1950 two-door sedan. He'd seen him the night before he reported it, and while he may have believed it was Buchanon, the State Police couldn't verify it. Yet another man, who had served time with the now-killer, was tipped off by a friend and was certain Buchanon had broken out of prison to 'get him.'

The Michigan State University Police investigated the theft of a 1951 two-tone green Chevy from the Kellogg Center parking lot, thinking Buchanon might be responsible, because there had been three other additional attempted thefts nearby. They quickly concluded it couldn't be Buchanon, as the front seats in each car had been moved forward, and it was unlikely Buchanon could have fit into the front seat because of his height. They quickly concluded it had to be the work of three recent escapees from the Boys' Vocational School in Lansing.

Even the railroads were affected when the State Police halted a Grand Trunk train in Perry, northeast of Lansing, because someone saw a transient on the train. A quick check verified he wasn't the killer. Searches were also made of the train yards in Battle Creek and in Grand Rapids.

As the fear continued to grow across the entire mid-Michigan region, spreading far beyond Ingham County, reports of further escapes from the prison were reported, fueling the frustration and anger:

> "Underneath the tension, under which women have quit their homes to live with relatives, and children refuse to go upstairs to bed in typical two-story farm homes, lies a smoldering resentment towards law enforcement and prison officials."[19]

With constant reports of additional escapes from the prison, whether real or rumored, people were taking note.

With the investigation ongoing, even Captain Babcock was going above and beyond his normal duties. Twelve-year-old Harvey Clark was standing in his yard when a police car pulled into the drive. Captain Babcock got out, asking, "Is your dad here?" Harvey quickly got his father, and Babcock went on to tell the young boy's dad about Buchanon escaping from prison. He told young Harvey's dad the escapee was a suspect in something, but Harvey couldn't quite hear what was said. Babcock continued on, asking Harvey's dad if he worked security and if he had a gun. Harvey watched as the Captain of Detectives asked his dad to raise his right hand, then swore him in as deputy sheriff.

Hopes of a quick arrest in the hamlet community were quickly dashed less than a week after the gruesome discovery. On September 10, while the investigation was still active, the Lansing State Journal reported, "Police have apparently reached a dead-end in their search for Buchanon, an escapee from Jackson prison and a prime suspect in the murder of Howard and Myra Herrick of Stockbridge."[20]

Even two weeks after the murders, Bruce McGlone, an Inspector with the Michigan State Police, who served as president of the Southern Michigan Law Enforcement Association, was driving with his wife to a meeting for the association, and as they crossed some railroad tracks in Jackson, McGlone's wife saw a man walking along the tracks. "Isn't that a convict?" she asked. The trustee, who had just walked away from the prison, was quickly apprehended.

Captain Edward Johnson, spearheading the Herrick murder investigation for the State Police, said, "If I were Buchanon, I would try to reach a large city like Chicago, Detroit, or Toledo." Johnson never realized Nealy Buchanon had done just that.

CHAPTER **5**

Bundles for Buchanon

"I believe every citizen within this county would freely give to the cause of raising a goodly [sic] *reward, but I think eight of ten people in the area feel the law is lax in its attempts to apprehend prison escapers. The Herrick suspect was free in this locality* [sic] *for approximately 36 hours before the crimes were believed committed."*[21]

-Harry Doesburg

The morning couldn't go any slower. It was Friday, September 9. Mourners began to gather early at the Gorsline Funeral home in Williamston for Howard and Myra's double funeral, scheduled to begin at 2:30 pm. The funeral home was on Middle Street in the midst of several family homes. Cars lined both sides of the street as relatives and friends arrived. With the autopsies done on September 6, the bodies had been moved from Sparrow Hospital to Williamston. The funeral had been delayed for a short time until special arrangements could be made through the Lansing chapter of the American Red Cross to speed the return of the Herricks' grandson from Sandia Air Force Base in Albuquerque, where he was stationed in the Air Force. Some of the mourners didn't even know the Herricks, but because they were elderly, and the murder was so brutal, they felt the need to pay their respects.

In front of the two closed caskets, Howard and Myra's granddaughter, Rosie, sobbed as she sat with her brothers. Trying to suppress their own grief, her brothers lightly teased her about the tears.

The small funeral home could barely contain the number of people who filed in as Reverend Frank Cowick, pastor at the Millville Methodist Church, delivered a beautiful eulogy. Afterward, the long, silent procession of cars following behind two black hearses made its way slowly to Fairview Cemetery in Dansville. The parade of mourners came to a slow stop near the back of the cemetery along the east side. The family huddled together as the final prayers were recited, and Howard and Myra Herrick were silently laid to rest.

The day before the funeral, Myra's will was filed in Ingham County Probate Court by Lester. He had been named executor of the estate, and the media reported the house had been willed to both him and his brother, with instructions that he should live in the house until his death, while all the household goods were left to Myra's daughter-in-law, Maxine.

On the same afternoon, Ingham County Prosecutor Charles Chamberlain announced he would issue open murder warrants for Nealy Buchanon. There was no question the evidence produced by law enforcement justified the warrants and included Buchanon's blood-spattered prison clothing and his fingerprints found at the scene. In addition, a federal warrant was also issued out of Michigan's Western Federal District for Buchanon's capture after it was believed he had crossed state lines. Sheriff Barnes had introduced some sort of evidence the escapee had crossed into another state but refused to tell the media what the evidence was, still fearing it might tip Buchanon off if he heard about it.

Howard and Myra Herrick.
Photo courtesy of the Ingham County Sheriff's Office.

A SLAYER WAITS

Police had formulated their theory as to how the murders had occurred. Basing his theory on the timeline from when Nealy Buchanon escaped, when the truck was found, and what had been learned from the witnesses, Sheriff Barnes believed Buchanon had slept in the Herricks' barn on Friday night. Barnes thought Buchanon had watched Howard leave the following morning for work. He also believed the killer had lain in wait for the elderly farmer to return from work later in the day and had appeared from his hiding place when Howard pulled his Desoto into the barn, striking him on the head with the ball-peen hammer. Barnes' conclusion was that the elder Mr. Herrick was hit twice with the hammer, and as Buchanon was dragging Mr. Herrick's lifeless body behind a small partition in the barn, Mrs. Herrick heard the commotion, came in to investigate and was likely attacked at that point. In his summation to the media, Barnes said the first strike to Mrs. Herrick's head was likely a glancing blow. The killer probably chased her, striking her two more times in the head, and there was likely a fourth blow to the side of her head after she fell. He also revealed Mrs. Herrick, although unconscious, was probably alive from four to eight hours after the attack. Barnes was basing part of his theory on Dr. Charles Black's forensic analysis from the Herrick autopsies.

Dr. Black was well known in the community and lived in Williamston on West Grand River Avenue. His home and office sat behind a small pond decorated with a small Dutch windmill, and the pond was a favorite ice-skating destination for local kids during the winter.

As the head of Sparrow Hospital's Pathology Department, Dr. Black had held the position for eighteen years. The doctor, basing some of his opinions on witness statements regarding the time of death, believed the attack occurred shortly after 3:00 pm on Saturday, when Howard stopped at Oakwood and Margaret Doesburg heard screams shortly after he left. He also opined that Howard was killed first, after being struck in the head twice, and he died almost instantly. He continued on concluding that Myra Herrick had put up a struggle with her killer. Black did microscopic studies of tissues and smears from Myra's body, noting several bruises from the encounter with her attacker. He determined that as the killer rushed her, she was able to fend off many of the blows. She had a large bruise on her right hip where she was either struck by the killer or thrown against some sort of hard object in her struggle just prior to being killed. Dr. Black also said she had several cuts and bruises on her hands which was evidence she had attempted to defend herself from the murderer. He also concluded the "wiry farm woman" was able to fend off the attack for a short time as the killer rushed her. Basing his opinion on the numerous areas of bruising, he suggested the struggle wasn't a momentary thing. Dr. Black noted a large gash above her left eye, and he thought it was made either by a hammer or the axe recovered by the police. In addition, he thought one or two of the four blows to her head likely caused her death. Another very violent, crushing blow caused an extensive fracturing of her right temple. Either one of those two injuries could have caused her death. Dr. Black, in his final opinion, surmised Myra Herrick, although unconscious, had lived for eight to ten hours after the attack while buried beneath the hay in her family barn.

The Ingham County Sheriff was frustrated because the killer had a 51-hour head start on the police, and Barnes knew he could be anywhere. On the other hand, he could be closer than they thought; he could still be in Detroit, Flint, Lansing, or any other place in mid-Michigan.

Sheriff Barnes wasn't the only person frustrated with the murders and the dead ends. Guilt and frustration permeated the Doesburg's lives following the murder of their neighbors. Hearing the blood-curdling scream as her neighbor was being murdered, while thinking it was their television and ignoring it, had started to take its toll. Harry Doesburg wanted to do something about it. With word of the murder investigation becoming stalled, Harry knew what he had to do next.

Harry had thought about it since the murder of Carolyn Brown in 1951. He told reporters, "I guess the murder of Carolyn Drown [sic], a Stockbridge girl, first started me thinking about doing something about crime." He continued, "It wasn't just that these people were my neighbors. I think the Herricks could have lived 50 miles away, and I still would have started this campaign. I just got so fed up with crime in Michigan, I couldn't sit idly by any longer."[22]

Doesburg's own solution to finding Nealy Buchanon first appeared in the local paper. The headline read *"Reward of $500 is Offered for Crime Solution,"* when several area township officials offered a resolution authorizing a $500 reward. Alva Cronkite of Stockbridge, Clarence Puffenberger of Onondaga, and Fred Marshall of White Oak Township, in addition to Austin Cavanaugh of Bunker Hill Township, offered the wording, and it passed unanimously. In part, the resolution read:

> *"For information leading to the apprehension, arrest, and conviction of the person or persons responsible for the murder of Mr.*

and Mrs. Howard Herrick."[23]

Harry had seen the article. He had already been contemplating the idea of a reward. Surely the offer of cash would be an incentive to anyone who might have information about Buchanon, and Harry knew he had a daunting task before him.

At 6'1", with his large frame, thick hair, and glasses, Harry Doesburg had originally come from Detroit where he had owned a laundromat and a few houses. After selling those, he moved to the small town of Dansville and purchased The Dansville Tavern. After a few years as a saloon keeper, he sold the bar. After the sale, he purchased Oakwood, just a few miles north of Stockbridge, settling in the small house next to the store with his wife, Margaret, and their kids. A chronic smoker who enjoyed three packs of Lucky Strike cigarettes daily, the local business owner occasionally wrote a local column for The Ingham County News. At different times, he had even run for a few local government positions. But finding his neighbor's killer was his biggest task.

Doesburg decided he needed to add on to the reward put forth by township officials, and he decided to put in much of his own money. It was overwhelming, and he knew it would take much more than money. The reward would serve no purpose unless people knew about it. Harry would need to publicize the reward, not just in mid-Michigan, but across the entire country. But first things first.

Doesburg began to solicit funding for the reward from his friends and neighbors in the Stockbridge community. Each evening after he would close Oakwood, Harry headed out going door-to-door asking for monetary contributions for the reward. He continued on through the weekends and whenever he had some free time. As his funding began to slowly grow, so did the media attention, while folded money and coins began to flow in.

Doesburg's friend, Lt. Murray Peek, who worked at the Detroit Police Department, after hearing of his valiant efforts to catch the Herricks' killer, endorsed the reward fund. Harry received even more publicity when the FBI also offered an endorsement for the reward. By the time the endorsements came, the reward had already risen to $2,200, with a large portion of the reward being added by himself.

In Harry's mind, the reward had to be more. He desperately hoped it would reach $3,000. After the endorsements, Harry was assured by the Detroit Police they would continue to assign their top detectives to continue the search for Nealy Buchanon in their city.

With the reward money set, more had to be done and Doesburg knew it. It wouldn't do any good to simply publicize the reward in the local media, because Buchanon could be anywhere in the United States. Immediately after the reward was set, Harry increased his efforts by sending the wanted posters and reward postings to large cities with concentrated populations of black people. Then he decided it wouldn't be enough, so he pushed his efforts one step further. Using even more of his own money, he began to contact federal, state, and local law enforcement agencies across the country. Law enforcement offices everywhere, including provincial and city departments across Canada, were notified of the murders and the identity of the killer, in addition to the reward being offered. Newspapers across the country became intrigued by Harry's persistence and his commitment to finding his neighbors' killer, so they donated space in their papers for "wanted" ads.

When the Michigan State Police heard about Doesburg's efforts to capture the killer by spending much of his own money, Harry received a letter from Captain Edward Johnson. In the letter, Johnson wrote:

> "Be assured that we will forever pursue this case until the fugitive is captured and brought to justice. We are employing many police methods throughout the country that we are not at liberty to divulge, lest the publicity defeat our purposes."[24]

Continuing, Johnson commended Doesburg for his efforts. He assured Harry several men had been continuously assigned to the case and no angle was being overlooked in the search for Nealy Buchanon.

Ingham County Prosecutor Charles Chamberlain also endorsed Doesburg's appeal for publicity by mentioning the murders and the reward on the Gang Busters radio program.

Gang Busters was known as "the only national program that brings you authentic police case histories," and it was sure to bring much needed publicity to the murders of Howard and Myra Herrick. Originally, the radio broadcast was known as G-Men, having premiered in 1935 and featuring only FBI cases. A year later, the title changed to Gang Busters. The opening of the show featured wailing police sirens, squealing tires, and the sound of gunshots, in addition to a dominating voice announcing the title of the night's program, saying, "Tonight, Gang Busters presents the Case of the..." The popular phrase "came on like gangbusters" became common after the show had run for several years.

Prior to 1945, leading into each night's case, the former head of the New Jersey State Police, Norman Schwarz-kopf, Sr., provided a short narrative of the circumstances surrounding each case featured. After 1945, because of other commitments, he was replaced by New York City Police Commissioner Lewis Joseph Valentine. Over the twenty or so years it was on the air, Gang Busters ran on NBC, then CBS, moving on to the Blue Network and finally returning to CBS, while being sponsored by Grape-Nuts and Wrigley's chewing gum.

Besides the national publicity Prosecuting Attorney Chamberlain was giving to the investigation through Gang Busters, and the local publicity Harry was receiving for his efforts, Doesburg also received assurances from the national detective tabloid, Fingerprint Magazine, that a "wanted" notice would be published, and it would include certain information, such as, Buchanon's prints being found in the Herrick auto.

Every chance Harry got, he would mention the reward and his attempts to raise it even further. He produced 12 x 20-inch wanted posters to be sent out to law enforcement, and he paid much of the postage himself. Each packet of wanted posters being sent out was titled "Bundles for Buchanon," and there were days when the cost for mailings would be close to, or even exceed, $100. Besides using the US mail, he would hand them out to truck drivers heading to different parts of the country, asking that they be given to local police, restaurants, motels, or any place where they might be seen. Each time a "Bundles for Buchanon" packet was handed out, another link was formed in a chain that could one day trip up Nealy Buchanon.

If friends of Harry were traveling somewhere around the country, the store owner would give them a stack of wanted posters and ask them to deliver the

"Bundles for Buchanon" to the local police.

An ad placed by Harry in several papers read:

> *"If your name is not listed in this ad, then it's up to YOU* [sic] *to give to the reward fund for the capture of the murderer of Mr. and Mrs. Howard Herrick. The fund is well on its way to the $3,000 goal which law officers feel is necessary to seek out the hammer-slayer of our dear friends.*
>
> *It has been a difficult and costly battle to raise the necessary money. The hunt is on from coast to coast. Our reward fund will help make the hunt even bigger.*
>
> *You shall do much in the years to come, but what have you done today?*
>
> *You shall give your gold in a princely sum, but what did you give today?*
>
> *You shall lift a hand and dry a tear, you plant a hope in place of fear.*
>
> *You shall speak the words of love and cheer, so what will you give today?"*

Listing all the donors, the ad ended with the phrase *"Those Who Have Heeded the Call."*[25]

It had been five months since the brutal murders, and Doesburg met with all four of the Herrick children. It was very difficult for him and for them. Yet he carried on, spreading the word every day so people wouldn't forget about the murder of his neighbors. Harry wrote about the meeting in one of his columns in The Ingham County News:

> *"I am not a newspaper reporter but I had*

a visit with the 2 sons and 2 daughters of the Herricks which proved interesting.

At Jackson Prison was housed a prisoner by the name of Nealy Buchanon. About 4:45 on September 2, he was given a truck and told to go the Jackson county fairgrounds [sic], and of course, return to prison. He headed east and made a stop on M-106 at Munith. He pulled away from there and left for Stockbridge, and there at the athletic field, he left the prison truck and fled into cornfields.

It was stated that an officer of high standing made the statement that the community had been scoured, and that it was decided that Buchanon had made his getaway, that there had been a close watch left on the alert until late on Saturday, September 3. The Herrick family disagrees. The night of September 2 was what one might call the dogs' night. They barked, they howled, and they barked some more. Farmers left their beds to look around. But who left the barn door open was what was mostly in the minds of the Herrick family. Nobody knew Buchanon was on the loose. In other words, officers must have believed he would go back to the prison. That was not the case. He made his hideout in the Herrick barn.

We talked about how their father filled the gas tank of his car at my store Saturday afternoon. He had no inkling that he was on his last mile, no suspicion that he and his wife would, within a few minutes, be joined in death.

Lester Herrick recalled the tense moments when he wondered at the absence of his father and mother, how he finally discovered their lifeless bodies in the barn at 11 pm on September 5. The sons mentioned the savagery of the killer; how after the killings, he took off his bloodstained garments and tossed them into a corner of the barn, replacing them with clothing of the victim. They speculated with what calmness the killer walked through the fields to reach M-36, stopped in the Millville store, got a ride to Mason, and there hired a cab to go to Lansing. Who has seen him since?

The visit with the Herricks was not pleasant. They discussed many things they had heard and what they had thought.

Harold Herrick brought up for discussion a letter I had answered in the Ingham County News. He stated he did not understand the editorial. When some people had asked "Why doesn't Harry leave it to the F.B.I.?" he wondered if some wanted Harry Doesburg to pick up his hat and head for home, leaving the F.B.I. alone. It would be far-fetched for anyone to think that the F.B.I. could or would be interrupted by what we have been trying to do.

Lester Herrick stated his belief that I

have not been a deterrent in the search for the killer.

'If the search is not successful, Harry Doesburg will have the satisfaction of knowing he did all he could,' the son said. 'This neighbor has taken a sincere interest in finding the slayer. He has persistently, untiringly and unselfishly worked the clock around to try and get the message about the crime before the American people, so that someone may reveal information leading to the capture of the killer.'

They took a look at the calendar and the proof was there that their mother and father had been gone for 5 months. The sons brought out this point, and they said they wondered why officers have not apprehended the killer. They stressed the point of this killer being on the loose, that each and every citizen should take interest and that all should be forever on the alert, thinking, planning, suggesting, maybe through this paper. And they asked readers to send clippings to friends, everywhere.

Lester Herrick is now employed by an interstate trucking company and his work takes him to many different states. He told of being in a large city recently and how he came in contact with an officer. While they were visiting he noticed this officer had a circular right out in the open in his police car. Lester said to the officer, 'You see that circular? This is the killer who took my mother and father from me.' This startled the officer, and he remarked upon what a small world this is, and little did he think that he would get so close to one of the family.

The officer said, 'You can be sure I shall do everything in my power if it comes my way, and I shall spread the news of this crime wherever I can.' How effective it would be if all officers could be so informed.

The Herricks asked that their thanks be extended to all who have aided in the search, to every person in every law-inforcing [sic] unit who is watching for the killer. They asked me to urge people wherever they go to spread the word about the crime and those aiding in the apprehension of the slayer."[26]

Harry Doesburg, neighbor to Howard and Myra Herrick, continued to wage his reward campaign almost single-handedly. Speaking to the media, he said, "If we can make Buchanon known as a criminal throughout the country, he will have no place to hide. With the reward as an incentive, I figure we should soon have a lead on his whereabouts."[27] Oftentimes, the only news about the investigation centered on Harry's own efforts to find the killer.

Four months after Harry's letter appeared in the local paper, he drove slowly to the Fairview Cemetery in Dansville. It was 6:15 am and in the cool, early morning haze he found himself standing at Howard and Myra's gravesite. He glanced around at the hundreds of headstones surrounding him, thinking to himself, other than the military veterans buried in the cemetery, Howard and Myra had paid the ultimate price. It wasn't the price for freedom, but the price for fear. He imagined them both asking what he was doing to bring their killer to justice.

Doesburg had heard others asking why he wouldn't give up. As he stood in the chilly morning air, he silently wished he was the chairman of a political group or even a sheriff. If he held one of those positions, he could direct all the resources to finding his friends' killer. Instead, he decided he was happy enough being the chairman of the Hunter's Club; hunting Nealy Buchanon. More than that, he knew he wasn't alone. He knew in his heart there were still people searching.

Even imagining his Hunter's Club, Harry was concerned; it had been several months since the killing, and there was still no sign of Nealy Buchanon. He figured by now the fugitive should be on the Ten Most Wanted list.

The Chairman of the Hunter's Club knew the only way to catch the killer was to go beyond law enforcement. The search had to include ordinary citizens; both men and women. He believed the world was a very small place for the killer to hide and the search had to go on.

In his heart, Doesburg knew law enforcement within the United States was the best anywhere and every resource was being put toward finding Buchanon. He was confident the escapee would eventually be caught. Yet he wanted more. He wanted Michigan Governor G. Mennen Williams to spearhead the hunt, and he wanted every local public official in Ingham County to play an active part in the search.

As Harry left the cemetery, he turned back toward Oakwood. As warm sunlight streamed through the front windows of the store, he walked to the back room and opened a large cardboard box. He began taking inventory; he had 5,000 "wanted" posters bundled, ready to distribute to whoever was willing to take them. Harry Doesburg was a man who would not give up, once saying, "Everything helps. Sometime, someplace, the murderer will turn up."

Harry Doesburg's passion and his commitment were unending. He was relentless in his efforts and continuing quest. More and more of the cost came from his own pocket. If someone or some organization needed posters, he would mail them with his own money, at no charge to whoever was receiving them. His obsession was to dig the killer out of hiding. And while his determination was largely supported, there were still those in the community who felt he was wasting his time and money saying, "Stop spattering the blood of the Herricks across the pages of newspapers throughout the nation." Others said, "Enough's enough, Harry. You've made a good try. Why don't you forget it? You're not getting anywhere."

Those same friends and neighbors couldn't have been more wrong.

One of the wanted ads placed by Harry Doesburg.
Photo courtesy of the Lansing State Journal.

CHAPTER 6

Caught

The bus ride seemed unending. The 40-foot GM Greyhound Scenicruiser bus lurched at every stop and go. The two-level coach was similar to the stainless steel American railroad dome cars, except the aisle was much narrower at only 14 inches. The silent killer said little, sitting in the back, choosing one of the 33 seats on the upper level. Only nodding to the person sitting next to him when he first took his seat, he kept to himself. With all the stops along the way, the uncomfortable ride was extended more than twelve hours.

The further the large coach traveled from Michigan, the more at ease Buchanon began to feel. Passing through Port Huron, the bus crossed into Canada before reentering the country in Buffalo. The border agents had questioned all the passengers, but only about their intended destinations. They knew nothing about a murder in Stockbridge, Michigan. Nealy knew the game and he was calm as they inquired about where he was heading. When they asked his name, he told them it was Howard Herrick. He used the dead man's stolen social security card as identification. Continuing on across the eastern seaboard, the killer was relieved when he finally began to see signs for New York City.

As the bus approached the huge metropolis, Buchanon could see a familiar landmark. He had seen it before, but only in pictures. The Empire State Building, rising far above the other skyscrapers in the New York City skyline, was an impressive sight.

Passing through Newark, then northwest up to West New York, the driver maneuvered the bus through the Lincoln Tunnel and into mid-town Manhattan, squeezing through the tight city streets, finally arriving at the 34th Street Bus Terminal. Buchanon, like the other passengers, slowly stood up, stretching after the long ride from Lansing.

The killer's first order of business was to find a place to stay. He chose a seedy hotel in the city, charging next to nothing for the week. He still had the money he had taken from Herrick's wallet after killing him. It would last a few days until he could find a job of some sort. Buchanon, now in the midst of a large city with over 7 million people suddenly felt as if he were a free man unknown to anyone; nothing more than a face in the crowd. It had been less than twenty-four hours since the murders, and he didn't even know if the bodies had been discovered yet.

The accommodations at the State Prison of Southern Michigan were superior to Buchanon's temporary residence in New York's Bowery District. Catering to transients and alcoholics, the smell was almost unbearable, and the shared bathroom with the other tenants was atrocious, in addition to having to step over an occasional drunk passed out in the doorway. The sleeping accommodations were nothing more than a very large room with several beds lined along the walls and a locker next to each bed. In the lobby, there were several chairs and a couple of cigarette vending machines. Buchanon hoped he wouldn't be staying long.

After his first night in New York, the killer headed to the closest employment office. He quickly found work in Brooklyn at a small diner using the identity of the man he had murdered. Having no experience in the restaurant trade, he was delegated to washing dishes. It wouldn't do.

The next day, Buchanon began looking for another job. At 6'1", his size alone made him the perfect choice for unloading fruit trucks on Washington Avenue. Each morning, he would grab the elevated train from the Bowery heading out to Brooklyn.

At the end of Buchanon's third day, he arrived back at the flophouse. He sat quietly on his bed in the large room writing out a postcard to his wife, Jeanette, simply to let her know he was okay. Not that it would have mattered. She hadn't spoken to him since he was first sent to prison. He dropped the card in a nearby mailbox. Three days later, it finally reached his wife, and the postmark read New York, New York.

With his first week in the large metropolis behind him, he was starting to relax a little. Never thinking about the postmark on the card he had mailed to Jeanette, he believed there wasn't anyone in the entire world who knew where he was.

With the weekend arriving, and having little money, Buchanon sat in the lobby of the cheap flophouse thumbing through a magazine. As he sat there, he could hear some of the conversation around him. No-

A SLAYER WAITS

body knew his real name and the few residents he did associate with only knew him by the name Howard Herrick. He listened as one of the transients described a visit earlier in the day from a New York City police detective looking for a man named Buchanon. He had killed two people in Michigan, and the police were asking if anyone might have seen someone who looked like him, as they showed a picture of the killer.

Buchanon paused. How could the police possibly know he was in New York? He thought again. Word must have reached across the country about the murder, and he quickly realized he had to get out of New York. The police were too close and eventually someone would recognize him. He quickly headed to his room before anyone took notice of him.

Nealy hadn't been paid very much for the three days unloading fruit trucks. Because he had to eat, his money was getting low. Still, he had to get out of New York. Trying to choose someplace in the country where he could blend in, he settled on North Carolina.

The following morning he packed what few clothes he had acquired since arriving in New York, and he headed back to the bus station on 34th Street, still not sure how far his meager wages would take him.

The second bus wasn't nearly as nice as the first coach he had taken from Michigan. Like his first ride, Buchanon stayed to himself. He had purchased his ticket under the name of his murder victim, knowing the police were looking for Nealy Buchanon. When he purchased his ticket, he realized he didn't have enough money to get to North Carolina; he only had enough for a one-way trip to Baltimore. It would have to do. He could blend in there until he could make more cash, then head to North Carolina.

The bus made its way south on Interstate 95 past

Philadelphia then curved to the west, past South Baltimore. Easing onto Russell Street, the bus driver turned the silver and blue Greyhound onto Haines Street. The brakes squealed as the large coach came to a stop in front of the terminal. Much like his first ride to New York, Buchanon stood and stretched as he tucked his arms behind his head.

On Tuesday, September 13, the Detroiter, now in Maryland, had to find a place to stay. Compared to the infested flophouse in New York, he found what he considered to be a pretty nice room for $2. Having someplace to sleep without worries was his first goal. After settling on the $2 room, he knew he would have to find work if he wanted to survive, and he only had to look across the street.

Two days after arriving in Baltimore and using Howard Herrick's social security card again, Buchanon was hired by the Bond Lumber Company as a temporary employee. Located at Baltimore and Bond Street, the established company had been started in the 1940s by Alvin Wolf and his father-in-law. Across the street, Nealy settled into his room at 12 North Bond Street.

Work at the lumber yard was better than washing dishes or unloading fruit. Buchanon thought he might actually be able to settle into a life away from Michigan and away from his past.

Ironically, a week after being hired at the lumber yard, Nealy was robbed. With the loss of his wallet and Howard Herrick's social security card, he knew he needed some other form of identification. He went to the Federal Building in Baltimore and got his own social security card under his own name. No one at the Federal Building had any idea of who Nealy Buchanon was or what he had done in Michigan.

After working at the lumber yard for a short time,

his temporary status had run out, and he found himself looking for work again. He checked the classified ads daily and eventually found work at Al Landy's Junkyard, but he had to take the bus every day to get there. It was just before Thanksgiving when the Baltimore city bus drivers went on strike; no transportation for the killer meant no job.

Nealy was persistent at finding work so he could continue his run to North Carolina. He had some experience unloading fruit trucks when he was in New York, so when he had the opportunity to get a job unloading a banana boat, he took it, but he quit the following day.

After more searching, Buchanon was hired by the Bohager Waste Paper Company. He settled into the job using Howard Herrick's name again, but had to use his own social security number because he couldn't remember his murder victim's number.

As Buchanon eased into his new life as Howard Herrick in Baltimore, Maryland, he began to make new friends, and no one had any idea of his past or what he had done to Howard and Myra. Buchanon knew nothing of a man named Harry Doesburg and his obsession with finding Howard and Myra Herrick's slayer.

In August 1956, Buchanon was confronted by a girlfriend who had a copy of a detective magazine showing a wanted poster for Nealy J. Buchanon, an escapee from the State Prison of Southern Michigan. Printed on the poster, it read Buchanon was wanted for the murder of an elderly couple in Stockbridge. The young female thought the photo looked like him. Nealy had grown a thick mustache after he left New York, so it was easy to discount his friend's claim, and he quickly denied there was any resemblance to the wanted man from Michigan.

It had been one year, one month, and twelve days since Howard and Myra Herrick were viciously beaten to death inside their barn amidst Michigan's gentle, crop-filled countryside, and the mid-October issue of Look magazine had just hit the newsstands. Actor James Dean looked odd in a cowboy hat. The hat was tipped slightly forward, and the young actor wore a gray shirt and black vest. His ensemble seemed more fitting for actors like Glenn Ford or John Wayne. Still loved by America, Dean's death in a car accident the previous year was still on the minds of Look magazine readers, and they were quickly buying up the October 1956 issue at every newsstand.

It didn't matter. That wasn't the magazine Seymour Hale was looking for. The 25-year-old man was looking for his favorite confession magazine. He knew right where it was kept at the small newsstand. He eyed the fresh stack of pulp fiction and his issue of Bronze Thrills. Under the title, he scanned the articles featured inside; *Sin by Degrees...I Stole a Husband...My Son Was a Dope Addict.* Hale picked up the October issue and admired the attractive woman on the cover. Anna Louise Pablo looked gorgeous adorning the front page, wearing a skintight, red-sequined dress with spaghetti straps, her hair gracefully combed back and framing her gorgeous smile. As he laid a quarter on the counter, he turned and walked into the morning sun.

Making his way toward work, Hale found it was much easier to walk along the crowded sidewalks rather than trying to negotiate the maze of streets in a car, especially this early. He didn't mind walking, and while the day's mid 40-degree morning temperatures would turn to below zero within a few months, the forecast for later in the day was calling for temperatures in the low 70s. The early morning fog had already started to lift, and the eight-block walk from his flat on Bond Street, then along Wolfe Street, didn't take very long. He couldn't wait to read his newly purchased magazine.

Fashioned after other true confession magazines, Bronze Thrills was geared specifically for blacks and was published by George Levitan, a high school drop-out who was white and Jewish. Located on the east edge of Fort Worth, Texas, the small, red brick building at 1220 Harding Street was home to the publishing magnate's enterprise.

Having little money when he arrived in Fort Worth, by 1950, Levitan had garnered enough money in the plumbing supplies business to purchase Good Publishing, which had formed in 1944. At the time, Good Publishing had only two magazines, Negro Achievements, and the true-confessions magazine, Bronze Thrills. As his business grew, Levitan expanded the small building housing his company to over 40,000 square feet. Of all the publishing companies around the country, Levitan's became the only self-contained publishing company for blacks.

As George Levitan's publishing empire grew, magazines like Sepia and Jive were added, and they often contained articles dealing with race relations, black politics, civil rights, and celebrity profiles, with some fiction mixed in.

Levitan's editorial staff relied on fictional stories mailed in by readers, and the staff would spice the stories up, adding details they felt their readers wanted. In addition to the articles, 'wanted' ads were placed in the pulp fiction magazines, hoping someone might recognize a wanted criminal.

As he sat in the small cafe sipping the cup of hot coffee he had ordered, Seymour Hale opened his new copy of Bronze Thrills. Like most people, he started by simply turning the pages of the fictitious rag while glancing at the article headlines and the photos pasted throughout. As he neared the back of the magazine, he paused to glance at the 'wanted' section. He quickly took note of what he thought was a $300 reward being offered. Having done time himself for assault with a deadly weapon, he knew what it was like to be on the wrong side of the law.

As he looked closer, Hale found himself staring into the eyes of a man who was wanted for killing an elderly couple in Michigan. The killer silently stared back at him from the page. He read the details of the killing and the description of the killer, taking note of the reward, and then his eyes met the killer's eyes again. Staring, he couldn't help but think he had seen the man before. He looked very familiar. The bar! He was certain he had met the wanted man a month or so before in a bar. He remembered now. They had had something in common. They both lived on Bond Street just a couple blocks from each other. Yes, now he was certain.

He knew where the man lived. He thought of heading back, hoping to find out if he still lived there. He decided it was unlikely, especially if the man was wanted for murder. Seymour Hale quickly got up and headed for the door, walking back down Wolfe Street, then toward Bond. As he made his way through the pedestrian rush, he paused, not believing what he was seeing. Walking toward him amid a mass of Baltimore's working class, he spotted the killer. As they walked toward each other, Hale looked away hoping the killer wouldn't spot him. As they passed, he reversed his direction and began following at a safe distance.

Now walking along in the northeast section of Baltimore, known as the Checkerboard section, he lost sight of the wanted man. Hale quickly looked around and spotted two Baltimore patrolmen walking a beat. Much to his relief, he recognized one of the officers as a friend of his. The crowd the killer had been walking in was now a block away.

Officer Henry Zukowski, at well over six feet tall, and Officer George Kidd, who was substantially shorter, were both proud members of the Baltimore police. With just under one million people in the Baltimore area, they were part of the city's 2,500 member police force. Their boss was a police commissioner who oversaw the entire department and was appointed by the Governor of Maryland. The officers' salaries were set by the state and paid by the city.

As one reporter spoke of the Baltimore Police, he described the city police garage as, "A used car lot." The detective cars were every color imaginable, and there were absolutely no identifying marks on any of them. One officer described the department as having gotten tired of identifiable detective cars being driven through rough parts of town and hearing kids yell 'dum de dum dum' in true Dragnet fashion.

Besides the multi-colored fleet of detective cars, their black squad cars were used for regular patrol, and their white cars were used for injury accidents, while the inspectors were relegated to large, black cars which were much like a limousine.

In 1955, there were 103 murders reported to the Baltimore Police Department. Of those, all but four had been solved. Like many other major metropolitan departments, the homicide division was clearly the busiest.

Officer Zukowski was a 43-year-old veteran of the Baltimore Police, and his partner, Officer Kidd, listened as the excited man pointed out the 'wanted' ad in the back of his newly purchased Bronze Thrills magazine. He also pointed out the man in the ad was now a block ahead of them in a crowd. The officers quickly headed out with Seymour Hale, collectively figuring this would be a wild goose chase.

Buchanon was standing at the traffic light at Fayette and Ann Street looking around and noticed two officers coming toward him. Mindful of his surroundings, he could tell they were watching him as they approached. There was no way they could be looking for him, but to play it safe while trying to mix in with several other people on the street, he casually walked into a candy store. Trying to look nonchalant, he began to peruse the selection of sweet treats inside the glass showcase when he heard the small chime over the door as it opened. He glanced out of the corner of his eye, trying not to look obvious, and his heart began pounding harder as his breaths became quicker.

While Seymour Hale waited outside the candy store, the officers cautiously approached their prey. Kidd stood to one side of the suspect at the ready as Zukowski confronted the man standing at the candy counter. Zukowski spoke first, asking the suspect for his name, and Nealy Buchanon replied, "Howard Herrick." The officer asked 'Herrick' for identification, or anything with his name on it, and Buchanon pulled some pay stub envelopes from his pocket showing the name of Howard Herrick, but he had no picture identification. Having been shown the wanted ad, which listed Howard and Myra Herrick's names, Zukowski had instant confirmation the man he was talking to was the wanted killer.

The pay stubs wouldn't do. There was no way Zukowski and Kidd were going to take his word. Zukowski politely told the suspect he would have to accompany them down to the station, so they could try to confirm his identity, telling him of the 'wanted' ad in Bronze Thrills. Kidd used the phone in the candy store and called for a patrol wagon.

Buchanon's breathing became even heavier. His heart was pounding stronger than it ever had before. He began to break into a cold sweat. He knew he was trapped and there was nothing he could do.

As the three men stood in the candy store, an obvious strategy to keep their suspect from running down a crowded street if he got the urge to try to escape, Patrolman Zukowski pressed Buchanon for more information, when he asked, "Are you wanted anywhere?" "Well, you've got me," the killer said. "I might as well tell you. I'm wanted for breaking and entering in Michigan. My name is Buchanon, and I escaped the penitentiary there." [28] Already knowing the answer, Zukowski was quick to respond, "Did you hurt anyone?" The two officers knew what Buchanon had done, but they received their expected response, "No." The veteran officer was persistent, and it wasn't long before Nealy Buchanon told the officers about the brutal crime in Michigan and how he had killed the Michigan chicken farmer and his wife.

The black squad car glistened in the morning sun with the red rotating beacon flashing, as the officer pulled to the curb to pick up Zukowski and Kidd's arrest. A large, bullet-shaped siren was mounted to the left front corner of the fender, with a speaker mounted on the right side. The Baltimore Police shield was displayed proudly across the door.

Nealy J. Buchanon was taken quietly into custody. Now in handcuffs, the 6-foot 1-inch man from Detroit ducked his head to slide into the back seat of the 1956 Ford sedan police car. With Zukowski and Kidd seated on either side of Nealy, the car silently slipped into the flow of morning traffic making its way to the Baltimore Police Headquarters.

Nealy Buchanon had been captured at 11:05 am without incident.

Later that day, the man who had been enjoying his monthly copy of Bronze Thrills magazine when he had spotted the killer, learned the reward posted in his favorite magazine wasn't $300. It was much more.

CHAPTER 7

The Extradition

It was Tuesday, October 16, 1956 when Harry Doesburg's phone rang at Oakwood. On the other end of the line was Captain Edward Johnson of the State Police. Captain Johnson said, "Mr. Doesburg, we have found your man."[29] The store owner paused. He wasn't exactly sure what he had just heard, so Johnson repeated it. Harry was stunned. He heard exactly what he had been waiting to hear for so long. Tears began to well in his eyes. The store owner glanced upward to thank God. While he didn't know the immediate details of the arrest, he knew in his heart it had involved some great police work over the previous thirteen months.

Across from Oakwood, the Herrick house had become a busy place in the year since the murders. Both Harold and Lester, along with their families, had moved into the house and renovations were underway to convert the home into a two-family dwelling.

Doesburg's son, Jerry, was in Oakwood when his dad received word of Buchanon's capture. While trying to make some phone calls to relay the good news, Harry told him to head over to the Herrick home and share the news with Harold, who was working on the house. Jerry sprinted from the front door and across M-92. "They've caught Buchanon," Jerry yelled. Hearing the news, Harold Herrick was overwhelmed. Like Doesburg, he could hardly believe what Jerry had just told him. "It kind of shocked me, even though I felt they would catch him someday," he said. "No punishment, not even the atrocities I saw in Korea, would be good enough for him. There should be capital punishment. I just hope I don't see him when he isn't under guard," he continued. And like his brother, he held undying gratitude toward Harry Doesburg, when he continued, "There just aren't any words that I could say that could express my deep gratitude to Harry Doesburg. I am so grateful that it was directly from the sending of his pamphlets that Buchanon was recognized."[30]

Lester was working in Mason and had gotten word the sheriff was trying to get in touch with him. He called the sheriff's department by phone and quickly received the good news. Lester was quickly quoted by the media when he said, "I was bewildered when word came that the sheriff wanted me to call him. Then the words I had playfully listed [sic] for came. I found they had already called my sisters, Mrs. William Foreman of Williamston and Mrs. Otto Foreman of Webberville. They were as excited as I was. I don't feel any punishment they could give him will be enough. This should show that capital punishment is a must in...There just aren't words made that could express the gratitude I feel to Harry Doesburg."[31]

"BUNDLES FOR BUCHANON"—Harry Doesburg and Howard
Herrick, Jr., son of the slain elderly Stockbridge couple, Howard
and Myra Herrick, look at one of the posters that Doesburg dis-
tributed throughout the nation in the successful search for Nealy
Buchanon. (Journal photo)

Harry Doesburg and Harold Herrick.
Photo courtesy of the Lansing State Journal.

"We were all so excited, we could scarcely talk. We think some pretty strong talk should be brought about capital punishment and about alerting every householder in the whole area whenever a prisoner gets out," said Lester's wife, after she heard of Buchanon's capture.

It seemed word of the killer's capture in Baltimore spread faster than word of the murder had. More than just Stockbridge, the entire mid-Michigan area collectively breathed a sigh of relief.

Robert Mackinder, a member of the Sheriff's Posse, was quoted in the papers saying, "They caught him in the wrong place. If we had caught him in Stockbridge, it wouldn't have cost the state another c-note [sic] for his keep."[32] Cecil Cobb, another member of the Sheriff's Posse with Mackinder, had only praise for Doesburg when he was quoted by the press saying, "I'm glad he has finally been caught. I think they should learn something from Doesburg's persistence."

Later that night, Harry spoke with reporters about the arrest and his continuous efforts to find the killer of his friends when he said, "I believe I have shown that rousing public interest is the best means of apprehending criminals. This case proves that relentless work brings results."[33]

A continuous stream of cars pulled into the driveway at Oakwood throughout the day and well into the night. Car headlights streamed across the front of the store after dark, and people poured in not for groceries, but to tell Harry of a job well done. Friends, neighbors, and strangers all wanted to say congratulations to Harry Doesburg. While some hadn't agreed with his never-ending pursuit in capturing the killer, they still wanted to congratulate him and say thank you. One said, "You made it Harry. I never thought you would. I just thought that Harry's a wonderful guy and really has his heart in it, but the United States is a big place."[34] Another neighbor said, "When I think of those stacks and stacks of Bundles for Buchanon you sent out, and the crime magazines you kept telling a murderer was somewhere to be picked up—well, it's just wonderful." Still others said, "Perhaps we all learn from you, Harry. Maybe we ought to get behind the law a little more." But most everyone simply wanted to convey their thanks to God and their thanks to Harry Doesburg.

The reporters flooded Harry's store, too. Harry explained his relentless quest to one of them when he said, "I've stalked this killer through every state in the nation…Chiefs of police, FBI, crime magazines, post office clerks…sometimes a single day's mailing cost over $100 in postage, but I kept on sending them. Sometimes, friends told me I was wasting my time, but I just kept on. Just this week, I sent another ad to the Ingham County News calling attention to the fact that the year was nearly up. It was last November that I started."[35]

While Harry made statements to the press and welcomed the congratulations from friends and neighbors, he had other details he had to attend to. Sheriff Barnes had contacted him, asking if he would go to Baltimore, with him and two deputies to give the $3,000 in reward money to the man who had identified Nealy Buchanon. Harry couldn't refuse.

Breakfast at the Baltimore Police Department was less than appetizing. Nealy sat in the small, dimly lit cell as he was handed his morning fare…a bologna sandwich and a cupcake. It was the same meal he had been given the previous evening. Still hungry, he choked down the dry bread with the slice of mystery meat. The previous afternoon he had been interviewed by investigators from the Baltimore Police about the killings. On this morning, he waited for his court appearance.

He hated the Baltimore Police Department jail. Knowing he would only be there a few days, he still hated getting up at 6:00 am, then being forced to sit on a bench, or stand, until 8:00 pm when mattresses were reissued. Prisoners were not allowed to be loafing on their beds for an entire day.

It was now Wednesday morning, October 17th, and while newspapers around the state of Michigan were reporting his capture, Nealy J. Buchanon was set to be arraigned in Baltimore Central Police Court. As he stood before Judge Meyer Cardin, the charges he faced were read to him, and he was told he would be extradited to Michigan unless he chose to appeal his extradition. Nealy was ready to put the murders behind him, stop running, and return to prison. His only response to Judge Cardin was, "I'm willing to go back to Michigan."[36]

Armed with warrants for each murder, Sheriff Barnes, Deputies Phil Maiville and Duke Jenks, reporter Richard Brown, and the man who seemed to have single-handedly led the campaign for Buchanon's capture, all left Willow Run Airport near Detroit by plane heading to Baltimore to pick up the Herricks' killer.

Before leaving, Harry Doesburg had made a quick trip to the bank to obtain the reward funds.

A SLAYER WAITS

The flight was scheduled to leave at 11:05 am but was delayed two hours. At 1:05 pm, the plane raced down the runway and gently lifted toward the sky. After a quick stop in Cleveland and then Pittsburg, the plane touched down at Friendship Airport outside Baltimore. The five men were picked up by the Baltimore Police and rushed to the sprawling, six-story building housing the Baltimore Police Department, located in the heart of Baltimore.

Sheriff Barnes had chosen Maiville, who wasn't very big, because he knew Maiville liked to 'mix it up' occasionally and wasn't afraid of anything. By the time they had finally arrived, Buchanon had already agreed to return to Michigan, so they would leave on Thursday morning. Barnes' hope was to get Buchanon back to Michigan and have him arraigned by Thursday after-noon.

Nealy was brought down from the maximum secu-rity section of the jail to an interrogation room where he was interviewed by Sheriff Barnes and Captain George Mintiens, chief of Baltimore's Homicide Divi-sion.

After the interrogation, the investigators all agreed Buchanon didn't hesitate at all when he confessed to the double murder and seemed relieved his running was over. He recited his social security number without any hesitation, and his demeanor was very calm. They even described the killer as being quiet while giving his confession to the murders. Barnes noted Buchanon had told them he had never made any effort to conceal his identity, but Nealy had grown a large mustache.

Harry Doesburg had his own business to attend to. He had already told reporters of his intentions. He was going to pay out the $3,000 in reward money to the man who had identified Nealy Buchanon from the pulp fiction magazine. A large portion of the reward was cash put forward by Doesburg himself, while the rest of the money was raised through the public's own subscription.

The Police Commissioner in Baltimore made a recommendation and suggested not only should Seymour Hale be paid the reward, but a small portion should be given to the officers who made the arrest. Harry agreed. Hale received $2,000, while both Zukowski and Kidd each received $200. The remaining balance of $600 was paid to the Baltimore Police benefit fund, a worthy cause in Harry's eyes.

DIVIDING REWARD MONEY—Harry Doesburg, fourth from right, presented $2,000 to Seymour Hale, right, and $1,000 to Chief Inspector Fred L. Fard of the Baltimore police department to divide between Officers Henry Zukowski and George William Kidd and the Baltimore police fund after the recapture of Nealy Buchanon.

(left to right) Baltimore Police Chief Inspector Fred Fard, Officer Zukowski, Officer Kidd, Harry Doesburg, and Seymour Hale.
Photo courtesy of the Lansing State Journal.

While Buchanon's arraignment in the Baltimore Central Police Court was taking place, Captain Mintiens was deluged with queries. Reporters wanted to know the name of the man who had identified Michigan's murderer. Stalling, Mintiens politely told them he didn't know the name, but it certainly wouldn't be difficult to eventually get the information to the press. They wanted an interview.

The Ingham County Sheriff and his entourage were up and ready to go early on Thursday morning. The deputies wore their uniforms, while their boss wore a matching beige-colored, double-breasted suit and pants. Three pens were pushed into the outer pocket of the suit and a small pendant in the shape of a revolver adorned his tie bar. They arrived at the Baltimore Police Central District just before 6:00 am to pick up Nealy Buchanon, and at 6:15, the killer was released to the sheriff and his deputies. Baltimore Police squad cars whisked the six men back to Friendship Airport.

At 7:10 am, the men walked across the tarmac to board their Capital Airlines flight with their final destination being Willow Run Airport.

Buchanon was wearing a black dress shirt opened at the collar, with a gray tweed suit coat and another coat folded over his secured hands. He hesitated as they approached the propeller-driven airplane. He had never flown before, and he was clearly nervous. After boarding, he sat between Deputy Maiville and Deputy Jenks. Sheriff Barnes and Richard Brown, the reporter from the Ingham County Democrat, sat behind the suspect and his guards. As the rest of the passengers boarded, Buchanon became more anxious. He wasn't sure what to expect or when to expect it. As the pilot began to start the engines, the propellers on both sides of the plane began to churn. Black smoke poured from the engines. As the propellers turned faster and faster, they became invisible as Nealy watched them. Buchanon, with his hands secured in front, quickly grabbed the back of the seat in front of him. Maiville and Jenks watched with interest as Nealy Buchanon never let go of the seat for the entire flight to Pittsburg.

Rain and fog had set in and Capital Airlines delayed their flights to Cleveland. Because of the delay, Barnes changed their flight to Northwest Airlines. An hour had been lost. While waiting for the Northwest Airlines flight, Barnes did an interview with the press over the phone. In the interview, Barnes said the killer, "Seemed relieved that it was over, but felt no personal remorse for the deaths of the Herricks."[37]

Barnes also phoned his department during their delay and told them of the change in airlines and their expected arrival time.

As the flight continued on Northwest Airlines, the weather had not improved in the Detroit area. Buchanon nervously looked out the window while still grasping the back of the seat in front of him with great trepidation. As the pilot began his descent, the fear in Buchanon's eyes became even more evident. The fog was thick and nothing could be seen until the plane dropped to within a few hundred feet of the ground. Fearing the worst, Buchanon spoke up saying, "Can that man find the ground?" referring to the pilot. In jest, Sheriff Barnes said from behind his prisoner, "One way or the other."[38]

It seemed the story of Nealy J. Buchanon, the double murder, his capture and his return to Michigan, must have been featured in every paper along the eastern seaboard. At each airport along the return trip, people paused and stared, while there were only silent whispers.

At 12:37 pm, the Northwest Airlines from Pittsburg carrying the killer of Howard and Myra Herrick touched down at Willow Run. It had only been 48 hours since his arrest and he was already back in Michigan. Two squad cars from the Ingham County Sheriff's Department were there to greet Sheriff Barnes and his prisoner. As soon as their baggage was collected, the two sheriff cars left the airport, heading west along M-112. When they reached M-92 west of Chelsea, they turned to the north and headed directly toward Stockbridge.

Buchanon and Sheriff Barnes at Willow Run Airport.

The two-car procession made its way along the two-lane state highway. As they approached the intersection of M-36, they passed a small family farm; the same farm where Howard and Myra Herrick were bludgeoned to death the year before. Buchanon stared forward, never acknowledging the landmark. The sheriff wondered to himself if his prisoner had even recognized the farm.

Because Nealy J. Buchanon had confessed to the murders and had seemed very cooperative, the plan was to move quickly. When they arrived back at the Ingham County Jail, the killer would be interviewed and then taken before Justice of the Peace Roy W. Adams in Mason, where he would be arraigned and afforded the opportunity of a preliminary examination. He could also waive the examination. If he chose to have it, it would be a simple hearing. The only purpose would be to determine if a crime had been committed and whether there was probable cause to believe Buchanon had committed it. If Nealy demanded the preliminary exam, Barnes and Prosecuting Attorney Chamberlain were ready to proceed. If he waived the exam, which everyone expected, the case would be forwarded to the circuit court in Ingham County. Buchanon would be arraigned there and given the opportunity to either plead guilty or demand a trial.

Sheriff Barnes asked Buchanon if he wanted to speak by phone with his wife, Jeanette. "I just don't want to talk to her now," he told Barnes. "I'll be glad to have her write me, or visit me in prison, but there's no point now in talking with her over the phone," he said.[39]

CHAPTER 8

The Confession

The Ingham County Jail had been built in 1927, and at the time, was the best of the best, but it had been almost thirty years since it opened. The sheriff's office and the lobby were located on the first floor in the front of the brown three-story brick building. In the rear of the main floor was an area referred to as the bullpen where prisoners were brought in after their arrest and booked. Prisoner cells for men were located on the second floor of the building. There was room for 48 prisoners, but at night, there could be up to eight prisoners sleeping in each cell. During daylight hours, the prisoners were divided into two day rooms. There were strict guidelines in place to prevent any contact between prisoners and the visitors, so voice contact was made using speaker boxes. The third floor of the building was reserved for female prisoners, laundry, and food services. An elevator was used to convey the laundry and food to different levels of the building.

The accused killer was brought down from his second floor cell to Sheriff Barnes' office on the first floor. Whatever fear Nealy Buchanon had when Officers Zukowski and Kidd approached him in Baltimore was now gone. He seemed genuinely relieved his days of trying to avoid the law were over.

He sat in the small room at the Ingham County Sheriff's Office smoking a cigarette as Sheriff Barnes met with Assistant Prosecuting Attorney Jack Warren privately.

Buchanon inhaled deeply on a cigarette as he stared at the wooden table in front of him. He was still dressed in the black shirt and tweed sport coat. Reaching toward an ashtray on the table, he rubbed the smoldering cigarette into the bottom of the tray and pinched the end as stale smoke slowly swirled upward.

It had been decided ahead of time that Warren, who would be responsible for prosecuting Nealy, would ask the questions during the interrogation. Sheriff Barnes and Captain Babcock would also be in the room, along with Peter Treleaven, another assistant prosecutor. Anything said would be recorded by Paul Skarstad, a court stenographer.

The door creaked as it swung slowly open, and the law enforcement officials walked in.

Nealy looked up, his maroon-colored eyes sizing the men up and down. Even though he recognized Barnes, there was a noticeable tension in the room. It was 5:24 pm.

Warren addressed the killer first by introducing himself, then telling him who Skarstad was and what his job would be. Buchanon already knew. Jack Warren continued by introducing everyone else in the room and making sure Buchanon understood who each person was. Buchanon nodded.

"Do you understand that this statement must be given by you voluntarily?" asked Warren.

"Yes," Nealy said.

Just in case the killer didn't understand, Jack Warren restated it differently, saying, "In other words, we cannot force you to give a statement, so if you want to tell us something, you must do so voluntarily."

Another yes from Nealy.

The attorney representing the People then told Buchanon the statement he was about to make might be used either for him or against him.

Again, "Yes," from Buchanon.

In the stenographic report, which Buchanon later signed, his answer to the statement being used either for him or against him had inadvertently been left out. When he was reviewing his statement for accuracy later, he placed his initials, N.J.B., after writing the word "yes" next to the question.

Warren continued his questions regarding Nealy Buchanon's ability and understanding of the proceedings and the voluntariness of his statements. He asked Buchanon if anyone had made any promises in return for him talking about the murder.

"No, sir," said Buchanon.

"Has anyone used any physical force on you to get you to give us this statement?" Warren asked.

Again, "No, sir."

Finally, the assistant prosecutor asked if he was giving the statement of his own free will.

Buchanon replied, "Freely and voluntarily."

Sheriff Barnes, who had sat down in one of the wooden chairs across from Nealy, slowly leaned back, crossing his arms.

Jack Warren's early questioning focused on Nealy's

full name and spelling and continued into whether or not he was married. When asked where his wife lived, he told Warren she lived in Detroit, then hesitated, looked over at the sheriff and said, "Pardon me, Sheriff Barnes, was that the same address in Detroit?" Barnes told him she had moved, and Buchanon asked if he could have the address where she was living now.

The assistant prosecutor interrupted, "As near as you know, she last lived in Detroit. Is that correct?"

"Yes," he replied.

"Nealy, do you remember September of 1955?" asked Warren.

Nealy did remember, saying he had been an inmate at Jackson Prison, then told Warren and the others in the room, as near as he could remember that it was on or about the 1st or 2nd of September when he left the prison.

The assistant prosecutor continued his line of questioning when he asked how Buchanon had accomplished leaving the prison.

Nealy didn't hesitate when he said, "Drove away a truck. An institution truck." He said it was around 4:00 am when he left the prison and he was headed away from Jackson.

"Did there come a time when you left the truck?" Warren asked.

Buchanon told Warren he had left the truck behind a large building. He thought it was a school building, and it was in a field behind the building. Asked about where he went after he abandoned the truck, he said he began walking through fields and wooded areas as much as he could.

Warren was getting close to the point in the interview where he wanted to be very specific in his questioning. He asked the suspect if there was a time after

A SLAYER WAITS

he abandoned the truck when he came across a farm.

Nealy said he had and told the lawyer it was on a blacktop road near an intersection. He continued answering the questions, saying there was a gas station, a barn, and a couple of houses at the intersection. He told Warren it had gotten dark by the time he reached the barn, and he had spent the entire day getting to that point.

Nealy continued his detailed statement to the lawyer who would lead the prosecution against him. He said, "Walked by the house and looked in, and I headed for the barn." He added the barn was open. "Well, there was a car sitting in the doorway, and I looked over the car and looked in it," he said. "I had some cigaretes [sic] I wanted to smoke, and I was mainly looking for a match in the car," he continued. He said after finding some matches, he smoked a cigarette.

He continued, "Well, I stood there for a while thinking, trying to figure out a way to get away from around that area, and I decided I would lay down and go to sleep that night…yes, I went in the back of the haystack and arranged it so I wouldn't be seen and laid down there, and I went to sleep after a while."

Warren wanted him to clarify where he had laid down. "Was that behind some bales of hay?" he asked.

Buchanon said it was, and he said he fixed the bales of hay so he could see the door to the barn. He described how he had slept that night, and he told his interrogator it was still dark when he awoke the next morning.

Nealy continued, "The first thing I did was come up and look out the doorway and try to figure out what time it was. It was still dark. I looked out there and it was dark and I saw the farmhouse. The light was on and the people were stirring around in there, so I decided I would fix things as I planned, to get this car and get some money so I could leave Michigan."

"Let me understand this: You figured and planned by which you could get a car and some money, right?" Warren asked.

The killer replied, "Yes."

Warren pressed him further by asking, "What was that plan, Nealy?"

"To knock out the man and take his money," was Buchanon's reply.

Jack Warren, knowing he was getting close to having the killer admit to premeditation, asked, "How did you intend to knock out the man? Did you take any step toward setting that situation up?"

Buchanon continued then with the description of his plot by saying, "It didn't look so hot, because he might see me or might hear me, and I thought of something else. They had a big chopping block to dress his chickens with or something of that sort, and I decided to move that up on the rafters, and when he come in [sic], I would drop it down on him and knock him [sic]. I would almost kill him."

Warren didn't give Nealy a chance to think about what he had just said. He continued, "You would almost kill him?"

Just as Warren hadn't hesitated, neither did Nealy when he replied, "If that block hit him, it would have killed him."

Jack Warren was curious if Nealy had been successful in moving the chopping block to the overhead rafters. He said, "Now, do I understand this: You moved that block up onto the rafter or beam? Overhead? Did you get up on the rafter or beam?"

"Yes," replied the killer.

"All right. Now, do you remember, or did there

come a time when a man came into the barn? And did he rummage around and work about the car?" Warren asked.

"He was removing some bags of some kind, food, from the car," Nealy said. He told the attorney the man hadn't seen him, and the man had left the barn, going back into the house. Buchanon said he stayed up there for another fifteen minutes or so until the man returned to the barn then drove off in the car. Buchanon got down from the beam, and the block remained where he had placed it.

Buchanon continued, "Well, I come down [sic] and walked around a little bit and said to myself: 'That has gone by. Couldn't do that,' so I decided I would stick around a while until I got a chance to get out. It was getting light then. I would stick around until I got a chance to get away, and during the course of that time, I kept my eye on the house, and I noticed the woman was getting ready to leave, was coming out of the house, and I said, 'Well, I will go in the house and get me something to eat and get some clothes and get ready to get out of there.'"

Buchanon relayed how he had gone into the house and had gotten clothes and food. He said he had found a pair of trousers, a shirt, and a jacket. He couldn't find any money. He told Warren had gotten a tomato and an egg, then a bottle of beer.

Buchanon said he went back to the barn and changed his clothes, then threw them in a closet, "...Somewhere where they kept the old dirty clothes. In a clothes closet."

Knowing the bloody prison clothing had been found in the barn near where the bodies had been hidden, Warren immediately picked up on the discrepancy. Buchanon really wasn't quite sure where he had changed. Warren asked if he had changed in the barn or the house, and Nealy then told him he had changed in the barn.

The prosecutor moved on. Buchanon told him he decided to lay around until the man returned from work, so he stayed in the barn.

Jack Warren had to have Buchanon describe what he had used to kill Howard and Myra Herrick and where he had gotten it from. He continued the interrogation by asking, "Now, were there certain tools in that barn?"

"Yes, sir," Nealy said.

Warren continued, "Did you take any of those tools?"

As Buchanon looked at some photos from the crime scene, he said, "Yes...I think I took that hammer there, and laid it somewhere. I rummaged around the barn for a while looking around in there and sat down and smoked and laid down and rested. You know, just laying around in there doing north [sic] much. Just laying in there."

Again, Warren asked, "Was that waiting for the man to come back?"

"Yes," the killer said.

Buchanon continued, describing how he had waited all day for the farmer's return.

The questioning attorney continued to build his case of premeditation. He asked Buchanon if there was time when the man did come back.

"He came back that evening...It was daylight," he said.

Warren slowed his pace a little. Being very specific now, he asked, "Now, where were you when you first became aware that he had returned?"

Buchanon continued without hesitation, saying,

"Over by the tool bench."

Warren, again, very specific in his questioning, asked, "Do you know what you did with it [the hammer] when you took it away?"

Nealy's glance turned toward the ceiling as he tried to remember, saying, "I think I laid it somewhere near where I could get at it in case he came in. I would be at the advantage, where I could see him and he couldn't see me."

"Now, when you first saw him and you were standing by the tools, where was he?" Warren asked.

Buchanon described how his victim drove into the barn. He described the car as a green Desoto and how Howard Herrick was alone.

Asked what he did when Herrick drove in the barn, Buchanon said, "I realized he was in. He stopped the car, was opening the door and he came a...I came around the tool bench and walked around him and met him as he was getting out."

"Did you walk around the front or the back of the car?" asked Warren.

"I walked around the back," was Nealy's reply.

"And you say you approached him as he was getting out of the car?" Warren continued.

Another yes from Buchanon.

Warren casually led the killer through the crime scene so he could remember exactly what he had done thirteen months earlier. He asked, "Did you say anything to him or did he say anything to you?"

Buchanon straightened up in his chair, and looked down toward the table as he continued, "He spoke to me and asked me what I was doing there...I told him I was admiring his tools and I had that in my hand."

Up to this point, their assumption was Buchanon had bludgeoned the Herricks with a ball-peen hammer.

"By 'that,' what do you mean?" asked Warren.

"The grinder," Nealy replied.

"You had a grinder in your hand?" Warren asked.

Another yes.

"And you told him you were admiring his tools, is that right?" Jack Warren said again.

Again, another yes from Buchanon.

Buchanon continued to describe the scene. He said, "I asked him, did he want to sell it [sic]…No, he didn't want to sell it…He sort of turned his head and I struck him with it."

Warren, keeping his cool, asked, "Where did you strike him?"

Nealy paused, trying to remember exactly where he had struck Howard Herrick with the grinding wheel. He said, "In his forehead, I think…With the grinder…He fell down."

Warren slowed his pace once more when he asked, "Now, at the time you struck him, Nealy, what were your thoughts or intentions? Why did you strike him?"

"To knock him out and get his money and his keys to his car and leave," Nealy confessed.

Buchanon continued describing the scene and describing exactly what Howard Herrick was wearing when he was attacked, including the baseball hat.

"After the man was struck, you say he fell to the floor?" asked the prosecuting attorney.

"Yes, sir…He was breathing…I reached down and turned him over so I could get his wallet," said Nealy, showing no remorse as he described his own actions. "I started to get the wallet…I just felt it and reached in to grab it. That is when his wife came in."

Nealy described in detail what Myra Herrick was wearing, though he had difficulty in estimating her age. When asked if he could recall the color of her hair, he said, "I am not certain. It seemed to me like it was brownish, sort of like, like his hair," as he pointed toward Sheriff Barnes.

Asked if Myra had said anything when she came into the barn, Buchanon continued, "She said, 'What is happening here?' I didn't say nothing to her [sic]. I just started hitting her."

Barnes unfolded his arms as Buchanon continued to describe the gruesome scene.

Warren asked, "Was she standing right at the side of you?"

"Right behind me. She come up on the side. I was facing him this way. She came in about from here to that doorway there, and asked what was happening. I rose up and started towards her and she sort of looked around and seen him [sic] and started screaming."

Warren, still keeping his professionalism, asked, "What did you tell her?"

Buchanon, without hesitation, said, "I struck her...It was either that weapon or that thing there. I am not sure."

Jack Warren tried to clarify by asking, "Either the grinder or the hammer?"

Buchanon replied, "Yes, or the hammer."

The questioning continued when the prosecutor asked, "What did the woman do you [sic] when you approached her?"

Nealy continued, "She put her hands up, she seen [sic] me get ready to strike her. She put her hands up like that...She kept on screaming...I hit her again."

Surprised at Buchanon's willingness to describe the murder in such detail, Warren knew he couldn't stop. He continued, "Did she fall after the second time?"

"She fell, yes," was the reply.

Warren wanted more clarification. He pressed

Buchanon for more details by asking, "Now, do you specifically remember whether she was hit two times, or could she have been hit more times?"

"She could have been hit more times, but I know it was two times because the first blow didn't hit her right or something, and she started screaming and I hit her again. I could have hit her again. I am not sure...I could have hit her more than two times, but I know I hit her twice," he said.

Warren knew Howard Herrick had been struck at least twice. He led Nealy back by asking, "What else happened then?"

"Well, after she fell, I looked around and he was getting up and coming towards me...I hit him," the killer said. When asked with what, he said, "Whatever I had. I think I had...I still think I had that thing."

"You are referring to the grinder?" Warren asked of the prisoner.

Buchanon acknowledged the grinder, then continued, "After I hit him, he fell down again and laid there...Seemed like he was breathing to me at that time."

Warren wanted more. He wanted to prove Buchanon knew he had killed Howard Herrick. He asked, "Was there anything unusual about that breathing?"

Buchanon knew Warren wanted him to describe what his victim's breathing sounded like. He said, "Sort of a rattle."

When asked about Myra's breathing, he said she was quiet.

More specifics. Warren wanted as much as he could get. He asked the killer, "Were either of these people bleeding?"

The killer replied, "They were bleeding slightly about the head...I went through the man's pockets and got his money, his wallet, cigaret [sic] lighter and his watch...I thought I would move out of the doorway in case anybody would see them. I pulled them around some bales of hay there in the barn...After I pulled them around I put some hay on them...Covered them up."

Jack Warren, knowing he would have enough to convict Nealy J. Buchanon, continued his questioning. He asked for more specifics on the Herricks by asking the killer, "Were both of them breathing at that time, do you know?"

Buchanon, again without any hesitation, or any attempt to lie, said, "I don't think so. Both of them were quiet. I am not sure whether they were breathing or not."

Asked to tell what he did next, he said, "I went through the car looking around for the keys...I tried to cross the wires but I didn't know how to do it."

Again, Warren knew every detail of the crime scene and led the suspect through the crime scene in minute detail, asking, "Did you ever succeed in starting the car?"

"No sir. I walked out of the barn and crossed the field, crossed the cornfield," he said.

Again, Jack Warren knew what had been recovered, but he wanted to verify Buchanon's story by seeing if he had kept anything he had taken from the barn. He continued with, "Now, you have indicated that you removed certain items and things from the man's person. Did you keep all those items or did you discard any of them?"

Buchanon nodded as he said, "I discarded his bank book and his check book, I think, in the field." He confirmed to the assistant prosecutor it was in the field. He continued, "I cut across the cornfield over to a store across the highway on the right hand side...I bought a pie...I caught a ride going into Mason."

Warren asked him what kind of vehicle it was he

had ridden in.

"In a pickup truck," Buchanon said, describing two men in the truck.

The lawyer continued, "Where did you go in Mason?"

"The bus terminal. The bus station," he said. "To catch a bus to Lansing," he continued. When asked how he had gotten to Lansing, he told the men he had caught a cab. He described two men in the cab he had taken from Mason, confirming it was still daylight. Asked where he went when he arrived in Lansing, he told them he had gone to the bus terminal.

Pressing him further, Warren asked, "What was your intention when you went to the bus terminal?"

"To get a ticket to Chicago...I just thought Chicago would be a good place to go."

Asked about his reason for wanting to go to Chicago, he said it was a big city, and he figured it would be more trouble trying to find him in a big city than there would be in a small one.

Now asked to elaborate, Buchanon said, "The bus was leaving too late. I decided on one to New York."

"You mean you didn't want to sit around the bus station?" Warren asked. "Did you go to New York?" he continued.

"Yes," said Nealy.

Jack Warren shifted gears in his questioning, turning to finances the killer might have still had by that time. He asked Buchanon, "Now, as near as you recall, Nealy, how much money did you have on you when you drove this truck off?"

Buchanon said, "About $43."

"I don't think you understand me. When you drove away from Jackson," Warren said.

Nealy now understood the question and told Warren he thought he had two dollars. When asked how much money was in the purse or pocketbook of the man on the farm, he said $43. Warren clarified he was referring to the man Nealy had killed. It was.

Buchanon was then asked if he had used some of the money to go to New York. He answered yes.

The questioning now turned to what Nealy Buchanon had done when he arrived in New York. He described getting a job at a cafe-diner in Brooklyn. He said he only worked a day then come back into New York. He described how he had stayed three or four days until he had enough money to leave. He told the investigators he was heading to North Carolina but stopped off in Baltimore to get a job and raise more money so he could continue on to North Carolina.

Warren, now refocusing on the date of the murder, asked the killer, "Now, just reviewing for the moment, Nealy, you would have been at this farmhouse on either September 2nd or 3rd, is that right?"

"Right," he said.

Asked if he could be more specific on which date it was, he said he couldn't be sure but it would have been one of those two days.

Refocusing on the clothing change, Jack Warren asked Nealy, "In regard to the changing of your clothes, Nealy, could it have been that you hit this man and this woman first and then changed your clothes?"

"Might have but I don't think so. I think I changed my clothes...my clothes first."

Warren asked if there were any other items taken from the scene.

"Yes, an identification card and a union card and some more stuff. He had a driver's license, I remember...I kept it," said Buchanon.

Asked if he ever made use of it, he acknowledged he had used it in both New York and Baltimore.

He was then asked to clarify what the name was on the card. His reply was, "Howard S. Herrick."

Warren then asked about physical characteristics listed on the identification card, and Buchanon said "The union card didn't show anything and the license didn't show anything. None of that had anything on it."

Jack Warren was satisfied. He and Sheriff Barnes made eye contact, then glanced at Captain Babcock. His attention turned back to the killer. He asked Nealy, "Is there anything further, Nealy, which you would care to tell me about these facts or this incident?"

As Nealy Buchanon lit another cigarette, inhaled and blew smoke into the air, he said, "I think that about covers it all as far I can remember."

Assistant Prosecuting Attorney Warren wanted to make sure Nealy J. Buchanon understood everything when he said, "Now again, I want to make certain that you understand that what you have told me has been voluntary on your part, is that right?"

Buchanon acknowledged it was.

Warren continued, "And no one has made you any promises to get you to tell me that, have they?"

Nealy answered, "No."

Again, Warren asked, "And you have told me of your own free will?"

Another yes from Buchanon.

"And no one has used any physical force upon you, have they?" Warren asked him.

"No," was the reply.

Nearing the end of Nealy J. Buchanon's confession to the murder of Howard and Myra Herrick, Warren said to the slayer, "Now, after these notes have been transcribed and you have had an opportunity to read the transcript, will you be willing to sign the statement?"

Nealy said, "Yes, sir."

Nealy Buchanon's confession ended at 6:00 pm.

After the transcription of the confession, Nealy read it through, then signed and dated the form under a statement that read:

> *"I, Nealy Joseph Buchanon, being first duly sworn, on oath, state: That I have read the above and foregoing statement, consisting of 27 pages, in addition to this one on which my signature appears; that I understand each of the questions therein contained, and that each of the answers as given by me and set down in this transcript of testimony is the truth."*[40]

After the 36-minute confession, Buchanon was taken back to his cell. A photographer took one last photo as he stood near the front of the small, confined area in his black dress shirt and gray tweed coat, with black suede shoes. He slowly inhaled on another cigarette as the flash from the camera went off, never flinching, and completely at ease.

Buchanon was allowed to be interviewed by reporters as he stood in the cell. He was calm and described as being almost impulsive as he spoke of the murders. He offered advice to the reporters saying, "Stay close to your mother and don't drink." He also told them he was tired of running.

In his brief interview with reporters, Nealy said at one point a girlfriend had recognized his photo in a wanted ad and had confronted him about it. He was able to convince her it wasn't him, and immediately after that, he left for Philadelphia. He was only gone a short time, then came back to Baltimore.

In retelling the story of his capture, Buchanon told the reporters he had negotiated a ride out of state and was only six hours away from leaving for California when he was caught.

The Honorable Roy Adams, Mason's Justice of the Peace, waited patiently in his office. He had received a call from the jail letting him know Nealy Buchanon would be brought over for his arraignment. Meanwhile, Buchanon had finished eating in his cell. It was almost 8:00 pm.

Ingham County Prosecuting Attorney Charles Chamberlain conducted the arraignment of the killer. The 39-year-old chief law enforcement official for Ingham County had been born on the east side of Ingham County in 1917. He had earned his bachelor's degree and his law degree from the University of Virginia. He first served in World War II, and after earning the law degree, he worked in private practice, then as an Internal Revenue Service agent in the United States Treasury Department. Before taking over as the Ingham County Prosecutor, he worked as an assistant prosecuting attorney and had served as legal counsel to the Michigan State Senate Judiciary Committee. While Buchanon's case was before the public eye, Chamberlain was actively running a campaign for Michigan's 6th Congressional District seat.

A SLAYER WAITS

Buchanon speaks with reporters upon his return to the Ingham County Jail. Photo courtesy of the Ingham County Sheriff's Office.

Buchanon stood before the local Justice of the Peace in handcuffs while deputies stood nearby. Both Prosecuting Attorney Chamberlain and Sheriff Barnes were there also. The magistrate began the brief court appearance by checking to see if Nealy had been made aware of his rights. Adams asked the prosecutor and was told Buchanon had not been made aware of his rights at this particular hearing.

Adams addressed Nealy when he began the hearing by asking, "You are Nealy Buchanon?"

"Yes, sir," was Buchanon's reply.

Adams continued, "I have a complaint by Willard P. Barnes that on the 3rd day of September, 1955, at the Township of Stockbridge, County of Ingham, Nealy Buchanon did then and there murder one Myra Herrick in violation of Section 316 of Act 328, Public Acts of 1931, Compiled Laws of 1948, Section 750.316, Michigan Statutes Annotated Section 28.548. In other words, you are charged with murdering the lady out there on the 3rd of September, 1955. Now at this time you can ask for an examination in my court, or you can take your choice to take this directly into circuit court. Do you understand that?"

Another yes from Buchanon.

"You have been through this procedure at previous occasions, have you, so you understand what it is," Adams asked.

Still another yes from the killer.

"Now which do you wish to do? Do you wish to have an examination, or do you wish to waive that examination?" the magistrate asked.

Buchanon said, "I wish to waive examination."

Adams made sure he understood what Nealy was saying, when he asked, "…And take it directly into circuit court?"

"Yes, sir," was Buchanon's reply.

The Honorable Roy Adams repeated the charge again for Nealy Buchanon, stating the second charge was for the murder of Howard Herrick.

Buchanon understood by saying, "Yes, sir."

Adams continued, "That was the man. Out in Stockbridge Township, the 3rd day of September, 1955. The same charge. Now what do you wish to do in respect to that charge?"

Buchanon, without any hesitation said, "Waive the examination."

Again, Adam's wanted to be sure he understood what Buchanon's wishes were, so he asked, "Do you wish to waive examination?"

Another affirmation from Buchanon.

The hearing was almost over. Adams said, "Well, it is the order of this court that on each of these charges, you shall be held without bail to appear in the Circuit Court for the County of Ingham on the 19th day of October 1956 at 1:30 pm at the courtroom in the City of Lansing."

The prosecutor interrupted, saying, "May it please your honor, we would like to have that at 9:30 am. In the morning."[41]

The entire arraignment took no more than five minutes, and Buchanon was returned to his cell. The following day would be a busy day for the double murderer, and pivotal for years to come.

CHAPTER 9

The Degree of Guilt

Nealy Buchanon was up early. The morning breakfast at the jail was scant, but it would have to do. He was allowed to shower, dress, and then sat on his bunk waiting for his escort to Lansing, a quick 20-minute drive from Mason. He didn't know it, but the route to the court in Lansing would be the same route the cab had taken thirteen months earlier.

While Mason was the county seat and part of the Ingham County Circuit Court was located there, there was another part of the Circuit Court located at the Lansing City Hall.

Two deputies met Buchanon at the door to his cell and placed handcuffs on him. He was escorted downstairs and took his seat in the back of an Ingham County sheriff's car. The deputies made the short drive to the corner of Capital Avenue and Ottawa Street in Lansing where Lansing City Hall stood, escorting their prisoner into the circuit court courtroom of the Honorable Marvin J. Salmon. Nealy was instructed to take a seat at the defense table.

The prosecuting attorney entered the dingy courtroom. In addition to the prosecuting attorney, there was a Deputy Court Clerk already in the room and a court officer. Just as the prosecutor took a seat at his table opposite the killer, Judge Salmon entered the courtroom. Everyone stood until the judge took his seat.

Chamberlain began the arraignment much like he had the night before in front of Justice of the Peace Roy Adams by asking the killer if he was Nealy Buchanon. He reread the same charges Nealy had heard the night before.

Judge Salmon cut in, asking if Nealy understood the charge.

"Yes, your honor," he said.

Salmon was a strict judge and he ran a tight courtroom. He expected attorneys appearing before him to be prepared. He had been raised on a farm in Livingston County during the early 1900s and had obtained his law degree from Wayne State University. In 1934, he settled in Lansing, and in 1939, he was hired as an assistant prosecuting attorney in Ingham County. He held the position for six years, and in 1945, he was appointed as a municipal judge in Lansing. Two years later, Governor Kim Sigler appointed him to fill a circuit court vacancy after Judge Paul Eger had passed away. When Salmon was appointed as the circuit judge for Ingham County, he was the youngest sitting judge on the bench.

Judge Salmon continued, "The Court wishes to advise you that you are entitled to be represented by a lawyer, and if you are not financially able to employ one, and will so advise the Court, the Court will see that you have a lawyer. Do you understand that?"

Again, Nealy said, "Yes, sir."

The Honorable Judge Marvin Salmon, circa 1950.

The judge followed up saying, "The Court also wishes to inform you, you are entitled to have a trial, either before a jury, or before the Court without a jury. Do you understand that?"

"Yes," the defendant said.

"How do you wish to plead, guilty or not guilty?" Judge Salmon asked.

Nealy said, "Guilty, your honor."

The judge, as a matter of procedure, wanted to make sure Nealy hadn't been promised anything, or been threatened in order to plead guilty. He continued his follow-up questioning of Nealy by asking, "Has anyone made you any promise of any kind to induce you to plead guilty?"

Buchanon said, "No, sir."

"Has anyone stated to you if you would plead guilty he would secure leniency from the Court?" the judge continued.

Again, "No, sir."

"Then you are pleading guilty because you actually are guilty?" Salmon asked.

"Yes, sir," Nealy Buchanon said.

Judge Salmon, like many other circuit court judges around the state, took a recess from the proceedings to have a conference in his chambers with Nealy, and no one other than Nealy. It was an accepted practice, and there was no court record made of the in-chambers conference. Speaking privately with Buchanon would allow the killer to explain why he was guilty without the pressure of the victims' family, the police, or other attorneys listening.

After a short time, Judge Salmon and Nealy Buchanon returned to the courtroom in Lansing City Hall.

Judge Salmon, now back on the record, said, "Let the record show that the Court has conferred with the accused relative to the circumstances in each one of these crimes, is convinced that he committed the crime, and that his plea was freely, understandingly, and voluntarily made, without undue influence, compulsion, or duress and without promise of leniency. Therefore, his pleas are accepted, and he is remanded to the custody of the county sheriff to await the taking of testimony of witnesses to determine the degree of the crime, and for sentence."[42]

The judge and the prosecutor, after a brief discussion, decided the time of the defendant's next hearing, to determine the degree of guilt, would be at 11:00 am. It was less than two hours away.

The prosecutor was prepared. He wouldn't be the only attorney asking questions of the witnesses. He would be assisted by another assistant prosecutor, Peter Treleaven, who had sat in on Nealy Buchanon's confession at the sheriff's department when Jack Warren had been interviewing the defendant the previous night. Jack Warren was also present at the circuit court for Buchanon's arraignment. His witnesses were ready. He would take testimony from Captain Babcock, Dr. Charles Black, Paul Skarstad, and Sheriff Barnes. In addition, he intended to have Buchanon's confession read into the court record, and he would present some of the evidence collected in the case, including photos taken at the murder scene, the ball-peen hammer, and the grinding wheel.

The Lansing Police Department was located in the basement of the city hall and served as a holding facility for the killer until the degree hearing began.

Buchanon had not asked for an attorney to represent him at his arraignment, even though he had been told by Judge Salmon all he needed to do was to advise the Court he wanted one, and the Court would appoint one for him.

The hearing to determine the degree of guilt was about to begin.

It was 11:10 am.

The prosecuting attorney opened the hearing by making a motion to consolidate both cases for purposes of the hearing, and Judge Salmon granted the motion.

Chamberlain called Captain Babcock to the stand.

Captain Versile Babcock began his testimony by telling the prosecutor he had known the Herricks, having met them in September of 1954.

Continuing on, Babcock told the Court he had gone to the Herrick residence on September 5, 1955 at about 11:00 pm at the request of the Herricks' son to help locate Howard and Myra.

The Captain of Detectives described going to the house first. He said one of the Herricks' sons was with him the entire time they were in the house, and they looked around to see if there was any indication the missing couple had just gone away for the weekend. Everything seemed to be in order. He described the windows being open and the doors being unlocked.

Babcock continued, "While we were checking the house, Deputy Gannaway and one the [sic]—Howard Herrick, or Harold Herrick [sic], went out into the barn to check the barn on routine investigation."

The detective continued to tell the Court he had finally gone to the barn himself and had found the Herricks' 1952 Desoto just inside the door of the barn. He also said that underneath some baled hay, the bodies of Howard and Myra Herrick were found.

"Were you able to identify the bodies there as the Herricks'?" the prosecutor asked.

"I did, yes, sir," Babcock replied.

Asked to describe the condition of the bodies, Babcock continued, "The bodies were...Mr. Herrick's was extremely bloated. It had started to decompose. It turned, what we say black [sic]. He had been...his head had been beaten, and there was quite a bit of blood around. Mrs. Herrick was laying face up, and she had extremely...quite a few blows on her head."

Captain Babcock was then asked about his search of the barn. He said, "I found a bloody hammer. I found a grinding wheel. I found some clothing. Also Mr. Herrick's driver's license in the northeast part of the barn. I found some book matches on top of the hay loft. Also found some foreign cigarette butts."

The prosecutor handed a piece of the evidence to the captain, asking, "What is it?"

Babcock replied, "That is the hammer that was at the Herrick barn on the night of September 5th...It has been—was in our custody and turned over to the State Crime Lab, Dr. Muehlberger."

A second piece of evidence was handed to the law enforcement witness. Babcock looked at it saying, "That is a grinding wheel for sharpening knives and so on, and that was at the barn on September 5, 1955, and it has been in our custody ever since."

Then the prosecutor handed Captain Babcock the photos taken at the crime scene. Babcock identified them as the pictures he took on the morning of September 6, 1955 inside the barn. Asked to describe a couple of the pictures, Babcock said, "Exhibit 3 shows—the photograph was taken from the top of the barn looking down. It shows the entranceway to the barn coming in from the north. It shows a hay loft, a fork. It shows a block of wood up on a rafter in the barn."

The prosecutor quickly made sure Babcock was the

photographer who had taken the pictures.

Chamberlain re-addressed the picture showing the block on the rafter when he said, "You say that they show a block of wood up on the rafter in the barn. Did you see that there yourself?"

Versile Babcock replied, "I did."

He was asked to describe the block of wood, and said, "It's a—it looks like a tree trunk, a large tree trunk, perhaps 2 to 3 feet across the top of it. It had feathers on it from chickens and blood. And it was approximately 3 foot in height. I don't know what kind of wood it was."

Asked if he found any identification with Howard Herrick's body, Captain Babcock said he had not.[43]

Chamberlain didn't have any further questions for Captain Babcock. Judge Salmon didn't either.

Assistant Prosecutor Peter Treleaven stood to address the Court, and Nealy sat at the defense table watching intently as the next witnesses were called. Treleaven called Dr. Charles Black to the stand.

The Williamston doctor was first asked what his occupation was and then his specialty. He replied, "My occupation is the practice of medicine...My specialty is pathology...Pathology has to deal with the diagnosis of disease, the determination of the cause of death and examination of...."

Treleaven interrupted, "And how many years have you been actively engaged in that occupation?"

Black continued his testimony, saying he had been involved in pathology for eighteen years, and he was the head of the Sparrow Hospital Department of Pathology.

Dr. Charles Black confirmed he had performed the autopsy on Myra Herrick on September 6, 1955, and was then asked about the condition of her body.

"Well, the body showed advanced postmortem changes. The abdomen was particularly swollen; face swollen," the doctor said.

Asked if there was any evidence of physical violence, he confirmed there was.

"The right side of the head showed a very violent crushing injury with very extensive fracture, and brain tissue was exiting out through the defect," he said.

Assistant Prosecutor Treleaven continued, "In your opinion, Doctor, was that injury sufficient to have caused death?"

"Yes," he said, "That is my opinion that it was the cause of death."

The prosecutor led the medical expert into the examination of Howard Herrick's body, and asked, "Did you find any injuries on that body?"

"Yes. I found a very violent crushing injury of the left side of the head with extensive fractures and brain tissue also exiting from the defect of the skull," he replied.

Again, the same question that had been asked about Myra's cause of death was asked about Howard's death, "And was that injury, in your opinion, sufficient to have caused death?"

The doctor answered yes.

The prosecutor continued his line of questioning, eliciting information about bruising on either Howard or Myra.

The doctor said, "Yes, I found numerous injuries about the entire body of Mrs. Herrick. She had several hammer-like blow injuries to both eyes, and one in front of the ear, and she had numerous bruises about the hands and wrists. She had a wrist watch on the left wrist, and that was broken, and her glasses were broken."

Treleaven wanted more. He asked, "What, if anything, did the injuries on the arms indicate to you, Doctor?"

"Well, it indicated to me that she had been involved in a very violent, prolonged struggle," he answered.

The prosecutor wanted to be sure the judge understood. He asked, "Apparently trying to ward off blows?"

"Yes, that would be my opinion," the doctor replied.

Judge Salmon interjected with a question of the doctor. "In your opinion, Doctor, could either one or any of the wounds that you saw on either, or both, of the persons here involved, be caused by either one or both of the instruments that you see before you there?" he asked.

Dr. Black replied, "Your Honor, it is my opinion that the ones on the skull could have been inflicted by a hammer. They were very violent, and the fractures of the skull radiated in all directions, and the marks on the forehead particularly had the oval shape of a hammer."

Treleaven picked up where Judge Salmon had left off by asking, "Doctor, if the record should later indicate that certain blows were delivered to the skull of Mr. Herrick by that grinding wheel, would that be consistent with your findings?"

The doctor answered, "Oh, I think it could be yes."[44]

The prosecutor didn't have any more questions.

Assistant Prosecutor Jack Warren stood and called to the stand, Paul Skarstad, the court reporter who had transcribed the confession of Nealy when it was taken at the Ingham County Sheriff's Department.

Skarstad testified he has been a court reporter since 1931, telling the Court he had transcribed the confession of Buchanon. He also told the Court it was taken at the sheriff's department and what time it had been taken.

After Skarstad was finished, Charles Chamberlain introduced the transcribed confession of Nealy J. Buchanon to the Court. The entire confession was read into the court record of the degree hearing by Chamberlain.

Chamberlain had one more witness to call for the degree hearing and it was Sheriff Willard Barnes.

The sheriff walked to the witness stand, raised his right hand and was sworn in before the Court.

Chamberlain would handle the questioning of the sheriff, and began by establishing Barnes was indeed the Sheriff of Ingham County in September of 1955, then continued by asking if he had been present at the interrogation of Nealy Buchanon on the previous evening. He also asked the sheriff if he had witnessed Nealy Buchanon sign his own confession after it had been transcribed. Each time, the sheriff's answers were short when the Barnes replied, "I was...I did...I have."

The prosecutor moved directly to Buchanon's apprehension in Baltimore and the conversations he may have had with the killer.

The sheriff was asked if he had any conversation with Buchanon about a chopping block that had been mentioned earlier and was shown in the crime scene photographs. Again, Barnes' initial answer was, "I did." He continued, "I asked Mr. Buchanon about the block and if he put it up on the beam. He stated that he did. And I asked him why he put it up there, and he said, 'To shove off to knock Mr. Herrick out.'"

The prosecutor asked him to continue.

"He explained to me that on this particular morning, that he laid up on top of the beam, and laid there waiting for Mr. Herrick to walk around, to give the opportunity to shove the block off on Mr. Herrick's head, or on his body, some place or other," said Barnes.

Asked if he had examined the block of wood, he said he had. He was asked to describe it and said, "I would say that the block was approximately 2 1/2 feet tall, smaller at the top than at the base, probably 2 foot across at the top, and probably 2 1/2 foot across at the bottom, and consisting of some kind of hard wood."

He was asked if had tried to lift it, and he acknowledged he had, guessing it weighed around 50 lbs.

Prosecutor Chamberlain glanced at Judge Salmon who was listening intently to Sheriff Barnes' testimony. He led into questioning Barnes about the murder weapons.

The sheriff continued his testimony, "I was interested in finding out what he had hit the victims with, and he told me of this grinder, which he called a blower at the time, but he identified it later. He told me that when Mr. Herrick drove in, he was over the tool bench looking the tools over, and he had this grinder in his hand. Mr. Herrick said to him, 'What are you doing there?' and he said, 'I was looking at the tools.' He walked around back of the car, and Mr. Herrick was getting out of the car, and Mr. Buchanon said that Mr. Herrick turned and he said, 'I was just admiring this tool. Would you like to sell it?' and that he waited until Mr. Herrick looked away, 'when I had a chance to hit him, and I hit him in the back of the head with the grinder.'"

Not forgetting about the hammer, the prosecutor asked the law enforcement officer about any conversations he had with Nealy regarding the hammer.

Again, the sheriff said, "We talked to him about the hammer, and this was one of the tools that he picked from the bench and used it in hitting Mrs. Herrick. That's a ball-peen hammer, weighs about 2 pounds. I think in the trade they call it a 2-pound ball-peen hammer."

The prosecuting attorney, wanting to establish Nealy Buchanon's premeditation, asked the sheriff if he had any discussions about the killer waiting in the barn all day.

Once again, the sheriff continued, "Yes. He told me about waiting there all day long. He told me that he waited, and he wanted to knock Mr. Herrick out to get his money, and he wanted to get out of Michigan."

Asked about Howard Herrick's wallet, the sheriff continued, "…He told me that after he hit Herrick, Herrick went down. He was attempting to roll him over to get into his hip pocket to get his pocketbook when he heard a noise, and Mrs. Herrick walked around the back of the car. He told me that she said, 'What's going on here?' and, of course, he got up, and when he turned around to look at her, she screamed, and he said he walked to her, and hit her in the head with this grinder."[45]

Judge Salmon slowly turned toward Buchanon. Chamberlain asked if the Court had any questions. Salmon turned back, and said he didn't.

Charles Chamberlain had completed the degree hearing. In closing the hearing, he said, "May it please the Court, we have no further witnesses to present at this hearing at the present time…If the Court please, we have nothing further to offer on behalf of the People."

Judge Marvin Salmon had been taking notes as each witness testified and said, "It is the judgment of this court that the murder of Myra Herrick was murder in the first degree, and it is also the judgment of this court that the murder of Howard Herrick was murder in the first degree."

The judge addressed Buchanon now saying, "Will you step up here, Mr. Buchanon? The Court will sentence you."

Nealy J. Buchanon stood before the Honorable Judge Marvin Salmon in the 30th Judicial Circuit Court of Ingham County, prepared to hear the sentence the judge was about to impose. There was apprehension, but no fear. The time was 12:30 pm.

"In the case of the People versus Nealy Joseph Buchanon, for the murder of one Howard Herrick, the Court is about to sentence you, Mr. Buchanon. Is there anything you have to say why sentence should not be pronounced against you?" asked Judge Salmon.

Nealy replied, "No, sir."

The judge continued with the sentencing saying, "It is the sentence of this court that you be confined in the State's Prison of Southern Michigan at Jackson, Michigan, for life."

Moving to the murder of Myra, Salmon said, "In the case of the People versus Nealy Joseph Buchanon, for the murder of Myra Herrick, the Court is about to sentence you, Mr. Buchanon. Is there anything you have to say why sentence should not be pronounced against you?"

Again, Nealy replied, "No, sir."

Sentencing Buchanon to life, again, for the murder of Myra Herrick, the judge continued by saying, "And let me say this for the record. This was a very cold, calculated, premeditated killing, with malice aforethought. Having in mind the manner in which you committed the crime and the purpose for you which you committed the crime, the Court is satisfied that you would commit murder again if you thought it would serve you in any way. Therefore, and for the record, it is my opinion that this sentence should never be softened or decreased, and that you should remain in prison for the rest of your life. That is all."[46]

Judge Marvin Salmon was satisfied Prosecuting Attorney Charles Chamberlain had established the elements of first-degree murder against the defendant in the degree hearing. It had quickly followed his arraignment in Circuit Court. The sentencing took only minutes.

Nealy Buchanon was now back in his cell at the Ingham County Jail awaiting his transportation back to Jackson and the world's largest walled prison from where he had escaped just thirteen months before.

CHAPTER 10

A Slayer Waits

After his escape and his recent conviction for a double murder, Nealy Joseph Buchanon was issued a new prison number…C-88620-JM.

As the squad car neared the prison, the 52-acre brick fortress with its pentagon shape looked all too familiar. He knew the prison system would be his home for the rest of his life.

All four of Howard and Myra's children were in the courtroom when Buchanon had received his sentence from Judge Salmon. It was the maximum the judge could impose, but to Howard and Myra's children, it would never be enough. While they wished Michigan had capital punishment, they knew otherwise.

The Michigan legislature had abolished the death

penalty in 1846 with the last public execution occurring in 1830. It was 125 years later when the Herricks were bludgeoned to death on their Stockbridge Township farm.

It was September 24, 1830, when Stephen Gifford Simmons was convicted of murdering his wife, Levena, and was hung in a public execution in Detroit. It was Michigan's last such execution.

Stephen and his wife were heavy drinkers by all accounts, and drank quite freely on Sunday, June 13. On Monday, they continued their imbibing during the morning hours, then slept until just before sunset. Simmons was a 50-year-old tavern owner in Wayne County, and he had suspicions about his wife's infidelity with a stagecoach driver who stopped daily at the tavern on his way to Ypsilanti. After waking late in the afternoon, Simmons tried interrogating his own daughter in an effort to confirm his distrust about Levena. Whatever was said between the two did nothing to allay his suspicions. Simmons became enraged, stormed into the bedroom and began beating his wife unmercifully. At some point during the assault, she confessed her marital betrayal, but the beating continued and became even more severe. Finally, leaving his bloodied spouse unconscious, Simmons returned to the other room to continue his drinking.

Two guests at the tavern quickly entered the bedroom in an effort to help the poor woman. Deciding to take her outside to the fresh air, they removed her from the bedroom, but soon discovered it was too late. Levena was already dead.

Other patrons at the tavern quickly restrained Simmons, who became overwhelmed with grief at the news he had killed his wife. He begged those same patrons to help her. Simmons was held until he could be delivered to the law the following day, when he was bound and transported to Detroit in his own farm wagon, along with his wife's body.

The trial for Stephen Simmons began on July 6, 1830, and after his conviction, his sentencing was set for July 26. Judge William Woodbridge passed sentence saying:

> "Your days on earth are numbered; a few brief days, and you will appear before that God who made you, the Creator of all things! Employ this short time, we beg of you, in making your peace with that God, whose laws you have so despised. Approach him with contrition and remorse; with repentance and with prayer. Approach him with a contrite heart and a proper spirit through the meditation of the blessed Redeemer, and hope may still beam upon you; for upon such terms has he not promised you his forgiveness, and that your sins shall be washed away, although they be as scarlet!"

In closing, Woodbridge continued:

> "Whereupon all and singular the premises being seen and by the said Court here fully understood it is considered by the Court here, and it is accordingly adjudged that the said Stephen G. Simmons

> be taken to the Gaol of the County of Wayne from whence he came and from thence on Friday the twenty-fourth day of September now next ensuing to the place of execution, and that between the hours of ten o'clock in the forenoon and four o'clock in the afternoon of said
>
> twenty- fourth day of September he be hanged by the neck until he be dead...And may God Almighty have mercy on your soul."[47]

Because the appointed Wayne County Sheriff Thomas Knapp had resigned his position on September 10, 1830, a mere two weeks before the scheduled hanging, and absent any undersheriff, by law, the responsibilities of the sheriff fell to the county coroner:

> "Whenever the office of sheriff shall become vacant in any county, either by death, resignation, or otherwise, and there shall be no under-sheriff therein, the coroner of such county shall perform the same duties, be vested with the same powers, and liable to the same fines, penalties, and other proceedings as, are or may be, provided by law in the case of sheriffs, during such vacancy."[48]

Local businessman Benjamin Woodworth had been appointed as the Wayne County Coroner in 1815. His only responsibility at that time was to summon a jury of men who would conduct inquests in front of dead bodies.

Woodworth was known in the area as 'Uncle Ben,'

and as a sort of entrepreneur, he ran a local hotel, a ferry to Windsor, Canada, held the position of Captain for an artillery company, ran several stagecoaches between Mt. Clemens and Detroit, and ran a grist mill in Rochester. He was eventually appointed as Wayne County Sheriff in late December of 1830, but was still only the coroner at the time of Simmons public hanging.

Woodworth knew the defendant's execution would bring large numbers of spectators to Detroit and would likely fill every hotel in the city of 2,200 people.

In planning Simmons' final farewell, he decided to hold the execution outside the jail in the middle of Gratiot Avenue. Stephen would only have to take a few steps to the gallows before being hanged.

The coroner planned accordingly for the crowds by having grandstand seating built on three sides of the scaffolding where the prisoner would stand. A military band would entertain the crowds prior to the hanging, while a militia of soldiers would stand around the scaffolding as a sort of honor guard. The final preparation for Simmons' execution included vendors selling food and alcohol to the throngs of spectators.

On September 24, 1830, entire families of men, women, and children came by every means to Detroit to watch the condemned man hang. When it was over, many left disgusted by the gruesome spectacle they had just witnessed. It was suggested Simmons' demeanor at his execution 'changed the tide of public opinion' toward execution.

On May 18, 1846, almost sixteen years after Simmons' public execution, Michigan Governor Alpheus Felch signed a new law which read:

"All murder that shall be perpetrated by

*means of poison or lying in wait, or any
other kind of willful [sic], deliberate and
premeditated killing, or which shall be
committed in the perpetration or attempt
to perpetrate any arson, rape, robbery, or
burglary, shall be deemed murder of the
first degree, and shall be punished by sol-
itary confinement at hard labor in the
State Prison for life; and all other kinds of
murder shall be deemed murder of the
second degree, and shall be punished by
confinement in the penitentiary for life, or
any term of years, at the discretion of the
Court trying the same."[49]*

Now, 110 years after the abolishment of Michigan's
death penalty, Nealy Buchanon's life had been spared,
in part, because of Stephen Simmons' dark place in
Michigan's history.

Nealy Buchanon was home again. The 6 x 9 foot
cell was furnished with a wash basin, a toilet, and a
bed identical in every other cell. As he sat on a prison
bunk for the first time in over a year, he had all but forgotten about some of the daily prison routine. Inmates
at the world's largest walled prison began each day to
the sound of buglers. Six polished horns were located
in the rotunda and select inmates with at least some
degree of musical talent would signal the start of each
day with a rendition of reveille. Meals and recreation
time were also signaled with the sound of the buglers,
and taps was played to signal the end of each day.

The convicted killer was smart enough to know he was there to stay. There was no way he would ever be part of the minimum security trustee division outside the walls of the prison, like he had before.

For inmates at the State Prison of Southern Michigan, whether new or returning, before being moved into the general population, a ninety-day quarantine period was required. There was no association with the general population inmates at the prison, and the quarantine allowed the prisoner just one hour of recreation time per day.

It wasn't the same for Buchanon. Because of his escape from the prison a year before, and the murder of an elderly farm couple, forty days after being sentenced to life in prison by Judge Soloman, Nealy boarded a prison bus for the long ride to Michigan's Upper Peninsula. He was being transferred to the State House of Corrections Branch Prison in Marquette located near the southern banks of Lake Superior. As Buchanon walked toward the prison bus, he shivered and could see the moisture of his breath in the frigid 22-degree temperature. It was Wednesday, November 28.

The ride along Michigan's US-27 toward the Straits of Mackinac was filled with rural scenes, many like the setting in Stockbridge Township, where Buchanon had killed the elderly farm couple. Harvested fields of corn, wheat, and soybeans dotted the sides of the highway, while homes and wooded areas filled in the gaps between small cities and towns along the way. The colorful fall foliage, sought after by tourists from around the state and beyond, had long since dulled to a faded brown with many of the trees now bare as winter was slowly setting in.

Arriving at the Straits of Mackinac, a narrow shipping lane connecting Lake Michigan and Lake Huron, the prison bus made its way onto a ferry to cross the five miles of waterway. The Mackinac Bridge, still under construction after two-and-a-half years, wasn't scheduled to open for another year.

Now in Michigan's Upper Peninsula, the temperature hadn't changed much since leaving Jackson, and as the bus made its way west across US-2, the wind had picked up to a crisp 20 mph. Reaching Highway 41 in Rapid River, the bus turned to the north toward Marquette for the final hour of the drive.

Nearing the prison along Highway 41 with Lake Superior on the right and forest land on the left, the bus slowed to make the sharp left turn into the secured area. The prison sat on the west side of the highway, and it was located north of the small town of Harvey and south of the larger Marquette.

As the bus made its way along the entrance to the Branch Prison grounds, the inmate from the State Prison of Southern Michigan could see the castle-like structure come into view.

The large, stone castle-like structure stood behind manicured walkways greeting new inmates and visitors alike. Much like structures from medieval times, the center of the 'castle' towered above the rest, and it was known as the keep, with a small battlement extending even further above. The stone building itself, three stories in height, had large octagon towers on each corner with stone walls extending to the east and west, and enclosing an inner ward or yard. This was the killer's new home, albeit temporarily.

'Lifer' was the term used to describe an inmate who had no chance of ever receiving parole. It was as simple as that for Nealy Joseph Buchanon. While the location of his incarceration occasionally alternated between Jackson and Marquette, he knew he would always be an inmate in the Michigan prison system.

Buchanon spent his first year in the system quietly. As a lifetime resident, he kept a low profile like the other lifers, and he listened intently to their stories of wrongful convictions mixed with appeals.

Within every prison system, there were inmates known as jailhouse lawyers who assisted other prisoners with legal work, most of the time with some sort of compensation required. The compensation was often cigarettes, food, or even protection. Joe Kelly was one of those, and, over time, Buchanon sought out his services behind bars, though it wasn't immediate.

It wasn't until early in 1966, ten years after his plea-based conviction and sentencing, when Buchanon found out about Kelly. With nothing but time, Buchanon wondered if there might be some sort of technicality affording him the chance for an appeal. With only a limited education, Buchanon arranged to have Kelly, the 'legal beagle,' help him with the paperwork required. The first thing Nealy needed was court-appointed counsel, but he had no idea how to go about getting an attorney appointed to represent him. Kelly drew up the request and Buchanon submitted it to the Ingham County Circuit Court on July 5, 1966.

It was just short of three months later when the Ingham County Circuit Court appointed 40-year-old Lansing attorney Hannibal Abood as the killer's appellate counsel.

Nealy was encouraged. It had only been since early July when he made the request for counsel, and by late October, he had an attorney to help file an appeal. Four days later, upon his request for transcripts from the court proceedings, the Court granted that request, too. There was no time wasted. On October 28, Abood filed a Delayed Motion for Appeal with a Writ of Habeas Corpus and a Writ of Certiorari, all on behalf of his client, in the Ingham County Circuit Court. With those legal documents, Abood was asking his client to be brought before the Court, in addition to having the complete file reviewed by the Court, so he could appeal Buchanon's case. In late December, he also filed a motion with the Circuit Court for a new trial on the basis that the Court had failed to ask Buchanon if he wanted an attorney present at his sentencing. He also alleged in his motion that the Court failed to take an adequate waiver of counsel, failing to advise Buchanon of the consequences involved in his plea. His final point alleged a failure of Judge Salmon to make a record of the discussion he had with Buchanon in his chambers just prior to imposing the life sentence.

At the same time Abood was filing the motion for a new trial, there was another appeal before the Michigan Supreme Court, and on January 13, 1967, Judge Marvin Salmon, who had originally sentenced Buchanon to life in prison, was now expected to either grant his motion for a new trial or deny it. Judge Salmon knew the pending case before the Supreme Court could affect his decision, and he decided to have Buchanon's case held in abeyance pending the decision of the Court in *People v. Winegar*.[50]

Oddly, the case paralleled Buchanon's in more ways than one and involved the actions of Judge

Marvin Salmon in the sentencing of a man involved in the 1961 kidnapping of two Jackson police officers and the shooting of an Ingham County deputy.

On October 27, 1961, Jackson Police Officer Norm Richmond responded to a call of a suspicious vehicle on Sparks Street inside the city. At around 10:00 pm, Officer Richmond hadn't been heard from, and another officer was sent to the same location in an effort to locate him.

Officer Frank Miller headed up North West Avenue, turning onto Sparks Street where he saw Officer Richmond walking toward his squad car with two men. As Miller approached them in his car, he slowly stopped next to them, and Richmond handed him what appeared to be a small shaving kit. It was packed with tools. It became clear to Miller that the two men with Officer Richmond had planned to break into a nearby business. As Miller tried his radio to call for some assistance, he looked up suddenly to find a gun pointed at him. Only moments before, the two men had disarmed Richmond.

Both officers were handcuffed by the two suspects and put into the back of the squad car. While the kidnapping of the two officers was taking place, a gun held by one of the suspects accidentally fired. Officer Miller was grazed, but not seriously injured. Nearby neighbors heard the shot, noticed a brief scuffle of some sort, and notified the police.

Before any help could arrive, the two officers were driven north of the city and taken off the road into a wooded area where they were handcuffed to a tree.

One of the two suspects, Richard Mauch, wanted to shoot the two officers, but his partner, William Winegar, had already gone through the officers' wallets, noticing a picture of Richmond's wife and child. Winegar had a wife and child of his own, and he convinced Mauch not to shoot them. They left the two officers handcuffed to the tree and fled in the squad car.

It was about 9:00 am the next morning when a tip led Ingham County Deputy Phil Maiville to a confrontation between the two suspects near a farm south of Mason. As Maiville tried to arrest the men, they opened fire and two rounds hit the deputy. The first round was stopped by Maiville's badge, and the second was stopped when it hit his checkbook. Deputy Maiville returned fire, shooting several times, and striking Mauch in the stomach with his last round. Quickly searching for cover, the deputy retreated behind a barn to reload while Winegar fled in his squad car.

Living on the south end of Lansing, Winegar headed to his own house on Reo Road and was quickly captured when more than 50 officers surrounded his house. After his arrest, officers found over $50,000 in stolen merchandise from Michigan, Ohio, and Indiana in the Winegar home.

On November 3, 1961, William Winegar was arraigned before Judge Marvin Salmon in Ingham County Circuit Court, barely five years after Nealy Buchanon had been sentenced in the same court. Winegar was facing a charge of assault with intent to commit murder for the shooting of Deputy Maiville.

After the charge was read to Winegar, Judge Salmon asked if he understood, and Winegar acknowledged he did. Salmon continued the hearing by telling Winegar he was entitled to have an attorney represent him, and if he was financially unable to employ his own attorney, the Court would employ one for him. Again, the judge asked him if he understood, and Winegar said he did, but all his money was "tied up." Salmon asked him one more time if he understood what he had just been told, and again, Winegar said he did.

Judge Salmon moved on. He told Winegar of his right to a trial either before a jury or before a judge and asked if he understood that. Once again, the defendant acknowledged his understanding.

Salmon asked Winegar how he wished to plead...guilty or not guilty? Winegar replied, "I have no contest of it. I don't wish to contest it at all." The judge repeated his question, saying, "How do you wish to plead...guilty or not guilty?"

"I am stuck in Ohio, too," was his reply.

Salmon pressed him even further by asking, "Will you just answer my question please? Do you wish to plead guilty or not guilty?"

Winegar appeared to be confused when he said, "I plead guilty, I guess. I don't know."

The judge wanted a more definitive answer, saying, "What is it you don't know?"

Winegar tried to explain to Judge Salmon his confusion when he continued, "I don't understand the laws at all in this state, Your Honor. I mean in Ohio, where I come from, they are entirely different."

Ever so patiently, the honorable judge tried explaining it again to Winegar when he said, "Well, you have had this charge read to you, and you are entitled to plead guilty or not guilty, or you may stand mute. Now, whatever you wish to do is up to you."

Winegar chose the latter, standing mute to the charge, and Judge Salmon entered a plea of 'not guilty' for him.

It was two weeks later, on November 17, when

Winegar entered Judge Salmon's courtroom again to plead guilty. The exchange was much like the discussion between the judge and Nealy Buchanon in October of 1956.

The hearing began with, "Mr. Winegar, you were before the Court on the third day of November, 1961. The Court then advised you of your rights, at which time you said you preferred to stand mute, and the Court entered a plea of not guilty for you. Now it is your desire, as I understand, to plead guilty, is that correct?"

Winegar, now standing before the judge, was respectful in his reply when he addressed the judge saying, "Yes, Your Honor."

Salmon wanted to make sure there was no confusion in Winegar's intentions. He asked, "And that is what you are doing now is pleading guilty to this offense?"

Winegar answered, "Yes."

The judge continued by asking the defendant if anyone had made any promises to induce him to plead guilty, and Winegar told him no.

Salmon pressed him further by asking if anyone had told him if he pled guilty he would 'secure' leniency from the courts. Again, Winegar said no.

The judge finally said, "Then you are pleading guilty because you actually are guilty?"

Winegar said yes.

Again, as Judge Marvin Salmon had done when he sentenced Nealy Buchanon, he held a conference in his chambers with Winegar. When the two men returned to the courtroom, Judge Salmon continued, "Let the record show that the Court has conferred with Mr. Winegar relative to the circumstances of the crime, is convinced that he committed the crime, that his plea was freely, understandingly, and voluntarily made without undue influence, compulsion, or duress, and without promise of leniency. Therefore, his plea is accepted, and he is remanded to the custody of the county sheriff to await sentence. That is all."

On January 4, 1962, Winegar returned once again to Judge Marvin Salmon's courtroom for his sentencing. The judge began, "You are here for sentence this morning, Mr. Winegar. Is there anything you have to say why sentence should not be pronounced against you?"

When the defendant said no, Salmon continued, "It is the sentence of this court that you be confined to the State's Prison of Southern Michigan at Jackson, Michigan for life...And I think you know why the Court is doing it. I don't think I need to explain to you. That is all."

On January 29, 1965, four years after his sentencing, William Winegar filed a motion to withdraw his plea of guilty. Two months later, the Court denied his motion.

An amended motion was filed on April 6, 1965, and it was denied a second time on April 26. The Michigan Court of Appeals eventually reversed Winegar's conviction based on two issues raised by the defense: The first issue was whether or not William Winegar had waived his constitutional right to the assistance of counsel. In reversing the conviction, the Court of Appeals said, "The record shows that the defendant was informed of his right to have counsel appointed if he was financially unable to employ counsel, but it further shows that the trial court failed to give the defendant an opportunity to so request."

The second issue raised by the defense was whether Winegar's plea of guilty was invalid because the court record didn't include a verbatim transcript of the discussion between Judge Salmon and Winegar in the judge's chambers immediately preceding sentencing. In reversing the conviction on that point, the Court of Appeals cited Court Rule 35(a) (1945), which said under Section 2:

> *Sec. 2. Imposing Sentence. If the accused pleads guilty, after such plea and before sentence, the Court shall inform the accused of the nature of the accusation and the consequence of his plea; and regardless of whether he is represented by counsel, the Court shall examine the accused, not necessarily under oath, and as a condition of accepting the plea of guilty and imposing sentence shall ascertain that the plea was freely, understandingly and voluntarily made, without undue influence, compulsion or duress, and without promise of leniency. Unless the Court determines that the plea of guilty was so made, it shall not be accepted."*

Continuing on, the Court cited Section 3:

> *Sec. 3. Record. The trial court shall cause a stenographic record to be made and promptly transcribed of the proceedings had under sections 1 and 2 above, and shall certify over his signature thereto that the same is a true record of the proceedings had. Thereupon the record so made shall be filed with the clerk of the court and become and be kept as a part of the record in the case. In any subsequent*

proceedings such record shall be competent evidence of the facts and circumstances therein recorded.

Finally, the Court cited Section 35:

Whenever any person shall plead guilty to an information filed against him in any court, it shall be the duty of the judge of such court, before pronouncing judgment or sentence upon such plea, to become satisfied after such investigation as he may deem necessary for that purpose respecting the nature of the case, and the circumstances of such plea, that said plea was made freely, with full knowledge of the nature of the accusation, and without undue influence. And whenever said judge shall have reason to doubt the truth of such plea of guilty, it shall be his duty to vacate the same, direct a plea of not guilty to be entered, and order a trial of the issue thus formed.

The Court of Appeals continued by saying Winegar never said he didn't understand the nature of the charge or the consequence of his plea. He was no stranger to the criminal justice system based on his criminal record, and he simply claimed the Court did not comply with the court rule because there was no verbatim record of the conference in Judge Salmon's chambers.

With regard to Winegar's appeal based on the lack of a verbatim record, the Court of Appeals stated, "If the arraignment proceedings, which culminate in a plea of guilty, fail to comply with the appropriate rule, there is no standard by which they could be said to be valid...Reversal of the lower court for noncompliance with Court Rule No 35A (1945), or GCR 1963, 785.3 is the only method an appellate court has of enforcing the court rule...The plea of guilty in this case should not be allowed to stand because the record does not show substantial compliance with former Court Rule No 35A, § 2 (1945), now GCR 1963, 785.3(2)."

After Winegar's conviction was reversed by the Michigan Court of Appeals, it ended up before the Michigan Supreme Court, who disagreed with the lower court's reversal. The Supreme Court opined, "First of all, a conviction based upon a plea of guilty is a judgment of the trial court. If the Court has jurisdiction to enter the conviction, it is presumptively valid."

Citing Court Rule 35(a), the Michigan Supreme Court said, "This rule is mandatory but failure to comply therewith shall not be considered jurisdictional." Additionally, citing Harmless Error, the Court said:

> *"No error in either the admission or the exclusion of evidence and no error or defect in any ruling or order or in anything done or omitted by the Court or by any of the parties is ground for granting a new trial or for setting aside a verdict or for vacating, modifying, or otherwise disturbing a judgment or order, unless refusal to take such action appears to the Court inconsistent with substantial justice. The Court, at every stage of the proceeding, shall construe these rules to secure the just, speedy, and inexpensive determination of every action so as to avoid the*

consequence of any error or defect in the proceeding which does not affect the substantial rights of the parties."

The Court continued, citing Section 26:

"No judgment or verdict shall be set aside or reversed or a new trial be granted by any court of this state in any criminal case, on the ground of misdirection of the jury, or the improper admission or rejection of evidence, or for error as to any matter of pleading or procedure, unless in the opinion of the Court, after an examination of the entire cause, it shall affirmatively appear that the error complained of has resulted in a miscarriage of justice."

Continuing with their opinion, the Supreme Court indicated the basis of the statutes under Michigan law were to deny a convicted felon the benefit of judicial oversights or 'miscues,' which don't apply to the conviction. The only thing contained in Winegar's filings was a motion to withdraw his plea.

In Winegar's case, since the motion was made after his conviction and sentence, the motion had to be made based upon a miscarriage of justice. The only thing appearing in the motion was a simple statement made by the defendant stating, "I am innocent of the charge lodged against me as I understand the law of the State of Michigan."

The Court concluded the statement by Winegar that he was innocent of the charge against him didn't constitute the showing of a miscarriage of justice.

Secondly, the Michigan Supreme Court continued:

"Reversal of a lower court is not the only method an appellate court has of enforcing the court rule. The superintending authority of the Supreme Court is sufficient to assure compliance by the trial courts with a mandatory but non-jurisdictional court rule. There is no need to release or retry criminals in order to enforce the court rule."

The Court also concluded there was no reason to set aside Winegar's guilty plea simply because a verbatim record didn't show compliance with GCR 1963, 785.3(2).

In opining further and citing an earlier court appeal, the Court said a convicted defendant no longer enjoys the presumption of innocence. That person has the burden of showing something more than technical noncompliance with a rule. Absent a showing of violation or denial of constitutional rights, he has the obligation of alleging in a motion to withdraw plea facts that would, if true, substantiate a finding that there was noncompliance which resulted in a miscarriage of justice.

Finally, the Court said, "It is in this light that we must view the affidavit of William Winegar attached to the motion to withdraw his plea. The affidavit is quoted in the margin. It does not state facts which, if true, would substantiate his claim that the plea was not freely, voluntarily, and understandingly made."

Judge Salmon had made the right decision to wait for the Supreme Court's opinion regarding Winegar's case. In addition to Salmon holding Buchanon's appeal in abeyance, Assistant Prosecuting Attorney James Ramsey had filed the appropriate paperwork in opposition to Nealy's appeal, asking the Court to deny his motion. The appeal filed by Winegar included the same appeals eventually made by Nealy Buchanon. Winegar's conviction, based on his appeals, though originally overturned by the Michigan Court of Appeals, were eventually upheld by the Michigan Supreme Court.

Based on the Michigan Supreme Court's decision on May 16, 1968, Judge Marvin Salmon denied Nealy Buchanon's motion, but it was only the beginning.

CHAPTER **11**

The Process

It was a fierce presidential election year when shortly after midnight on June 5, 1968, Senator Robert Kennedy, the democratic hopeful for the 1968 presidential election finished a speech in the Ambassador Hotel in Los Angeles, California. Kennedy, seeking the democratic presidential nomination, was running against Vice President Hubert Humphrey. Only two months before, the nation was rocked by the assassination of civil rights leader Dr. Martin Luther King in Memphis, Tennessee, with race riots following across the country and opposition to the Vietnam War growing across college campuses. As Kennedy made his way through the hotel kitchen after his speech, a Palestinian/Jordanian immigrant named Sirhan Sirhan used a .22 caliber Iver-Johnson revolver and fatally shot the democratic hopeful as he was shaking the hand of seventeen-year-old Juan Romero. Kennedy died twenty-six hours later. His body lay in repose for two days at St. Patrick's Cathedral in New York City before his funeral was held on June 8. He was laid to rest in Arlington National Cemetery.

Three days after Senator Kennedy's funeral, while the nation still mourned the young senator's death, Nealy Buchanon filed an Application for Delayed Appeal alleging errors at his arraignment, degree hearing, and sentencing. Given Judge Salmon's denial of the previous motions, the next step for the convicted killer was the Michigan Court of Appeals. After his previous appeal to the Ingham County Circuit Court was denied, Hannibal Abood no longer represented Buchanon.

The Michigan Court of Appeals was formed under the Michigan Constitution in 1963, but didn't begin hearing cases until 1965. Prior to that, if an inmate was appealing a case and there had been no remedy in the lower courts, the case was automatically forwarded to the Michigan Supreme Court. Beginning in 1965, however, the Intermediate Court of Appeals added an additional step for an inmate to present the case for appeals.

There was a problem with Buchanon's motion to the Court of Appeals. There were contradictions between his new appeal and the appeal Abood had made on his behalf to the Ingham County Circuit Court.

Within three weeks, the Ingham County Prosecutor's Office filed a Brief in Opposition to Buchanon's Application for Leave to Appeal, noting his former appellate counsel Abood had admitted in his previous motion that Buchanon was present in the courtroom when Judge Salmon had conducted the degree hearing. On page three of Abood's brief, he wrote:

> "The record is clear that the trial court then took the accused back into open court for a hearing on October 19, 1956 to determine the degree of guilt. At said hearing, a prosecutor and two assistants alternated taking the testimony from witnesses, and again, the accused was totally without representation."

There was a second problem with Buchanon's own affidavit attached to his former appellate counsel's pleadings, because it showed Buchanon knew when he was arraigned before Justice Adams that he was facing an "open charge of murder," and he failed to claim in his own affidavit that he wasn't present at the Hearing to Determine the Degree of Guilt. In fact, it implied he was present.

On August 26, 1968, the Michigan Court of Appeals denied the appeal, "...for lack of merit in the grounds presented."

Nealy would not be deterred in his efforts to appeal his plea-based conviction. Working with the prison "legal beagle" Joe Kelly, he filed another Delayed Motion for Appeal Joint with Writ of Habeas Corpus, including a Writ of Certiorari with the Michigan Supreme Court, asking the Court to review his appeal. This time, Buchanon alleged errors in the "sufficiency of the complaint, the plea-taking process, the voluntariness of his confession, and the lack of grand jury indictment."

Three days later, Buchanon received a letter stating his pleading would be considered as an Application for Leave to Appeal, and a month after he received the letter, the Ingham County Prosecutor's Office filed a Brief in Opposition to his appeal. On November 12, he filed an additional brief, specifying his arguments.

This time the convicted killer raised eight issues with the Supreme Court, including the errors in the plea-taking process, the voluntariness of his confession, the waiver of counsel, failure to advise him of the consequences of his guilty plea, and being subjected to "quick justice."

Two things stood out in Buchanon's brief. This time, he acknowledged at the time of his arraignment before Justice Adams that he knew the offense was "an open charge of murder." Secondly, he said he never alleged in his previous appeal to the Michigan Court of Appeals that he wasn't present at the Hearing for Determination of Degree of Guilt; he simply implied he was present, but he wasn't qualified to conduct any cross-examination of the witnesses.

Winter had set in, and the new year had already begun before the Michigan Supreme Court responded. It was on January 14, 1969 when the appeal was denied. The Court indicated Buchanon, "Failed to persuade the Court that he has a meritorious basis for appeal or that the decision of the Court of Appeals was erroneous."

Buchanon was not giving up. In March, he filed a Petition for Writ of Certiorari to the Ingham County Circuit Court in the Michigan Supreme Court. Again, he alleged improprieties in the plea-taking procedures. As in his previous appeals, he indicated he was present at the Hearing to Determine Degree of Guilt when he wrote:

> *"Petitioner did not take the stand, nor did petitioner poses [sic] the legal knowledge*

*to object to any of the proceedings as
occurred on October 19, 1956. Therefore, no cross-examination of the witness
was made by petitioner."*

While convicted murderer Nealy Buchanon's appeals were being considered by the courts, the United
States was making great strides in the space race. As a
dress rehearsal to the first moon landing, Apollo 10
came to within 8.4 nautical miles of the lunar surface
with the goal of refining what was known of the
moon's gravitational field. The rehearsal was needed to
calibrate a powered descent to the surface of the moon
for the upcoming Apollo 11 mission. With a crew of
three astronauts, Thomas Stafford, John Young, and Eu-
gene Cernan, the command module, called Charlie
Brown, and the lunar module, labeled Snoopy, began
the mission on May 18, 1969.

Stafford and Cernan were able to test the ability of
the lunar module to ascend toward the lunar surface,
but, as planned, only to a height of approximately
50,000 feet. After surveying the landing site for the
scheduled historic mission in July, the descent stage
was separated, and they began their ascension back
toward the command module.

On May 26, 1969, amid the fanfare of the Apollo
10 astronauts returning to earth, the Michigan Supreme
Court denied Nealy J. Buchanon's petition. It was denied a second time on October 13.

After having gone through the entire appeal process, first with the Ingham County Circuit Court, then
the Michigan Court of Appeals, and finally the Michi-

gan Supreme Court, Buchanon realized he would have to start anew, alleging some of the same things he had in the past and adding even more.

His second appeal to the Ingham County Circuit Court was filed on November 19, 1971. This time, Buchanon tried to withdraw the guilty plea he had made fifteen years before and asked for a new trial. For the first time, he claimed he was innocent in the killing of Howard and Myra Herrick. As in the past, he claimed the guilty plea was improper because he did not knowingly waive his right to have an attorney present, but he did admit, again, that he was present at the Hearing for Determination of Degree of Guilt by writing, "Did not testify on his own behalf and did no [sic] cross-examine the witnesses."

A week later, the Ingham County Prosecutor's Office again had to file a Brief in Opposition to Buchanon's motion. Two days later, Judge Salmon once again denied Nealy Buchanon's appeal.

Months before Nealy Buchanon escaped from the Southern Michigan Prison at Jackson in 1955 and killed Howard and Myra Herrick, the United States had begun sending military advisors to Vietnam, with the first advisors arriving in February. President Eisenhower had promised to ensure a non-communist government for the country. Over the next several years, the amount of advisors grew, developed into direct US military involvement in the war with North Vietnam, and over 58,000 United States military personnel lost their lives during the Vietnam War.

On March 19, 1973, two months after the Vietnam

Peace Agreement was signed, the last United States troops left South Vietnam, and Hanoi released the last United States prisoners of war. The move ended the United States direct military involvement in a war that had started, at least in part, almost twenty years prior.

On the same day the last of the United States troops started their journey home from Southeast Asia, Nealy Buchanon filed another motion for the withdrawal of his guilty plea in the Ingham County Circuit Court. His motion was also asking the Court to Vacate Judgment and order a new trial. In his new motion, Buchanon attacked his own guilty plea stating he lied to the trial court in tendering his guilty plea. In addition, this was the first time he claimed he wasn't present at the Hearing for Determination of Degree of Guilt.

On April 10, the appellate attorney for the Ingham County Prosecutor's Office, Corbin Davis, filed a brief in opposition to the Motion to Withdraw Guilty Plea or Hold an Evidentiary Hearing. On May 1, Judge Salmon again entered a written order denying the killer's motion.

Early on the morning of June 17, 1972, there was a break-in at the Democratic National Committee Headquarters at the Watergate Building located in Washington, D.C. With the arrest of several men, it developed into a major political scandal resulting in the resignation of President Richard Nixon.

Though there was some question about whether the president knew of the break-in ahead of time, he took several steps in an attempt to cover it up which ultimately led to his resignation in August of 1974. Before the president's decision to resign was made, he outlined his involvement to the American people on May 22, 1973. In his statement, Nixon said:

> "I had no prior knowledge of the Watergate Operation...I took no part in, nor was I aware of, any subsequent efforts that may have been made to cover up Watergate...At no time did I authorize any offer of executive clemency for the Watergate defendants, nor did I know of any such offer...I did not know, until the time of my own investigation, of any effort to provide the Watergate defendants with funds... At no time did I attempt, or did I authorize others to attempt, to implicate the CIA in the Watergate matter... It was not until the time of my own investigation that I learned of the break-in at the office of Mr. Ellsberg's psychiatrist, and I specifically authorized the furnishing of this information to Judge Byrne...I neither authorized nor encouraged subordinates to engage in illegal or improper campaign tactics."[51]

On the same day President Nixon made his statement to the American people, Nealy Buchanon was filing another Application for Delayed Appeal to the Court of Appeals after Judge Salmon's May 1 decision. One month later, Assistant Prosecutor Corbin Davis again filed a Brief in Opposition to Application for

Leave to Appeal. Once again, the Court of Appeals denied Buchanon's appeal for 'lack of merit in the grounds presented' and under authority of *People v. Taylor*.

By 1977, Buchanon, now back at Jackson Prison, had another chance to perfect his motion to the Ingham County Circuit Court in his bid for a new trial. In his Affidavit of Non-Culpable Negligence, he cited three points for the Court to consider. He indicated in his filings that he was a layman and had never known about these points he was bringing to the Court's attention. He also wrote, "Defendant/appellant was threaten [sic], and so was his relatives, and that he only told the truth of all the circumstances that had happen [sic] now, because he no longer has to protect anybody but hisself now [sic]." Buchanon included an affidavit about his arrest in Baltimore and the entire process he went through after being released to Sheriff Barnes, including allegations that he was threatened by Judge Salmon during the discussion in chambers:

> *"When I was arrested by the Baltimore City Police. I was taken to the city jail. There I was locked in a blood spattered cell, around 2:00 P.M. About an hour or so later, three men in plain cloths entered the cell and began to question me about the murder of Mr. and Mrs. Herrick. I refused to say any thing and asked if I could see a lawyer. One big fat bellied (name unknown) officer, hit me accross the back with a black jack, and told me that I couldn,t have a lawyer, and that I was going to need a doctor when they got through with me. Then they all start-*

ed to beat me all across the back, shoulders, arms and accross my knee caps. The pain was more than I could stand, and I couldn,t move bedause my hands were cuffed behind my back. I beg for them to stop, they did. Then one of them left the cell, saying that he would be back and that I,d better be ready to make a statement. While he was gone, the other two officers began to tell me what it was that they wanted me to say. About an half hour later the officer came back with another man, who told me that he was a member of the F.B.I. He asked me if I wanted to make a statement, the other officers nodded to me to comply. I then told him what the officers said I was supposed to have done. Then they left me alone in the cell.

Later that evening, two of the same three officers came back to my cell and told me that I had to sign a paper partaining to extradition. I didn,t know what it was, but at the time, I would have signed any thing. I was then takened to another jail to wait for the people from Michigan to pick me up and take me back.

Early the next morning, four people came. One introduced himself as sheriff Barnes. He said that he and his other officers were going to take me back to Michigan, one way or the other. Dead or alive, and he didn,t give a damn which. As we were driven to the airport, I was questioned again about the murders.

When we arrived in Michigan, I was taken to Stockbridge city jail. There was a large crowd of people around the jail and we had to push our way through. I was taken to a cell and locked in. After an hour or so, I was taken into the sheriff,s office. There was another man there, but I don,t who he was. Sheriff Barnes told me that they had my statement. He asked me if I saw all those people out there as we came in. I said yes. Well, he said. 'They want to hang your black ass, so you had better stick to this statement that you made in Baltimore. Then I was taken to another courtroom before a judge. After that, I was questioned again. This time by news reporters. An hour or so later, I was taken back to a cell.

The next morning I was taken to Lansing to appear befor the Circuit Court. There the statement that I had been forced to make, was presented to the court. During the trial, Judge Marvin J. Solmon stoped the procedeings and took me into his office. There he told me, that if I wanted to protect my family and myself. I had better go along with the program. Or, he,d send me back to Stockbrigge and let the mob have it,s way with me. He said we,ve had the police staying in your home with your wife and children for some time. Then I said, wait a minute Judge. I didn,t do this and I don,t want to hang for it, and I want a lawyer. He then told me, 'we don,t have

*the death penalty here in the state of
Michigan so you wont need a lawyer.
You,ll be out in about ten years, if you
keep your nose clean, and be able to get
back to your family. So you had better go
along with this, because we can,t [sic]
have you niggers going around killing
white people, we can,t have that. A nigger did this, and we,ve got you.'*

*I,ve never said any thing before now,
because of my family. All these years, I,ve
kept it inside of me. Now I no longer
have to keep it a secret. My wife has re-
married and I no longer have a family, or
any to protect, other then myself.*

Thats about it."[52]

He concluded the motion, writing that he had never been appointed counsel to perfect his appeal to the Court.

It became clear he was filing the motion by himself, even though he had used jailhouse lawyers to help him write it. The paperwork was sealed in an envelope, postage attached, and mailed to the Ingham County Clerk and the Ingham County Prosecuting Attorney.

On April 1, Ingham County Circuit Judge Thomas L. Brown denied Buchanon's motion for a new trial. Judge Brown, in denying the motion, stated:

*"The defendant, having filed a delayed
motion for new trial, and the movant,
having shown no good grounds for the
setting aside of his plea, nor no reason,
excuse, or explanation for his failure to
raise the instant claims at an earlier date,*

*and the Court being fully advised in the
premises, it is HEREBY ORDERED [sic]
his application for leave to file a delayed
motion for new trial be denied, and his
conviction and sentence affirmed."*[53]

On April 15, Buchanon received his letter from Lee
Atkinson, who was now the Chief Appellate Attorney
for Ingham County, advising him of the order denying
his motion.

On May 3, two weeks after receiving notice of his
motion being denied, Buchanon was transferred back
to Marquette where he continued his efforts to appeal
his murder convictions. The spring air was welcome,
even if he was confined to a prison bus, and it made
the long ride back to northern Michigan at least beara-
ble.

On June 8, 1977, Buchanon filed another motion in
the Court of Appeals. It was a Delayed Application for
Remand to the Trial Court for an Evidentiary Hearing.
In his effort to have the case remanded back to the
Ingham County Circuit Court for an Evidentiary Hearing, he began by stating he was convicted of two first-
degree murder charges on October 19, 1956 and was
subsequently sentenced to life in prison. He also noted
on April 1, 1977, the trial court denied his motion for a
new trial, or in the alternative, failed to grant an evidentiary hearing, both of which he claimed were supported by the involuntariness of his plea. He alleged
the denial of his motion was erroneous, and he should
be granted an evidentiary hearing on the issues he presented. He continued by alleging the lower court had
violated the provisions of the Michigan Court Rules by
failing to ask if he, in fact, wanted counsel appointed to
represent him and failed to advise him of the conse-

quences of his guilty plea. He also wrote, as he had in the past, the Court had failed to make a record of his examination, and they had failed to provide counsel at his sentencing. In making his argument, he also wrote that a delayed motion for a new trial could be made at any time if the trial court granted it. In closing, Buchanon noted the lower court had refused to review the fact that court-appointed counsel failed to perfect his timely appeal, and it would be a miscarriage of justice if the Court didn't exercise its discretionary authority to consider the motion.

Included in his affidavit, Buchanon specified in separate paragraphs that when he was arrested on October 17, 1956, he was beaten by the police until he gave a statement, he was denied counsel at his arrest, and he was forced to sign extradition papers. He continued on by saying that when he arrived in Michigan, he was denied counsel again and was repeatedly questioned by officers, including Sheriff Barnes and even a newspaper reporter. He included he was forced to give another statement without an attorney, was ordered into Judge Salmon's chambers without the benefit of record, and was intimidated even further.

On July 8, Assistant Prosecuting Attorney Lee Atkinson's response to the motion highlighted each time Nealy Buchanon's applications for Leave to Appeal were denied by the Ingham County Circuit Court and Michigan Court of Appeals. Atkinson noted Judge Salmon's review of the appeal filed by Buchanon and holding the matter in abeyance for over a year to receive guidance on how to proceed with the matter while waiting for a ruling in the pending case of *People v. Winegar*, which mirrored Buchanon's appeal. He went on to point out that the Michigan Supreme Court had denied Buchanon's motion, not once, but on three separate occasions. Atkinson, in his response, wrote:

> *"Not only was the Defendant-Appellant properly convicted and sentenced pursuant to his plea of guilty based on the THEN EXISTING [sic] law (People v. Olson,[54] People v. Winegar) but he raises the same issues in this motion, as the Court has previously denied leave to appeal for lack of merit. Based on the law of the case doctrine, which this Court discussed, and followed in People v. Bergin, the Defendant-Appellant would not only be precluded from raising any issues already decided by the same court, but also from raising any new issue (if one existed) which <u>could have been raised</u> [sic] at the time of the original appeal."[55]*

It was only a week after he received the decision from the Court of Appeals when he was transferred from Marquette back to Jackson again.

By December, Buchanon was still alleging errors in the taking of his guilty plea twenty-one years earlier, and in another Delayed Application for Leave to Appeal, he noted because of the errors, it required setting the guilty plea aside, and he should have been granted an evidentiary hearing. The Application was made to the Michigan Supreme Court, and in February of 1978, he filed a Motion for Peremptory Reversal in Lieu of Leave to Appeal, again alleging errors in the plea-taking process, because he wasn't advised of the degree of the murder and was not present at the Hearing to Determine Degree of Guilt.

It was clear from the verbiage in his paperwork that

he had found another jailhouse lawyer to help him.

In his new pleadings, Buchanon made a motion to proceed 'forma pauperis,' or as someone who doesn't have money, to pursue his criminal defense. In the same pleadings, he submitted a motion for the appointment of an attorney to represent and protect his rights and privileges under the Fourteenth Amendment.

Mike Woodworth walked into the Ingham County Prosecutor's Office for his interview with the newly-elected Prosecuting Attorney Peter Houk. Houk, sitting behind his desk, looked up to see the young applicant standing before him. Woodworth, at well over six feet tall, shoulder-length hair, and a keen sense of humor, was undeterred by the elected official's question when he asked the lanky Woodworth, "What's a long-haired hippie guy like you doing applying for a job at the Prosecutor's Office?" Without hesitation, Woodworth responded, "What's an elected public official like you doing judging people by their personal appearance?"

Houk smiled, as did Woodworth, with both men cementing a lifelong friendship.

Mike Woodworth, the twenty-something young attorney, had been a school teacher from 1970 to 1973 in the Jonesville school district before deciding to go to law school. Having already earned his bachelor's degree from Central Michigan University, he began taking classes for his Master's degree at Eastern Michigan University while he taught high school. After deciding on law school, he ended up with his degree from Wayne State University.

The young attorney was hired by the Michigan

Court of Appeals as an appellate attorney in 1976. All he had ever wanted to do was to be a trial lawyer, but when he was offered a job by the Court of Appeals, he couldn't turn it down. His position lasted for one year and when he left, he heard about a job with Ingham County as the Chief Appellate Attorney. The larger prosecuting attorney's offices around Michigan, like Ingham, Wayne, and Genessee County, all wanted their own appellate specialists, and Woodworth's experience with the Court of Appeals made him the ideal choice.

Inheriting the Buchanon case, Woodworth knew nothing of the murder, let alone the appeal. A young paralegal, Gina Melvin, who would later become Mrs. Woodworth, helped him research the case. Gina, at twenty-two years old and hired by the former prosecutor Ray Scodeller, searched for the original file in the basement of an old county building, while Woodworth went to the library in hopes of finding old news articles about the murder, in addition to reviewing Lee Atkinson's files. There was no way they would take the 'Statement of Facts' from Buchanon as proof of anything. They needed to be certain. Having nothing more than what Nealy Buchanon had submitted in his Application for Appeal, Gina was assigned to assist Woodworth in his quest for more than what Atkinson had.

Woodworth, along with many other appellate attorneys, believed appellate cases were made or broken based largely on the "statement of facts." When the paperwork was finished and filed, they simply tried to tell a story. Making it even more difficult, Woodworth was working under the gun. He was assigned numerous other appeal cases at the same time, with hard dates where briefs had to be in order and presented to the Court of Appeals.

While Gina Melvin was searching for the original file, Woodworth used Digests, which were publications highlighting various Supreme Court decisions from around the country. Each digest was indexed, and even classified by state. In order to argue against Buchanon's appeals, Woodworth had to find appropriate case law to reference. He was always skeptical of the cases highlighted in the digests, wondering who was choosing the cases highlighted in the digests, or who was actually preparing the index.

If Nealy Buchanon had begun filing his appeals in 1956 within the legally required time, he would have had an automatic Claim of Appeal if the Michigan Court of Appeals had been in existence at the time and an absolute right of oral arguments before the Court. Because he waited ten years, he had to begin his process by filing an Application for a Delayed Leave of Appeal.

Working with John Steele, another assistant prosecuting attorney, Woodworth's response to Buchanon's latest round of appeals was substantive. In their Opposition to Delayed Application for Leave to Appeal, Woodworth and Steele noted that the court rule in which Buchanon was basing his allegations of error on wasn't in existence at the time he pled guilty in 1956. Citing a previous court opinion from 1976, *People v. Olson*, they wrote, "A guilty plea should be examined in light of the law in existence at the time it was taken." Their brief continued, "A defendant who could have raised issues concerning his conviction for murder on his original appeal, as of right, is precluded from belatedly raising these issues on a subsequent appeal," again citing a case from 1975, *People v. Bergin*.[56]

The two attorneys highlighted a rule of law known as the law of the case doctrine, by noting, "It militates strongly against piecemeal litigation of alleged errors by means of successive and interminable appeals from a single judgment."

In their final point, they wrote, "When a criminal defendant has solemnly admitted in court that he is in fact guilty of the offense with which he is charged, he may not thereafter raise independent claims relating to the deprivation of constitutional rights that occurred prior to the entry of the guilty plea," citing *Tollett v. Henderson* and *People v. Peters*. In addition, "In any event, guilty pleas may not be set aside on the basis of newly discovered evidence...Even if the defendant's confession was illegally obtained, and therefore inadmissible, the guilty plea constitutes a waiver of the infirmity."

Having no success at an appeal for over 22 years, Buchanon knew he had nothing to lose and wasn't about to give up. Still representing himself, a Motion for Peremptory Reversal in Lieu of Leave to Appeal was filed. In his latest filing, Buchanon claimed he was never informed as to the degree of murder or the essential elements of the offense he pled guilty to. He continued, noting his guilty pleas were involuntary and must be set aside by the Court. On the same day of the original pleas, the Court conducted a hearing, took testimony, and admitted evidence without his presence, and then, only afterward, determined it was first-degree murder. Finally, Buchanon claimed he was denied due process of law when the Court held the hearing to take testimony, receive evidence, and determine the degree of the offenses without having him present or without a waiver of his right to be present.

Again, Woodworth and Steele were tasked with answering in opposition to the motion. While brief in their response, they noted the original record reflected the defendant was specifically informed he was charged with two counts of murder in violation of the first-degree murder statute, MCLA 750.316; MSA 28.548. Woodworth also wrote that the subject matter of the appeal did not involve legal principles of major significance to the jurisprudence of the state. With respect to Buchanon being absent from the Court, he noted the previous records showed the defendant was indeed present for the hearing.

This was the fourth round of appeals Nealy Buchanon had filed in an attempt to reverse his plea-based conviction. Each of the issues raised, and others, had already been raised in one or more of his prior appeals, and the rulings of the appellate courts had consistently denied the appeals. In fact, each of the issues raised by the killer in this appeal had already been rejected in previous appeals by the original trial court, the Michigan Court of Appeals, and the Michigan Supreme Court.

By the time Buchanon's appeals had been denied again, he had found another jailhouse lawyer to help him.

Ronald Larkins, an inmate who would tout himself as a legal assistant at the prison, suggested to Nealy he might be able to file a lawsuit in Federal District Court. It was the first time anyone had ever suggested anything regarding appeals with the federal courts. One of the requirements for the killer to file a petition in the federal courts was having all his previous appeals in the lower courts exhausted, which had been the case for Buchanon. He would have to make a constitutional challenge to his conviction, and he knew he would need Larkins' help in filing the paperwork. His challenge to the conviction would have to be framed in the context of a federal constitutional violation. The federal court could review the case but solely on constitutional grounds.

Larkins, working on behalf of Buchanon, filed a Petition of Habeas Corpus, a Motion to Proceed in Forma Pauperis, an Affidavit of Indigency, an Affidavit in Support of the Petition, and a Memorandum of Facts and Law. The paperwork was filed in the United States District Court, Eastern District of Michigan, Southern Division, on October 12, 1979.

Ronald Larkins had obviously been helping other inmates with legal paperwork. His petition for Nealy stated he had been 'unconstitutionally detained and imprisoned' by Charles E. Anderson, Warden of the State Prison of Southern Michigan. Larkins wrote that Buchanon had exhausted all available state remedies under 28 U.S.C. Sec. 2254 and outlined all the steps taken by Buchanon to remedy his situation by listing the numerous dates Nealy had filed an Application for Delayed Appeal, Delayed Motion for Appeal, Application for Remand to the Trial Court For an Evidentiary Hearing, and a Delayed Application for Leave to Appeal in the Michigan Supreme Court. Larkins continued by stating Buchanon's "restraints are unconstitutional" based on the Memorandum of Law and Facts. Larkins based the petition on records and files from the Michigan Supreme Court file and, in closing the killer's petition, asked the Court to "relieve Petitioner of the unconstitutional restraints of his liberty."

In the section of Buchanon's petition regarding the Statement of Facts, Larkins followed Nealy's previous allegations of having no record of the conference in Judge Salmon's chambers just prior to sentencing and having been "absent" during the degree hearing. Larkins, still on behalf of Buchanon, maintained because Nealy wasn't informed of the degree of homicide he was charged with, his plea was therefore not understandingly made, and it was accepted in violation of right to due process of the law. In validating the claim, Larkins wrote:

> "Proper advice in a plea procedure entials [sic] a defendant knowing the degree of the offense and notice (i.e. being informed of the charges against him) which has been described as the 'first and most universally recognized requirement of due process'....The importance of this right cannot be questioned. Its waiver cannot be presumed from a silent record."

Throughout Buchanon's appeals in the lower court, each time he made the assertion he was not present at the degree hearing held on October 19, 1956, the response was always clear in describing what had occurred during the hearing, and testimony was cited in the response to each appeal showing Buchanon was present at the hearing.

Larkins, in writing the petition of late, asserted again that Nealy Buchanon wasn't present at the hearing when testimony was taken, evidence was received, and the degree of the offense was determined. Larkins wrote:

> "In the instant cause, the record reflects that there is more than a reasonable possibility that Petitioner Buchanon was prejudiced by his absence during this hearing. It cannot be said that Petitioner's absence made no difference in the results reached."

It was only after he filed the paperwork in the Federal District Court when Nealy decided to withdraw his petition. Buchanon had been speaking with someone other than Larkins in the prison's Paralegal Services, and he was told his case wasn't strong enough. The suggestion was made that he withdraw the petition without prejudice, and the inmate in Paralegal Services would look it over for him. On January 14, 1980, a motion was made for the withdrawal.

Before the petition was withdrawn, the Michigan Attorney General's Office represented the state, and on August 29, 1980, Assistant Attorney General Keith Roberts filed a motion to dismiss the petition, or in the alternative, a motion for summary judgment in the matter saying the twenty-four year time lapse between Buchanon's guilty plea and his Petition for Writ of Habeas Corpus had prejudiced the State's ability to effectively respond to his claims.

To support his argument, Assistant Attorney General Roberts cited a Memorandum of Opinion written by Judge Charles W. Joiner discussing the standards for applying the argument:

> *"The standard for denial of writ is whether the delay denied the state the ability to fully respond to the petition. It is not whether the state may retry the petitioner successfully. Furthermore, even prejudice to the state's ability to adequately respond to the petition is sufficient for dismissal, unless grounds exist which the Petitioner could not have had knowledge by the exercise of reasonable diligence before the circumstances prejudicial to the state occurred."*[57]

In addition to the lapse in time between the guilty plea and the petition, the Ingham County prosecutor's file containing the information charging Nealy Buchanon with murder couldn't be located. Deputy Ingham County Clerk Mary Jo Graham had searched the files. The Herrick murder file was last known to exist in 1977, three years before, after it was checked out to the Ingham County Prosecuting Attorney's Office, but it was nowhere to be found. This added to the State's inability to respond to the petition, in addition to the unavailability of the former prosecutor Charles Chamberlain.

Arguing further, Roberts wrote that the validity of a guilty plea under the Fourteenth Amendment is whether the plea represented a 'voluntary and intelligent choice among the alternative courses of action open to the Petitioner.' It was the State's position that the record removed any doubt as to Nealy Buchanon's plea being voluntary.

Citing an additional decision by the United States Supreme Court in *Bute v. Illinois*,[58] Roberts referenced it, writing:

> *"Doubts should be resolved in favor of the integrity, competence, and proper performance of their official duties by the judge and state's attorney."*

In Nealy Buchanon's motion, he argued he was denied due process when the Hearing to Determine the Degree of Guilt was held in his absence. The State's position was that the hearing was not a trial or a trial-type adversary proceeding requiring the opportunity to confront and cross-examine witnesses. Buchanon had already entered a guilty plea to the murder of Howard and Myra Herrick. The trial court was correct under Michigan law by affording the defendant the Degree of Guilt hearing. On behalf of the State, Roberts maintained Buchanon had no right to participate in the 'non-adversary' proceeding.

In his final argument, Roberts wrote that the hearing was unnecessary. Citing the Prosecuting Attorney Charles Chamberlain's testimony, he wrote:

> "MR. CHAMBERLAIN: (Reading information charging a violation of Sec. 316 of Act 328 of the Public Acts of 1931, being C. L. 1948, 750.316; M.S.A. 28.548.)

Roberts wrote that as far as he could reconstruct from the record, the information cited in the court record contained only the charge of first-degree murder. The statute requiring a hearing to determine the degree of guilt was only applicable when a 'general' plea of guilty is entered, charging murder with more than one degree. Because of that, the hearing to determine the degree of guilt was unnecessary, and Buchanon's claim that he was denied due process was without any merit.

In closing, the Assistant Attorney General noted that even if Buchanon had the constitutional right of confrontation in the hearing, the transcript revealed his presence at the hearing, and no objection or 'attempted intervention' was ever made. Roberts wrote:

> "Indeed, Petitioner's silent acquiescence in the presentation of evidence serves only to further support Respondent's position that he knew the full consequences of the plea and intended the effect."

It wasn't until late October when an order was issued by United States District Judge Robert DeMascio to grant the request for withdrawing the petition, but on October 20, a letter was received by the Court asking the petition to be reconsidered and reinstated.

On December 9, there was an order from the United States District Court saying the Motion for Reconsideration and Reinstatement be granted, and Buchanon was given 20 days to respond to the motion for dismissal of his petition.

It was the day after Christmas when Buchanon's response was received by the Court. In his 'Counter-Statement of Facts', Nealy Buchanon revealed why he had withdrawn his earlier petition. On January 9, 1980, believing he would receive a Governor's Pardon, he withdrew it, after he was told by other inmates that the State would never release him if he didn't. He never received the pardon.

He continued in his denial of the State's Motion to Dismiss by citing the affidavit filed by Mary Jo Graham, indicating any fault for losing the file rested with the Ingham County Prosecuting Attorney's Office. Additionally, a mere lapse of time was not sufficient for the State to claim he failed to file his appeal earlier. There had to be some sort of prejudice on the State, and a loss of the file on the part of the Prosecuting Attorney's office wasn't enough to constitute prejudice.

Buchanon's petition went on citing the U.S. Supreme Court case of *Rice v. Olson*,[59] stating, "Although a plea of guilty waives many constitutional rights incident to a jury trial, it does not waive the right to due process." Continuing, some of the facts of his case were highlighted in the petition:

"Petitioner escaped from Trustee Division

in 1955. He thereafter proceeded to Ingham County where, while trying to steal a car he was surprised by the male owner of said car, in the barn of the latter owner. During a scuffle, Petitioner picked up a small object, believed to be a 1 1/2-2 pound hand-grinder used for sharpening small household items, and hit the male owner of the car in the head. Petitioner was trying only to prevent his capture and hit the deceased two or three times. Whereas, the deceased's wife discovered Petitioner standing in the barn, and Petitioner also hit her in the head, two or three times. There was no malice towards the two people by Petitioner. There was no premeditation. To be sure, the deaths were unjustifiable. Nevertheless, the deaths could be termed 'manslaughter.' The 'maximum' sentence for the crime of manslaughter is fifteen years. Petitioner has already been confined longer than twenty-four years. Had your Petitioner been allowed to be represented by counsel at the degree hearing to determine the degree of his crime, he would have been advised by counsel that should he choose to plead guilty, he would be pleading guilty to manslaughter, and not first-degree murder."

The petition went on to address the State's position of Buchanon's silence that during the presentation of evidence, it only furthered their belief that he knew the full consequences of his plea and the intended out-

A SLAYER WAITS

come. Citing the case of *Moore v. Michigan*, the petition read:

> "*Nothing could be further from the truth where the Petitioner was the object of an intensive hunt, and the general racial climate of the country necessitated his plea of guilty, where he was the only Black American present throughout the proceedings to determine his guilt, and 'common sense' demanded that he so plead.*"

Buchanon's petition closed, stating there was no coroner's report presented to show a cause of death for Howard and Myra Herrick, and his fingerprints were not found on the murder weapon. He maintained a hearing was required to allow the State to respond to his petition. At the end of his petition, he added that at the time of his arrest, he only had $3 on him, and it was 'sufficient proof' he could not have hired an attorney for his defense. He concluded by writing:

> "*Petitioner's indigency required that if Justice* [sic] *was to be done, counsel should have been appointed for the indigent accused Petitioner, unlettered and frightened out-of-his-wits* [sic].*"

With that, Nealy Buchanon, in addition to requesting a hearing, formally requested the assistance of counsel for the first time since his arrest 24 years earlier.

CHAPTER 12

Counsel

Frank Eaman had been practicing law for ten years when he took Nealy Buchanon's case before the United States District Court of Appeals in 1981. At thirty-six years old, criminal defense was his lifeblood in the beginning, having attended the University of Michigan Law School and obtaining his juris doctorate. His grandfather, a practicing attorney in Detroit for over fifty years, had been appointed as the Detroit Police Commissioner in the 1940s and had been tapped for duty by Detroit Mayor Edward Jeffries, Jr. in 1939 to route out corrupt officers and to bring racial integration and respect to the Detroit Police Department. His grandfather was also a part of the commission responsible for building the world's largest walled prison.

In the 1960s, Eaman was engaged in the civil rights movement, including marching with several thousand Detroiters down Woodward Avenue with Dr. Martin

Luther King. It was still early in his career when he was admitted to the bar in the Eastern District of Michigan in 1971 and to the Sixth Circuit Court of Appeals in 1978. Originally, he had worked for Gage, Burgess, Knox, Burgess & Eaman. By the time he took Buchanon's appeal, he was partnered in a small firm called Eaman and Ravitz, working with his wife, Allyn, who was also an attorney.

On July 2, Judge DeMascio ordered Buchanon's request for court-appointed counsel be granted and ordered an evidentiary hearing be held with the issue revolving around the taking of his plea.

Shortly after DeMascio's opinion, United States Magistrate Thomas Carlson called the young attorney. Eaman, who was on the Federal Assigned Counsel Panel, was eligible to take appeal cases and had met Carlson before. The magistrate asked if he would take an appointment to a habeas case. Eaman knew Carlson had been a Supreme Court Commissioner and had worked with his cousin, who was another practicing attorney. Frank Eaman agreed to take the case but knew nothing of the details.

On the seventeenth floor of the Ford Building in downtown Detroit, Eaman's office had certain historical significance, having once served as the office for Thomas Chawke, a Detroit attorney who defended Dr. Ossian Sweet in 1925 alongside attorney Clarence Darrow. Darrow had received notoriety for famous trials, including the Scopes Monkey Trial and the case of Leopold and Loeb in Chicago.

Dr. Sweet, who was black, had moved his family into a white neighborhood in Detroit, and when a mob surrounded his home, a shot was fired from inside, killing a man in the crowd. Dr. Sweet and three members of his family inside the home were charged with the man's murder, along with eight others.

Chawke, working with Darrow, defended Dr. Sweet and three others. In Clarence Darrow's argument before an all-white jury, he argued, "I insist that there is nothing but prejudice in this case; that if it was reversed, and eleven white men had shot and killed a black while protecting their home and their lives against a mob of blacks, nobody would have dreamed of having them indicted. They would have been given medals instead." It was Dr. Sweet's brother, Henry, who admitted having fired the shot, and he was acquitted on grounds of self-defense, while charges were dropped against the other defendants.

From Chawke's former office, Frank Eaman could see the Ambassador Bridge connecting the United States and Canada. As he began preparing for his new case, his first priority was to review Buchanon's file, then go to Jackson Prison and meet his newest client.

Normally, prisoners who met with their attorneys at the prison were put into a private area specifically for attorney/client meetings. At his first meeting with Nealy Buchanon, the two men were put in a large visiting room with other inmates and their families. Frank's sole purpose was to go through Nealy's personal background, discuss the case with him and the issues at hand. It was essential for Eaman to build a relationship with Buchanon where both men would trust each other.

As the two men met, Frank studied the face of the killer. He saw an old man sitting in front of him who had been in prison for a very long time and had never had a lawyer represent him. To Frank's knowledge, he would be the first attorney to ever represent Nealy Buchanon in a legal proceeding. All the previous legal paperwork written regarding Buchanon's appeals had been done by jailhouse lawyers, except for a very brief period in 1966, when Hannibal Abood filed the first appeal for Nealy.

It was shocking to Frank Eaman, and he quickly realized the incredible responsibility he had before him.

As the low man in seniority at the Michigan Attorney General's Office, Eric Eggan worked in an extremely small office on the first floor of the Plaza One Building on South Washington Street in Lansing and had one secretary who was also assigned to three other attorneys. Originally, the building had served as the Knapp's Department Store, but it had since been remodeled into state offices. Because the building still maintained much of its original architecture and the floors shook as people walked down hallways, there was concern over how many file cabinets should actually be brought into the first floor because of the aging structure and fear that the first floor might actually collapse. In his tight, cramped office, it was evident to the young assistant attorney general that the state had not put a lot of money into the renovations.

Eggan was from the Alpena area, and he had graduated from Alpena High School in 1974 with his high school sweetheart. He attended Central Michigan University in Mt. Pleasant and continued his education at Thomas M. Cooley Law School in Lansing, graduating in 1980. Eric Eggan was working as law clerk at the

Michigan Attorney General's Office in 1981 and had been assigned to help Assistant Attorney General Keith Roberts with the Buchanon file, doing much of the previous research for him on the appeals. Both Roberts and his law clerk, Eggan, were assigned in the Corrections Division of the Attorney General's Office, and cases were assigned randomly. Because there were so many other cases being handled, as soon as Eggan passed the Bar exam in 1981, Roberts asked if he wanted to take over Nealy Buchanon's case. Eggan jumped at the chance, having already done much of the previous research on it.

There was a problem. In an effort to prepare for the pending evidentiary hearing, Eggan asked for the entire file from the Ingham County Prosecuting Attorney's Office, which would include the police report and transcripts of Buchanon's confession, arraignment, degree hearing, and sentencing. The search was on, but the original case file, now twenty-five years old, was missing.

The evidentiary hearing would have to proceed without Eggan having it.

The assistant attorney general was confident and excited about handling the appeal and felt it was a strong case which might eventually go before the United States Supreme Court. In preparation, he never met Frank Eaman prior to the evidentiary hearing but spoke briefly by phone with him regarding procedural matters and witnesses each attorney would be having testify at the hearing.

Buchanon was finally getting the news he had waited for since he first began filing appeals in 1966. It had been almost twenty-five years since he was sentenced to life in prison, and now the Eastern District of the United States District Court was going to hold an evidentiary hearing based on Nealy's petition.

On August 14, 1981, two weeks prior to the evidentiary hearing, Frank Eaman submitted a brief supporting the amended petition for a Writ of Habeas Corpus on behalf of his client, Nealy J. Buchanon.

In his first argument, Eaman noted a book by Joseph Cook titled *Constitutional Rights of the Accused: Pretrial Rights* (1974), writing, "Few constitutional protections are as fundamental to insuring a fair trial to the accused as the right to counsel." He continued by mentioning the U.S. Supreme Court's description of the importance of the Sixth Amendment:

> *"The Sixth Amendment stands as a constant admonition that if the constitutional safeguards it provides be lost, justice will not 'still be done.' It embodies a realistic recognition of the obvious truth that the average defendant does not have the professional legal skill to protect himself when brought before a tribunal with power to take his life or liberty, wherein the prosecution is presented by experienced and learned counsel. That which is simple, orderly, and necessary to the lawyer — to the untrained laymen — may appear intricate, complex, and mysterious."*

Eaman also added a description of the requirements for a valid waiver of counsel and the judge's duty in determining it, which was provided by Justice Black in the case of *Von Moltke v. Gillies,*[60] Superintendent of the Detroit House of Correction:

> *"We have said: 'The constitutional right of an accused to be represented by counsel invokes, of itself, the protection of a trial court, in which the accused—whose life and liberty is at stake—is without counsel. The protecting duty imposes the serious and weighty responsibility upon the trial judge of determining whether there is an intelligent and competent waiver by the accused.' To discharge this duty properly in light of the strong presumption against waiver of the constitutional right to counsel, a judge must investigate as long and as thoroughly as the circumstances of the case before him demands. The fact that an accused may tell him that he is informed of his right to counsel and desires to waive his right does not automatically end the judge's responsibility. To be valid, such waiver must be made with an apprehension of the nature of the charges, the statutory offense included with them, the range of allowable punishments thereunder, possible defenses to the charges and circumstance in mitigation thereof, and all other facts essential to a broad understanding of the whole matter. A judge can make certain that an accused's professed waiver of counsel is understandingly and wisely made only from a*

penetrating and comprehensive examination of all the circumstances under which such a plea is tendered."

Eaman continued his position saying, based on that, the case should properly be compared to *Moore v. Michigan*. He maintained his client had been refused counsel out of fear and coercive suggestions made by authorities.

In addition, Eaman maintained that Buchanon's plea was not voluntarily and understandingly made because it was induced by coercive behavior and without counsel. According to him, it was inconsistent with due process, citing the U.S. Supreme Court's position:

> *"A conviction, following a trial or on a plea of guilty based on a confession extorted by violence or by mental coercion, is invalid under the Federal Due Process Clause. (350 US at 118)"*

To substantiate his claim, Eaman noted Buchanon's 1977 affidavit describing his treatment by the Baltimore Police Department when he was arrested and a statement allegedly made to his client by Sheriff Barnes, saying, "They want to hang your black ass." This treatment, along with Judge Salmon's in-chambers conference when he allegedly told Buchanon to "Go along with the program" or he'd send him back to Stockbridge, and, "Let the mob have its way with him," all occurred within 72 hours of Nealy's arrest. Eaman described them as coercive tactics, writing:

> *"It would be safe to say that a black man charged with the slayings of two white*

> *people in a predominantly white rural community in the 1950s easily could be motivated to plead guilty out of fear alone where he was physically abused in one jail and threatened by the prospects of facing a crowd seeking revenge by none other than a sheriff and judge."*

Frank Eaman also asserted his client's guilty plea might never have been made if he had been provided with counsel.

Moving to his next argument, the new court-appointed counsel for Nealy Buchanon wrote that his client was denied due process and the right to confront witnesses, because he was absent at the hearing to determine the degree of guilt, in addition to not being afforded the opportunity to participate in the hearing. Referencing a point in the hearing transcript where Buchanon was asked to approach the bench, Nealy claimed he was only brought into the courtroom at the conclusion of the hearing. Even if the Court found he was present, he still wasn't afforded the opportunity of counsel or the ability to participate. Eaman maintained, as Buchanon's attorney, that it was a "Gross violation of the due process clause of the Fourteenth Amendment and the Sixth Amendment of the Right to Counsel." He also wrote that Buchanon's sentence could have been mitigated had he been present at the degree hearing and had the opportunity to cross-examine prosecution witnesses.

While Eaman couldn't cite any cases addressing the constitutional right of a defendant to be present at a degree hearing, he wrote, "Concepts of due process and analogy to other cases strongly suggests that Petitioner's absence from a degree hearing was a violation of the Fourteenth Amendment's Due Process Clause."

In closing his brief, Eaman pointed out that the degree hearing held by Judge Salmon in 1956 was not a fair hearing, and thus, violated the Due Process Clause of the Fourteenth Amendment and was in violation of the right to counsel and confrontation clauses of the Sixth Amendment.

Nealy Buchanon's day had finally arrived, and he was represented at the hearing by his newly-appointed counsel. The hearing was held before Magistrate Thomas Carlson in Detroit, and though it had been scheduled for July 30, the hearing was delayed until September 3, 1981; oddly, twenty-six years to the day after the murders of Howard and Myra Herrick. Judge Carlson, a former assistant attorney general himself, made it clear in the beginning that the purpose of the hearing was to discuss the circumstances surrounding Buchanon's 1956 guilty plea.

Eric Eggan had spent a lot of time preparing for the case and knew it forward and backward, but he was concerned with what had happened in Mason twenty-six years earlier. His concern centered on Buchanon having been brought into court for his arraignment without an attorney to provide him guidance, as he pled guilty to two counts of first-degree murder. It didn't just concern Eggan; it gave great concern to the attorney general's office as a whole, and collectively, they felt there were certain issues which had to be addressed in order to affirm Nealy Buchanon's conviction. Though confident, he expected problems with the case because of previous decisions by the United States

Supreme Court, including *Gideon v. Wainwright*.[61] He also knew Frank Eaman would be very well prepared.

In the landmark case of *Gideon v. Wainwright*, the United States Supreme Court ruled unanimously, under the Sixth Amendment, that states are required to provide counsel to defendants who can't afford to pay for their own attorney.

A break-in at the Bay Harbor Pool Room in Panama City, Florida was the basis for the Gideon decision. It was in 1961 when the business was burglarized, with a cigarette machine and record player being smashed, along with cash being taken from the register. A lone witness saw Clarence Gideon leaving the poolroom at around 5:30 am with a wine bottle, and he was quickly arrested.

In an exchange with the Court at his arraignment, Gideon was denied an attorney:

> *"The COURT: Mr. Gideon, I am sorry, but I cannot appoint counsel to represent you in this case. Under the laws of the State of Florida, the only time the Court can appoint counsel to represent a defendant is when that person is charged with a capital offense. I am sorry, but I will have to deny your request to appoint counsel to defend you in this case.*
>
> *GIDEON: The United States Supreme Court says I am entitled to be represented by counsel."*

As a result, Gideon acted as his own attorney, was found guilty and sentenced to five years in the state prison.

During his time in prison, he appealed to the United States Supreme Court. He wrote in pencil on prison stationary, alleging in a suit; first, against the Secretary of the Florida Department of Corrections, H. G. Cochran, and second, against Cochran's retirement replacement, Louie L. Wainwright, that he had been denied counsel and his Sixth Amendment rights, as applied to the Fourteenth Amendment, had been violated.

The United States Supreme Court opined that the Sixth Amendment to the United States Constitution didn't differentiate between capital and non-capital offenses; thus, an attorney must be provided for an indigent defendant in all cases. They also said the "mere existence of a serious criminal charge in itself constituted special circumstances requiring the services of counsel."

On the morning of Nealy Buchanon's evidentiary hearing, the assistant attorney general picked up retired Judge Marvin Salmon at his condominium in East Lansing in the blue Chevy Chevette he and his wife had purchased while living in Alpena. They drove to Detroit together, as Salmon was the State's only witness.

At the same time, a writ had already been received by the prison ordering Nealy Buchanon's appearance at the Sixth Circuit Court of Appeals in Detroit.

For Frank Eaman, there was no hurry to drive anywhere. With his office in the Ford Building, he was within walking distance to the Recorder's Court, the Wayne County Court, and the Federal Court.

At the large, impressive Federal District Court House bordered by Ford Street and Lafayette Street, the magistrate's courtroom was small. While their work was important, the magistrates weren't afforded the larger, more luxurious courtrooms, like the federal district judges were. The magistrate sat on the bench at the front of the courtroom. There were two tables for the attorneys, no jury box, and a small gallery in the back.

It was the first and only time Eric Eggan would come face to face with Nealy Buchanon, and he had no idea what to expect.

At fifty-seven years old, Nealy Buchanon was still a hulking man with maroon eyes, and his black hair had long since turned to gray. Eggan was taken aback at how calm the now bearded Buchanon was, knowing what he had done to Howard and Myra Herrick so many years before. As he took a seat at the defense table, Buchanon seemed very quiet, unassuming, and almost grandfatherly to the young attorney. He didn't seem overly anxious about the proceeding at all. He was Frank Eaman's first witness.

In his first round of questioning, he acknowledged to Eaman that he had entered a guilty plea in Ingham County Circuit Court in 1956, and he told the Court he hadn't been represented by an attorney when he made the plea. He continued by answering Eaman's questioning about whether or not he ever received advice from an attorney, either before the guilty plea, during the plea, during the sentencing, or after the sentencing, saying he had not.

Eaman took Buchanon back to a time before the murders of Howard and Myra Herrick, having him admit he had been involved in the court system before and then asking if he had ever had a lawyer in any of his court proceedings.

Nealy replied, "No."

"This question relates to before 1956. Before 1956, in relation to your other court appearances or other matters, could you afford to hire an attorney for yourself?" Eaman asked.

Again, Nealy replied, "No."

Asked if he could afford an attorney in 1956 when he was charged with the Herrick murders, he again said, "No."

In fact, Eaman made it clear to the Court through his line of questioning that even after being sentenced to life in prison, his client still couldn't afford an attorney. That led into questioning him about when he first filed an appeal, and he told the Court he had used the services of another inmate to help him file his first appeal in 1966. Eaman quickly followed up having Nealy tell the Court he was provided with an attorney shortly after filing his first appeal in Ingham County, and Buchanon explained that his attorney discussed the case 'very little' with him.

Buchanon listed the appeals he had made to the higher courts and how he had done it by himself, using another inmate to assist him with the paperwork and eventually filing an appeal with the Michigan Supreme Court.

After establishing he had never used an attorney in any of the appeals after 1966, Eaman cut to the chase by asking, "Now, do you consider yourself to be a murderer under the law or not?"

Buchanon replied, "No."

Eaman followed up the question by asking, "Were you in 1956?"

Again, Buchanon answered, "No."

Buchanon told the Court the first time anyone had suggested he file an appeal in the Federal Court was in 1977 or 1978, and it was another inmate who had suggested it to him.

Eaman wanted the Court to understand why his client had withdrawn his petition in the federal court earlier, and Nealy explained the discussion he had with the inmate in Paralegal Services at the prison.

The attorney was quick to point out through his client's testimony that he had not withdrawn his petition in an effort to intentionally delay the process. When asked about the reason his petition was withdrawn, Nealy said, "I didn't—I didn't know. I didn't think I had a chance. I didn't think I had any rights, you know."

He was asked if he was aware of the prosecutor's claim that their file was lost, and then asked if he had anything to do with it, to which he replied, "No." He also told the Court he had not been given any prior access to their file or a chance to ever review its contents.

Frank Eaman then led his client into recalling his arrest in 1956. Buchanon detailed his confinement and his interview by the Baltimore Police. He told the Court, "Well, they were kind of aggressive and a little disrespectful...they shoved me around a little bit."

Eaman asked what he meant, and Buchanon said, "They beat on me with a blackjack across the back and shoulders." The attorney pressed him further by asking him what the police had told him. "They said that I was going to get beat up and killed, possibly killed, if I didn't make a statement...Said it would be easier [sic] for me," he explained.

Frank Eaman was sharp. He was trying to establish that Buchanon's confession was somehow coerced. He continued, "At the time you were arrested on the two counts of murder and held in the Baltimore jail, what was your understanding of the penalty for murder in the State of Michigan?"

"I thought you would get electrocuted. I thought they had a chair...I thought it would be easier for me and easier for my family. I was married then," said Buchanon. He continued by telling the Court the police had told him that unless he made a statement, he was in trouble and his family was in trouble.

Eaman moved his questioning into the convicted killer's state of mind when he was arrested in Baltimore. His client said, "Well, at best, I was a little mentally unstable, run down, tense, and I felt useless and alone."

Asked if he had the opportunity to speak with a lawyer in Baltimore, he said, "No."

"Did you, in Baltimore, at any time, have any feelings of fear in regard to anything?" asked Eaman.

Nealy continued, "Oh, yes, I was scared...Baltimore is a southern town, you know, with no black men, you know; the victims were white. That alone would be enough to hang you."

Buchanon's attorney asked him if he feared for himself at the time, to which he replied he not only feared for himself, but for his family. Buchanon continued, "I felt then, at that time, if I didn't make a statement, I was going to be killed."

Nealy Buchanon then described his encounter with Ingham County Sheriff Barnes, when he arrived in Baltimore, and statements he had made. Asked about the extradition papers he signed, Buchanon said he didn't understand it. When asked why he signed the extradition paper if he didn't understand it, Buchanon said, "Because they wanted to get out of Baltimore...I felt that I was—my future was finished, and if I survived this, it would be a miracle."

Frank Eaman now wanted to paint a picture for the Court about the mood surrounding Buchanon's return to Michigan. Asked to describe his return to the Ingham County Jail, Buchanon said, "Yes, it was a lot of people outside, 50 to 100, I guess. I don't remember how many. There were news reporters, a lot of yelling and a lot of pushing and shoving, a lot of excitement, I guess. And it was just a high-tensed situation."

Nealy described how some people were allowed to come in and look at him through a small window in his jail cell. Asked about how long it went on, he said he thought it went on until he was taken over to the courthouse sometime during the evening.

Eaman asked if anyone had come to him regarding making a statement, and Nealy said Sheriff Barnes was the only one who asked for a statement.

The defense attorney continued the questioning by asking, "How did he ask you, what did he say?"

As Buchanon began to respond, Eric Eggan stood up and interjected, "Your Honor, I'd like to object. I know there's been a lot hearsay here today; I haven't been objecting on hearsay grounds, but I'm going to start objecting on hearsay grounds."

Frank Eaman had anticipated the objection. He addressed the Court by saying, "It's not being introduced to prove the truth of the matter, but the witness's state of mind."

Judge Carlson addressed both attorneys, saying, "All right. With that understanding, we'll allow the Petitioner to continue questioning."

Eaman continued by asking his client what Sheriff Barnes had told him.

"He told me that unless I stuck to the original statement, he was going to turn me over to the mob outside," Buchanon said.

The attorney had just set up his next question asking, "Now, in your past, or in the recent past, had you known of any incidents, had you known of any incidents that had occurred regarding mob violence injury to someone similar to your circumstances?"

Eggan stood just as Buchanon replied, "Oh, yes."

Eric Eggan said, "Objection, Your Honor. That's certainly not in the record or anywhere other than Counsel's statement or what Petitioner has to say. That certainly has no relevance to this situation."

Once again, Frank Eaman had anticipated the objection and quickly responded, "It goes to his state of mind, his knowledge at the time. It's not being introduced to prove the truth of the matter."

Eggan was quick to reply, "Your Honor, much of what Petitioner has to say today is in his state of mind, but it's certainly prejudicial and absolutely irrefutable."

The Court allowed the line of questioning to continue, and after the question was repeated, Buchanon again replied, "Yes."

Eaman asked him about the incident he was thinking about.

"Emmet Till," said Buchanon.

"And what are the circumstances of that as known to you?" asked his attorney.

The killer replied, "Well, he was accused of looking at a white woman, and a mob killed him...It occurred down south. I think it was Carolina or Mississippi, one of those states."

Nealy Buchanon was referring to Emmet Till, who was just fourteen years old when he was kidnapped and murdered in 1955. What Buchanon didn't realize was Emmet Till's kidnapping and murder, his funeral, and his burial coincided with his own escape from the

State Prison of Southern Michigan and the two murders he committed in Stockbridge.

Living in Argo, south of Chicago, Emmett Till was a typical young teenager full of energy and ready to take on the world. At a young age, he contracted polio, and while his recovery was almost complete, a permanent side-effect from the disease was a tendency to stutter when he spoke, especially if he became excited. The young teen learned to cope with his disability by sometimes whistling in an effort to pronounce words properly.

In August, his great uncle, Moses Wright, had come to Chicago from Money, Mississippi, for a funeral. Emmet's cousins, Wheeler Parker and Curtis Jones, were going to travel back to Money for a visit with Moses, and Emmet wanted to go along. His mother, Mamie, was against the idea, but the fourteen-year-old boy was convincing in his argument for the trip. Mamie was cautious about sending her only child to Mississippi, so she had a talk with him about the culture in the south. She knew life was different in the southern states than it was in Chicago. She told him to only speak with white people if he were spoken to first. She told him if he were walking down the street and a white woman was walking toward him, to step off the sidewalk, bow his head and don't look her in the eye. Even more than that, she told him not to look back at her after she passed. She told him to answer 'Yes, sir,' 'Yes, ma'am,' 'No, sir,' or 'No, ma'am,' and she said to him, "If you have to humble yourself, then just do it. Get on your knees, if you have to.[62]"

Mamie's son didn't think it could be that bad, but she told him it was worse. She said if you were a black man in the south, not only should you never look at a white woman in the eye, you should never even look at a photo of a white woman.

The young man tried to reassure his worried mother. He reminded her she had raised him right and taught him how to act.

On August 20, 1955, the *City of New Orleans* left the Englewood Station in Chicago with Moses Wright, Wheeler Parker, and Emmet Till on board the passenger car. Curtis Jones would join them later. They were headed back to Money, Mississippi.

During the visit at Emmet's Uncle Moses' home, Emmet helped with the daily chores, which included picking cotton in the fields.

On the evening of August 27, after a long day in the fields, Emmet, Wheeler, and several other kids drove into town for some treats at Bryant's Grocery and Meat Market. While the owner, Roy Bryant, was out of town, his twenty-one-year-old wife, Carolyn, tended to the store.

Emmet had gone in at one point and paid two cents for some bubble gum, then left the store. All the kids were standing around the car laughing and talking about what they had bought with their earnings, when Carolyn Bryant walked out of the store and headed toward her car. It was at that point, a whistle was heard and, over time, several theories developed among the kids as to what that was. The stories ranged from Emmet whistling as he got stuck on a word, to his whistling at a checker game move on the porch, or simply to be "playful." Whatever the reason for the whistle, the kids quickly decided that Mrs. Bryant must be going to her car for a gun, and they wasted no time in fleeing.

At about 2:00 am on Sunday morning, two men showed up at Moses Wright's home where Emmet was staying. It was Carolyn Bryant's husband, Roy, and his half-brother, J. W. Milam. Milam held a .45 semi-automatic pistol. Wright knew what it meant when white men appeared at the door late at night with guns.

The two men demanded to see the boy from Chicago. They forced their way through the home and, waking Emmet from a sleep, took him away in the night.

Moses Wright was threatened with his life as the men left with his great-nephew in the back of a truck.

Six days later, on September 3, a young fisherman discovered the body of fourteen-year-old Emmet Till in the Tallahatchie River with a seventy-five-pound cotton gin fan tied around his neck. He had been beaten, tortured, and shot, with his eye gouged out.

On the same day Emmet Till's body was found, Howard and Myra Herrick were bludgeoned to death in their Michigan barn.

After his body had been returned to Illinois, Emmet Till's mother, Mamie, asked the funeral director not to do anything to prepare his body for a viewing. She wanted people to see what had been done to her child. Emmet Till's body lay in repose at a funeral home in Argo, Illinois, with a clear piece of plastic over the open coffin showing the grotesque, swollen, tortured body of the fourteen-year-old boy. Thousands of people passed by his coffin, and photos were published worldwide.

On the same day Emmet Till's body was interred, Howard and Myra Herrick's bodies were discovered hidden in their barn.

Roy Bryant and his half-brother, J. W. Milam, were charged with Emmet Till's murder. They were quickly put on trial. One month after the discovery of Emmet's body, the two men were acquitted of murder by an all-white jury after only sixty-two minutes of deliberation.

To Nealy Buchanon, after being captured in Baltimore and returned to Mason, Michigan, his fear of ending up like fourteen-year-old Emmet Till was legitimate.

Buchanon continued his testimony before Judge Carlson by saying Sheriff Barnes had taken him directly to his office for the statement.

Moving his questioning to Buchanon's trip to the jail, Eaman asked his client how many police officers were in the car with him when he was transported, and Buchanon told the Court, "There were two policeman [sic] and one reporter, and the driver."

Then his attorney asked if he was questioned in the car. When Buchanon said he was, Eaman asked him what he had been questioned about. Nealy said, "What I—the statement I had made, the statement I had made to the Baltimore Police."

Eaman quickly led back to Buchanon's state of mind after he had made another statement when arriving back at the Ingham County Jail. "Yes, I was scared. I was really scared. I was really tight and feeling very sorry for myself…scared," said Nealy.

Frank Eaman asked Nealy if he felt, by making a statement in Michigan, there might be some benefit, and he said, "I did think that I would get some relief from the fear I had and that my family would, you know."

Continuing his questioning, Buchanon's attorney asked him if he knew anything about the law regarding homicide in 1956, and his client said he didn't. Eaman took it a step further by asking, "You didn't know there were degrees of homicide, or manslaughter, or any of that...Were you knowledgeable about defenses to homicide, such as insanity?"

His client replied, "No."

In his calculated questioning, Frank Eaman led Nealy Buchanon directly to what had happened after he had made a statement. Nealy described being taken before the magistrate during the evening and described his understanding of the arraignment, including how much the bond amount was set at. Buchanon thought it was $50,000. Asked if he had a lawyer represent him at the arraignment, he told the Court he hadn't.

Eaman glanced at his notes, asking his client if any reporters were allowed to speak with him directly, and Buchanon said they were.

Asked about the timespan from when he was brought to the Ingham County Jail to the time he was sentenced in the Circuit Court in Lansing, Buchanon said he thought it was about 32 hours.

"Do you remember the Judge telling you you could have a lawyer appointed for you?" asked Eaman.

"Yes," his client responded.

"Do you know whether the Judge ever asked you the question precisely, if you wanted a lawyer?" the attorney continued.

"No," was Buchanon's reply.

The attorney continued, "Did you want a lawyer?"

"I didn't know—At first, I didn't think a lawyer would do me any good...Because I thought that lawyers and policemen—This is the attitude I had then—all worked together against me," Buchanon said.

Eric Eggan, listening intently to every answer Buchanon gave to questions posed by his attorney, wrote hurried notes on a legal pad.

Still leading his client in establishing his state of mind, Frank Eaman asked Nealy Buchanon about his understanding of his rights at the time he went before the Circuit Court.

Buchanon answered, "I thought I didn't have any rights."

Eaman quickly followed up by asking, "And what made you think you didn't have any rights?"

"Well, my past life, what I'd experienced in the Army, and elsewhere, getting a job, and elsewhere. I had always thought of myself as a second-class citizen, I didn't think I had any rights," was his client's reply.

In another follow-up question, Eaman asked, "Was there anything that was done by the law enforcement people in Baltimore and Michigan, or anything that reinforced these feelings about not having any rights?"

Nealy Buchanon said, "They were disrespectful, and they called me names…Black nigger, black son-of-a-bitch, things like that."

Judge Carlson was curious about the witness's answer to the question. He wanted more information about who might have made those statements to Buchanon. Carlson said the question was framed in a general sense, and it could have been anyone in Baltimore or Lansing.

Asked who used those words, Buchanon said, "They were detectives, because they had on plain clothes, but I don't know them by name. They didn't tell me their names…This was in Baltimore."

Nealy was asked if those same words were used against him in Michigan, and he said they were. When asked who used them, Buchanon said, "Sheriff Barnes and Judge Marvin—Judge Salmon." Buchanon continued his testimony by saying Judge Salmon had used those names when he had him in his chambers.

Buchanon described a conversation where the judge had told him he better go along with the statement he had prepared, or he and his family would be in big trouble.

Eaman pressed him further by asking in what context Judge Salmon had used those names.

Eric Eggan was on his feet interjecting, "Objection. He's about to testify as to the Judge's frame of mind at that time, and I don't think he's qualified to say what that is."

Frank Eaman didn't understand the objection.

Eggan continued, "He's about to say that the Judge thought he was some kind of a..."

Judge Carlson interrupted Mr. Eggan's objection, "Well, the witness can simply answer what it was that he heard the judge say."

Eggan continued by saying, "Well, could we have a restatement of what the last questions were then?"

Frank Eaman repeated the question, and Judge Carlson said, "Well, even apart from that, I think you can just simply ask the witness what he said and then what the Judge said."

Eaman backed up his questioning a little, first asking if Buchanon had said anything to Judge Salmon, to which he replied, "I didn't say anything. He said 'We got you, nigger, and we're going to hang you. A nigger did this, and we're going to hang you.'"

Asked by his attorney if he asked for a lawyer at any point, Buchanon said, "No, I didn't really. You know, my attitude at that time was a lawyer wasn't going to do me any good anyway. I was in trouble."

Eggan continued scribbling notes from the plaintiff's table.

Nealy Buchanon's affidavit describing his treatment in Baltimore was introduced by Eaman as an exhibit.

Nealy Buchanon was asked by his attorney about an answer he may have given to a question in the course of giving his statement in Michigan about whether he had been threatened or coerced in any way. Buchanon admitted he had answered 'no' to the question, but said it wasn't entirely true at the time. When asked to explain, he said, "I felt that there was a mental stress being put on me, and I was extremely frightened, so I believe now that should have been taken into consideration."

"Why did you say no?" asked Eaman.

"I mean, it would be easier for me and easier upon my family," he said.

Eaman changed his line of questioning, asking his client if he was aware, on the present date, that the offense to which he pled guilty was a premeditation and deliberate offense with intent to kill.

Judge Carlson interrupted, saying, "The question presupposes something that I don't think is necessarily accurate. I don't think he pled to first degree, did he? Didn't he simply plead to murder, and then they had the degree hearing?"

Frank Eaman rephrased his question, saying, "Are you aware today that murder in the first degree requires what's called premeditation, deliberation, and intent to kill?"

"Yes," replied Buchanon.

"Were you aware in 1956 that in order to be convicted of murder in the first degree, the Court had to find the existence of those things, were you aware of that or not?"

"No," said the witness.

Eaman continued, "Let me ask you, in your mind in 1956, had you, in 1955, done anything to the Herricks that you believed to be premeditated, deliberate, or with the intent to kill?"

Buchanon replied, "No, I don't. I don't believe so."

Now leading Nealy Buchanon directly into the killing, his attorney asked, "In 1955, did an incident occur between you and the Herricks?"

"Yes," said Buchanon.

"Did you then, during the course of that incident, strike anyone?"

Again, "Yes."

"And whom did you strike?" asked the attorney.

Buchanon said, "Herrick and his wife."

"At any time during the time that that happened, did you have an intent to do anything?" asked Eaman.

Eggan was on his feet, "Your honor, I'm not sure what the relevance of this is."

Carlson, treading lightly said, "Counsel, I think we're kind of getting afield a little bit, aren't we? What is it that you're trying to show?"

Frank Eaman responded to Judge Carlson's query saying, "I think under *Moore v. Michigan*, under the circumstances, the Court has to take into consideration the circumstances at the time he pleaded guilty and whether or not there were matters that could have, or should have, been raised by an attorney at that point so as to consider whether or not a voluntary waiver of counsel [sic]. Is the Court saying that going into the facts of the case as background or in relation to possible defenses is not to be considered at the time? Or, in fact, will the Court give me an opportunity to reopen on that?"

Skeptical, Judge Carlson said he thought it was of marginal relevancy but would allow a couple of questions and allow Buchanon to answer.

"My intent was to knock out Mr. Herrick and secure his car and his keys," Nealy said.

Asked if he had ever done anything like that before, he said he hadn't.

Eaman then asked if he knew what an 'irresistible impulse' defense was.

His client replied, "I never heard of it, but I think I understand it."

"Now you offered a plea of guilty in 1956. Why did you plead guilty without a lawyer," Buchanon's attorney asked. His client answered straightforward, "Well, I felt that I was guilty."

Eaman continued, "Guilty of what?"

"Of murder," answered Buchanon.

The defense attorney clarified once again that Buchanon felt he was guilty based on his lack of understanding of the various degrees of homicide or the insanity defense, and Buchanon agreed.

Leading his client into the court proceedings from 1956, he asked him if he recalled being present when testimony was offered by the police, the coroner, a court reporter, and others. Nealy said no. Asked if, while in chambers with Judge Salmon, he was told he would be brought back to participate in the hearing regarding the degree of homicide, he said no. Eaman reiterated the point that Buchanon was not afforded an opportunity to ask any questions of any witnesses presented at the degree hearing and was not afforded the assistance of counsel.

Judge Carlson interrupted the questioning, saying, "What do you mean by that, Counsel, about any questions? I understood him to say he wasn't there."

Frank Eaman carefully changed the question into two parts, asking first, "Were you afforded the advice or assistance of a lawyer before the degree hearing?"

"No," his client answered.

The attorney continued, "Do you know whether or

not, during the degree hearing, you were represented by a lawyer who spoke for you or participated in the hearing for you?"

Again, "No."

"And when you were brought back to court to be sentenced the same day, did you have a lawyer then?" Eaman asked.

"No," said Buchanon.

Satisfied, the attorney looked down at the legal pad in front of him to check his notes. With nothing else to ask, Frank Eaman was done with his questioning and sat down.

It was Eric Eggan's chance to cross-examine Nealy Buchanon now. As Eggan stood up, he apologized to Buchanon in advance for having to jump around during his line of questions.

Eggan began by having Nealy tell the Court about his previous convictions prior to the murders and the fact he had pled guilty to both the armed robbery and the breaking and entering. The assistant attorney general's strategy was to show the convicted killer was familiar with the legal system long before he had ever killed Howard and Myra Herrick.

Asked if he discussed the possibility of appeals with jailhouse lawyers, Buchanon said he had and also admitted he had the ability to confer with them over the ten-year period between 1956 and 1966.

Eggan continued, "Why didn't you then, prior to 1966, begin an appeal? Why didn't you begin proceedings prior to 1966? Why did you wait ten years?"

Buchanon, not sure of what Eggan was going to ask him, answered, "Well, there was a lot of reasons, but the main reason being that I felt that at the time I filed, I wasn't able to just go out and locate anyone. I had to sort of feel my way around, and meet people, and talk to people who wanted to talk to me."

"Did you ever, at any time in your incarceration, hear of a case called Gideon v. Wainwright?" asked Eggan.

"Yes, but not back in that time...I didn't hear about it until I came down here in Jackson about five or six years ago," said Buchanon.

Eggan was persistent when he asked, "Why didn't you bring your appeal at that time? Why didn't you come to federal court at that time?"

Buchanon told Eggan his appeal was in the state court at the time.

"What did you discuss with these jailhouse lawyers? Presumably, if these jailhouse lawyers were able to give you information regarding a possible appeal, they would have known about Gideon v. Wainwright," Eggan continued.

Frank Eaman stood, objecting to Eggan's questioning, saying it was argumentative.

Judge Carlson allowed the question, and Buchanon answered, "We discussed mainly their cases first. Any inmate—Well, you had to understand the makeup of the inmate body. Before I can get some help, I've got to be able to listen to his story and see if I can help him. That's usually the case, and in talking to the rest of the inmates, you've got to be selective and find to who you think [sic], based on your own knowledge, can help you the most. There's a lot of jailhouse lawyers in there. They messed up my case as it was."

Eggan knew where he wanted to go with his line of questioning. He got Buchanon to admit he did discuss his case with jailhouse lawyers in 1966. He continued, "But it wasn't until some 12 to 14 years later that you found out about a decision called Gideon v. Wainwright, Miranda v. Arizona?"

In the case of *Miranda v. Arizona*,[63] the U.S. Supreme Court made a decision which became relevant to all law enforcement agencies in the United States, requiring them to advise a defendant of their "Miranda Rights" when they were arrested.

It was on March 13, 1961, when the Phoenix Police Department arrested Ernesto Miranda. There was circumstantial evidence that he was linked to a kidnapping and rape of an eighteen-year-old woman.

After two hours of interrogation, Miranda signed a confession which stated:

> *"I do hereby swear that I make this statement voluntarily, and of my own free will, with no threats, coercion, or promises of immunity, and with full knowledge of my legal rights, understanding any statement I make may be used against me."*

Prior to writing out his confession, Miranda was never advised of his right to remain silent or that his statements could be used against him. Miranda was convicted anyway, and he was sentenced to 20 to 30 years in prison.

The United States Supreme Court overturned the decisions by the lower courts, when it opined:

> *"The person in custody must, prior to interrogation, be clearly informed that he has the right to remain silent, and that anything he says will be used against him*

in court; he must be clearly informed that he has the right to consult with a lawyer and to have the lawyer with him during interrogation, and that if he is indigent, a lawyer will be appointed to represent him."

The opinion continued:

"If the individual indicates in any manner, at any time prior to or during questioning, that he wishes to remain silent, the interrogation must cease...If the individual states that he wants an attorney, the interrogation must cease until an attorney is present. At that time, the individual must have an opportunity to confer with the attorney and to have him present during any subsequent questioning."

Buchanon answered, "Right. There was a lot of that learned up here in Jackson. You see, I was in Marquette at the time when I first went up there. They've got a law library that the books are obsolete, and then you don't—You're not able to get in, at least you wasn't able to get in there. They just passed the law where you have to have a law library here, in fact, the last few years."

Eggan, after discussing which prison Buchanon was in at different times, got him to admit he had access to the law libraries, regardless of which prison he had been at, and that he was able to read.

The young attorney switched his line of questioning to the Baltimore Police, asking, "Now, you say the police officer beat you, is that correct, with blackjacks?

"Yes," replied Buchanon.

"Did they leave bruises?" asked Eggan.

"No," said Buchanon.

"Did you ever receive medical attention for these beatings?" Eggan continued.

"No," was Nealy's answer.

Eggan persisted, "Didn't it bother you that they were beating you up at this time?"

"Some I took for granted. It always happens," said Buchanon.

Eggan paused, then continued, "You took it for granted that the police could beat you into a confession?"

"Yes" was the answer.

The young assistant attorney general continued his line of questioning when he asked Buchanon why he hadn't brought up the beatings to people he had spoken with in the news media.

"These people are white, just like you are. I'm the onliest black man in this whole city that looked like everybody was on me [sic] then," Buchanon said.

Eggan realized the killer seemed to think Baltimore was in the south and asked him if he could point it out on map. He couldn't.

The attorney wanted to know if the agent from the F.B.I. had beaten him, too, and the killer said he hadn't, which led directly to questioning about statements made to Willard Barnes when he arrived in Baltimore for extradition. Buchanon said, "He suggested if I didn't go along with the statement I made in Baltimore, he was going to turn me over to the mob outside."

Confused, Eggan reminded the witness he was referring to the statements made in Baltimore. He asked, "In Baltimore, did the Sheriff tell you he'd kill you if you didn't make a statement?"

"No, he didn't tell me anything like that," said Nealy.

Pressing further about whether Sheriff Barnes had threatened to kill him, Eggan continued his line of questioning about threats made to Buchanon, confronting him with inconsistencies in his statement, "Didn't you just testify that he'd be willing to bring you back dead or alive?"

Buchanon responded, "Well, yes, yes, he did say that."

"Well, then he wasn't going to kill you," the young attorney said.

"He said it in this context, 'We can go back, you can make it easier for yourself or harder, I'm going to take you back one way or the other, dead or alive,' that's the statement he made," replied Buchanon.

Eggan was still concentrating on the alleged beatings, and he asked who was present in the room when Buchanon made a recorded statement. Buchanon remembered four men, in addition to a woman. Asked if they had tried to beat him, Buchanon admitted they hadn't but said he felt coerced.

"So then did you make up statements to go along to quell your fear so that—in other words, was your statement made up? Were you telling the truth in your statement?" asked Eggan.

Buchanon answered, "As far as I know, I was telling the truth."

Eggan was well prepared, and he was leading Buchanon further, when he asked, "Well, why didn't you make a...If you were so scared, if they were so

ROD SADLER   245 mean to you or whatever, why didn't you make another statement that was to your benefit? Why did you embellish the statement with such lurid details?"

Frank Eaman stood up, objecting to Eggan's questions and telling the judge it was argumentative. The judge agreed. Carlson said, "You must distinguish between the argument you can make to the Court, the testimony, and the evidence you must get from the witness."

Eggan changed his line of questioning by asking Buchanon if someone had asked him if he wanted to see his wife after the interview. When Buchanon said the sheriff had asked him, he continued by saying he thought the sheriff wanted to show some concern. Eggan quickly continued, "This was the same sheriff who had threatened to kill you if you didn't make a statement, now showing concern?"

Eric Eggan, still pressing Buchanon about alleged threats made by the law, said to Nealy, "Now, you stated you were scared at the time. What do you mean by 'scared'? Throughout this entire proceeding, you were telling us how you were scared and..."

Buchanon interrupted the attorney, "Well, you would have to be in that position to know. I mean I was literally scared."

Eggan quickly responded, "Isn't it possible that this scare was just because you had just brutally murdered two people, and you were caught?"

"I suppose it is when you consider that they were white people, and I'm a black man," said Buchanon.

As the hearing continued, the young assistant attorney general again touched briefly on Buchanon's past experiences with the legal system prior to the Herrick murders. As he continued, he led into questioning Nealy about his arraignment before Judge Salmon. He

A SLAYER WAITS

first asked Buchanon if he could recall which day it was in 1956. Buchanon simply said it was somewhere around the 16th of October. Eggan quickly corrected him by telling him the arraignment was on the 19th of October.

Frank Eaman was on his feet again telling the judge the young assistant attorney general was testifying. Judge Carlson interrupted, telling Eggan to simply find out what the witness knows. Eggan's response was simple, "Your Honor, I'm simply trying to establish that this witness does not have as good a memory as he says he does."

Carlson corrected Eggan, telling him he was being argumentative.

Eggan moved on, asking Buchanon if he recalled being read something out loud at the arraignment, telling him he was about to be charged with murder. Buchanon didn't recall it, so Eggan showed him a copy of the information and complaint, asking if it refreshed his memory. It did.

Asked if he remembered the Court saying he was entitled to be represented by a lawyer, Buchanon said he did. Eggan then asked if he recalled the Judge saying, if he wasn't financially able to pay for one, one would be granted to him.

"Right," said Nealy.

"Do you think he was kidding when he said that?" asked Eggan.

Before Nealy could answer, Eaman was on his feet again accusing Eggan of being argumentative.

Eggan interrupted Buchanon's attorney saying, "Well, Your Honor, I believe the witness previously testified that he believed this whole thing was a sham."

Eaman quickly disagreed saying he didn't believe that was Buchanon's testimony.

Judge Carlson interjected saying he thought Eggan had asked the witness if he remembered clearly.

Eggan continued with Buchanon, asking if he recalled the Court telling him he was entitled to a jury trial.

Buchanon did.

Moving forward, the assistant attorney general then asked the killer if he remembered the Court asking him if he wanted to plead guilty or not guilty.

When Nealy answered yes, he was asked if knew what guilty meant, and again, answered yes.

Pressing him even further, Eric Eggan asked, "Then did you then plead guilty? Did you say, 'Guilty, Your Honor'?"

Another yes from Buchanon.

Eric Eggan was trying to illustrate to the Court that Nealy Buchanon had been afforded all the protections under the law at the time when he plead guilty to murdering Howard and Myra Herrick. He asked the witness if he recalled the Court asking him about any threats made to induce him to plead guilty, but Buchanon couldn't recall.

Eggan continued, "Do you remember anyone saying—Do you remember the Court saying, 'Has anyone stated to you that if you will plead guilty, you will secure leniency?'"

Buchanon said he didn't remember that, and Eggan showed him the transcript from the 1956 arraignment. After reading it, the killer answered yes.

In the interest of time, Carlson addressed Buchanon himself, asking if he had reviewed the transcript and if everything was accurate in it. Nealy told the judge as far as he knew, it was.

The assistant attorney general continued, "And it's been your testimony that Judge Salmon took you into his chambers and began to call you names. He just took you into his chambers, and he sat down, and he called you a stupid something or another, and he forced you to plead guilty?"

Buchanon disagreed, saying, "That isn't—I didn't say that."

With Frank Eaman objecting again, the Court interjected, "No, no. Ask the witness, Mr. Eggan, what it was that was said to him."

"Do you remember what specific questions were asked you in chambers...Did the Judge ask you whether anyone had coerced you...Did he ask you whether anyone had threatened you?" asked Eggan.

"Not in chambers," was Buchanon's answer.

Eggan had one more question, asking Nealy Buchanon, "Did you testify that you were not present at the hearing concerning your degree of guilt?"

"As a matter of fact, I don't remember being there, I really don't remember being there," said Buchanon.

Eric Eggan glanced down at his notes, having finished his questioning of the Herricks' killer.

Frank Eaman had a few more questions for the witness and began his redirect examination of his client by asking if, at the time the statement was made in Lansing, he was basically telling the truth and Buchanon said he was. He also said he didn't realize there were not any eyewitnesses to the murders in 1955.

Asked about his educational level, Nealy Buchanon said he had "about" an 8th grade education.

Eaman continued the questioning, asking, "Now, in response to questions from Mr. Eggan, you admitted saying all these things before Judge Salmon, that you were guilty, no one had promised you leniency, et cetera; what were you thinking at the time you made these statements?"

Nealy replied, "Well, I was really despondent. At that time, I figured I was just—my life was over anyway."

Buchanon's attorney had finished his questioning, but Judge Carlson had some questions of his own. He wanted Nealy Buchanon to clarify a few things, asking about where his family lived in 1956 when he was captured, and then asking what his argument was before the Michigan Supreme Court.

Buchanon replied, "Yes, I was arguing my constitutional rights. I went in there on a certiorari."

Asked if he was arguing to the Supreme Court the same thing he was arguing before Judge Carlson, he said he was.

Carlson continued, asking briefly about the discussions in chambers with Judge Salmon and asking if he told Salmon he hadn't committed the crime.

"No," said Buchanon.

Carlson, pressing him further, asked, "What specifically did you think that Circuit Judge Salmon could do if you just said, 'I'm not going to plead to anything; I want a lawyer'? What did you really think they could do to you?"

Buchanon stuttered as he answered, "I didn't think they'd—I didn't think they'd consider that. I thought that they would—if I didn't—At that time, I thought if I didn't go along with the statements I had made, and I'm not denying the statements, but if I wouldn't go along with the statements that I made, I could either be hung, killed, or you know, et cetera, and the family would be..."

Carlson interrupted, "Who would kill you or hang you?"

"The system, the people in it, you know, all them white people, in other words, is what I thought, you

A SLAYER WAITS

know, under that system," replied Buchanon.

Carlson was trying to find out whether Nealy was afraid of being turned over to a mob outside or if he was afraid of being hung, either by the police or by the courts.

Buchanon didn't think the courts would hang him, but he was afraid the Court might "make it convenient" for the mob to get him.

Judge Carlson ended his questioning, asking if either counsel had anything further.

Eaman addressed the Court and said if they were concerned about Buchanon's credibility regarding his racist fears, there were several things in Nealy's past where he was a 'rather unusual' victim of racism by white people, but Eaman would only make that as an offer of proof.

The assistant attorney general had nothing more to add.

Judge Carlson asked Frank Eaman about additional witnesses, and Eaman told the Court there were some stipulations between counsel regarding their witnesses and their availability.

The next witness was Judge Marvin Salmon, and he was already in the courtroom ready to testify.

Eaman continued, "It's also my understanding that the prosecutor named Warren is presently alive and is a judge now, I think, in Ingham County. And if he were called as a witness in this case to testify, he would testify. He has no independent recollection of the events surrounding Mr. Buchanon's arrest, statements, and guilty plea."

Eaman told the Court the former Prosecuting Attorney Charles Chamberlain was alive, living in Washington D.C., and would also testify that he has no recollection of the events. It was the same story for Treleaven, who was now working for the attorney general's office.

Eggan reluctantly agreed with the defense counsel. No one seemed to have any independent recall of the matter, and both attorneys knew Willard Barnes was dead.

There was no mention of the sheriff by either attorney. His career had started to spiral out of control in 1959, only three years after Buchanon had been sent to prison.

The beginning of the end for Willard Barnes started on October 7, 1959 at around 2:00 am. Bartender and part-time truck driver, Richard Goble, was driving eastbound on US-16 west of Williamston when a car heading westbound swerved across the roadway, almost striking his truck. Goble was able to catch a glimpse of a sheriff insignia on the door of the car, and when he reached Williamston, he called the State Police. They dispatched Williamston Patrolman Ellis Nemer to meet with Goble, and together they drove back along M-16 looking for the car. It wasn't long before they discovered the sheriff's 1960 sedan stopped along the side of the roadway about four miles west of the city with the driver passed out behind the wheel.

Patrolman Nemer woke the driver, only to discover it was Ingham County Sheriff Willard Barnes. Barnes told Nemer he had pulled to the side of the road to rest, as he had been working all day searching for an escapee from the county jail farm. Nemer, not wanting to arrest the sheriff, offered to follow Barnes back to Mason, and the sheriff agreed. As the two vehicles started heading west on US-16, Barnes made an abrupt U-turn and began speeding back toward Williamston. Patrolman Nemer tried to pursue him, but Barnes' vehicle was faster, and Nemer was outdistanced. The officer radioed ahead, and the sheriff was finally stopped in Williamston and arrested.

Sheriff Willard Barnes was charged by Jack Warren, who by then had become the Ingham County Prosecuting Attorney in the years following Nealy Buchanon's arrest. The 285-pound, burly sheriff stood mute to the charge when he appeared before Justice Robert Wood in Williamston, so Justice Wood entered a "not guilty" plea and set the matter for a trial on October 20.

Defense Attorney Benjamin Watson, representing Barnes, asked for a week's delay in the trial, telling Justice Wood his client wasn't properly prepared for the trial. Wood granted the delay.

A week later, the sheriff's trial began, taking place at the Williamston Fire Department, the only building able to hold the large crowd of over seventy spectators, press, and witnesses. Four prosecution witnesses testified, and Barnes's attorney didn't offer any witnesses on his client's behalf. Sheriff Barnes was found guilty on the drunk driving charge, and he quickly filed an appeal, hoping to take the matter before the Ingham County Circuit Court. In order to file the appeal, he also had to file an additional $500 appeal bond.

Two months had passed since his conviction, and on Christmas Eve, while Barnes was still waiting for his appeal, Michigan State Police Trooper Ralph Warnstrom was dispatched to a quiet county road on a report of a car stuck in a ditch southeast of the Michigan State University Campus. He arrived to find a drunken Willard Barnes, and the sheriff was arrested a second time for drunk driving. Barnes quickly issued a statement saying he was sick at the time and had taken an overdose of medicine, thus causing him to appear drunken.

By now, the Ingham County Republican Party and the Michigan Sheriff's Association were suggesting the five-term sheriff should resign from his position. At the time, Barnes was serving as the President of the Michigan Sheriff's Association and fourth Vice President to the National Sheriff's Association. There were rumors that if he didn't resign, a recall effort would be mounted. As the pressure began to build, Willard Barnes went into seclusion for a few weeks. When he reappeared in January of 1960, he agreed to resign his elected position as the county sheriff, in addition to his positions with the Michigan Sheriff's Association and the National Sheriff's Association.

When Sheriff Willard Barnes made his announcement to resign from his elected position, he said:

> "Today, I entered a plea of 'nolo contender' in the case against me in Meridian Township court. In making this plea, I do not admit guilt. I have been in ill health for some time and am in no physical condition to withstand another trial. I know that there are those who feel strongly about this incident. Nevertheless, I am convinced that those people who now think evil of me would continue to feel that way whether I was acquitted or not. Likewise, my true friends would not change their thinking regardless of the outcome. Under all these circumstances, and with the thought in mind of avoiding any further expense to the county, I have

*made this decision. I have this day ten-
dered my resignation from the office of
sheriff, effective April 30, 1960.*"[64]

Former Ingham County Undersheriff John Lechler, who had left the department when Barnes was elected ten years earlier was appointed to finish out the sheriff's term until the November election.

By March of 1960, the Lansing City Council had been notified by the state's Liquor Control Commission of Willard Barnes and his wife, Sophie, seeking a transfer of ownership for the Motor Bar located across from the Motor Wheel Factory in Lansing. By the end of April, the request had won approval by the Lansing City Council in a 7-1 vote, and the Liquor Control Commission approved the sale after that.

Later that same year, the Lansing Police Department received a report of a car traveling on the wrong side of the street and driving up over the curb. At 5:05 am, they were able to locate the car and driver, and for the third time in less than one year, the now former Sheriff Willard Barnes was arrested for drunk driving again.

In late December of 1960, Barnes' original drunk driving charge was dismissed when a circuit court jury could not reach a verdict in the case. Prosecutor Jack Warren said he wouldn't seek another trial due to the expense involved, and he felt Barnes had suffered considerable punishment through the adverse publicity he had received and his forced resignation from office.

Barnes died in 1965, a year before Nealy Buchanon had ever started his first appeal.

With no other witnesses, the discussion turned to the appeals Buchanon had filed before the Michigan Supreme Court in 1978 and the entire file being available at the time that was now missing.

Eaman, as counsel to Nealy Buchanon, addressing the Court said:

> "*I have to rely on what Respondent has related to me or what is contained in Respondent's brief filed with the Michigan Supreme Court in 1978. It's my understanding that there have been no opinions in this matter and when the Court asked Mr. Buchanon a question about whether the issues raised in 1966 were the issues raised today. In Mr. Buchanon's mind, they are. I would suggest to the Court that they are not. The issue raised in 1966 was specifically, and the pleading will show this, whether, on the record, there was an adequate waiver of counsel, and the Wineberg [sic] case, which was relied on by the trial judge in that matter for his decision held on the record that the plea was adequate.*
>
> *In 1977, following this, the Michigan Supreme Court found that the Michigan Court then, on file with the Michigan Courts, the issue raised regarding the circumstances surrounding the plea was raised, and relief was just denied on those particular grounds. That's why Judge DeMascio noted in his order that question was raised in at least '77 regarding circumstances surrounding the plea, and*

that he was entitled to an evidentiary hearing, and he did ask for that in 1977, but I do not believe he asked for that at any other appeal, including the one that went to the U.S. Supreme Court."

Eaman continued, telling the Court he didn't have any previous pleadings by Buchanon prior to 1977. He said his client had an unfortunate incident with another jailhouse lawyer, having trusted him with the copies of his pleadings, and they were destroyed.

Eric Eggan stood, telling the Court the attorney general's office didn't have copies of the pre-1977 pleadings either.

After the suggestion that Eggan check with the Court of Appeals for pre-1977 pleadings, the next witness, the former Judge Marvin Salmon, was called. It had been several years since he had looked Nealy J. Buchanon in the eyes.

CHAPTER 13

An Evidentiary Hearing

Marvin Salmon, the retired Ingham County Circuit Court Judge, had led a distinguished career in Ingham County's judicial system. After serving for twenty-six years on the bench, he retired on the first day of January in 1974, saying, "If I had to do it over, there's nothing I'd rather do. I've made some mistakes, and I've been reversed a few times, but I've always kept my eyes on the facts." During his career, he had served as the President of the Ingham County Bar Association and had been appointed to serve on the Supreme Court Jury Instruction Committee for several years. When he stepped down, he had the designation as being the longest serving circuit court judge for Ingham County. Now retired, instead of presiding from the bench, he would testify from the witness stand.

The assistant attorney general, in preparation for the evidentiary hearing, had called Salmon to let him know he would be subpoenaed to testify. The retired judge was distinguished-looking with his gray hair, was polite, and was everything Eggan expected of a retired circuit court judge. He was gracious and projected an almost fatherly image.

Eric Eggan began his questioning, asking the former judge if he remembered the crime in which Nealy Buchanon pled guilty, and Salmon said, "In a general way, yes, and some items I remember."

Asked if he remembered the guilty plea, the former judge said, "Some of it I remember distinctly."

Eggan asked Judge Salmon to explain the procedure used in 1956 to take a guilty plea.

Salmon began by telling Eggan and the Court that the procedure he used was also being used in most of the other circuit courts around the state. A defendant was brought before the Court, and the "Information" or the charge was read to the person. The defendant was then asked some questions and taken back into the judge's chambers where the judge would discuss the matter with the defendant. After a brief discussion, the person was returned to the courtroom where the Judge would place the matter on the record.

Frank Eaman wasn't clear if this was done each time a plea was taken or if Salmon was speaking with regard to Nealy Buchanon's case in particular.

Eric Eggan quickly clarified it when he told the Court the procedure used was done in "presumably" hundreds of cases.

Eaman objected, wanting the former circuit court judge to be asked specific questions about Buchanon's case and then more specific questions about the procedures. Judge Carlson disagreed saying it really didn't matter in which order the questions were asked, saying the former judge could tell the Court what the general purpose of the in-chambers conference was for.

Judge Salmon continued his testimony, telling the Court the reason for the in-chambers conference with the defendant was so the judge could "alone" determine if the person had been "taken advantage of." Salmon explained further, saying it was very difficult for some people to admit their guilt with the police in the courtroom, or with someone who might have come to court with them standing nearby, or with parents of victims in the court. Because it was so difficult for some people to go into specific details about their guilt, it was easier for them to do it behind closed doors with the judge, and that was the sole purpose of the in-chambers conference. Salmon went further, telling the Court it was also an effort on the judge's part to determine if the defendant may have been pushed into pleading guilty.

"Were you the only Circuit Judge who employed this procedure?" Eggan asked.

Salmon said, "Well, I know everyone in our circuit did, and we had at the time, at that time, I think we had three or four circuit judges. But my understanding is that they were doing this throughout the state."

Eggan continued his question, asking the former judge, "Do you ever recall rejecting a guilty plea based on this conference?"

Frank Eaman quickly objected, saying the question had no relevance.

Responding to the objection, Eggan told the Court the question was extremely relevant in an attempt to show the in-chambers conference was objective.

Judge Carlson asked Eggan to simply continue questioning Salmon about Buchanon's hearing.

Asked if he remembered taking Buchanon into chambers before accepting his plea, Judge Salmon said he did recall taking Nealy Buchanon back into his chambers alone.

Eggan asked, "Do you recall making any threats to Mr. Buchanon?"

Salmon answered, "No, I never did, and I want to emphatically deny that, and I also want to emphatically deny that I ever used the language 'nigger.' That's not in my vocabulary. I don't treat people that way."

Eggan continued, telling the judge he noted in the record of arraignment that he had said specifically he was convinced Buchanon's plea was freely, under-standingly, and voluntarily made.

Judge Salmon reiterated his point again, saying, "Yes, sir, and I go into sufficient facts, or did go into sufficient facts in chambers to cover that. That's the summary of what we did."

Asked if Buchanon had ever mentioned during the in-chambers conference about any police threats or coercion, and the former judge said no.

Almost done with his questioning, Eric Eggan asked the judge specifically about the language he used when he addressed the Court about Buchanon's plea. The judge had said on the record that the plea was "volun-tarily made without undue influence, compulsion or duress, and without promise of leniency." The assistant attorney general continued, asking if it was part of any court rule. Salmon said he thought those were the ele-ments of Rule 35(a) and that it was another reason for the in-chambers conference.

Leading the former judge into the degree hearing, Salmon recalled they definitely had a degree hearing but he couldn't remember any specific details about it.

Eggan was done with his line of questioning, and Frank Eaman took over to cross-examine Marvin Salm-on.

Eaman first wanted to know how long Salmon had been a judge prior to 1956. He asked the former magistrate if he could recall how many times in a year he was called upon to take a plea in a murder case.

Judge Salmon couldn't answer specifically, only recalling it seemed there were two or three murders in the community each year.

Not wanting to insult the former judge, Eaman explained to him he had to ask certain questions to lay his foundation and asked if he had continued his education beyond going to law school, and then asked if he read newspapers.

"Occasionally, yes," was his reply.

"All right. I'm going to ask you if you can recall any newspaper accounts you might have read about this case, the Buchanon case," Eaman said.

Salmon couldn't.

Buchanon's attorney showed the witness four newspaper articles published in 1956.

Asking about the newspapers specifically, Judge Salmon couldn't recall reading those specific articles and admitted he probably read articles in The State Journal, which was published in Lansing, but he couldn't remember any of the specifics from those.

Eaman seemed to be leading the judge to a more specific issue when he asked him, by looking over the articles he had just shown him, whether or not he recalled a little more about the Buchanon case. The attorney continued, "Well, let me ask you more specifically. In one of these exhibits, the reporter suggests that there were extra guards that had been posted at the jail."

Eggan was on his feet before the judge could answer, objecting to the question, telling the Court the news articles were hearsay evidence and they were not 'best evidence.'

Carlson directed his gaze to Eaman, asking what the purpose of his line of questioning was.

Frank Eaman, now addressing Judge Carlson, said he wanted to know if Salmon recalled extra guards being posted at the jail.

Carlson told him to ask the question first, then see if he needed to go any further.

Eaman turned back to Judge Salmon, asking if he recalled if there were extra guards posted at the jail. He didn't.

"Do you remember the fact that Mr. Buchanon was an escaped black convict accused of killing two elderly white farmers? Do you remember that?" asked Eaman.

When the former judge acknowledged he did, Eaman continued, "Let me ask you about that for a minute. You say there were two or three homicides a year in Ingham County at that time, approximately, and I won't hold you exactly to that. How many of those, at that time, involved an escaped black convict allegedly killing two elderly white farmers?"

After a brief objection by Eric Eggan, Carlson told the former judge he could answer.

Salmon didn't know.

Eaman quickly followed up, asking, "Can you recall any other case involving the same circumstances that you just said you remembered?"

"No, sir," Salmon said.

The attorney pressed further. He wanted to know if Judge Salmon remembered if the arrest of Nealy Buchanon was the result of a magazine article.

Salmon knew it was, but he hadn't known it at the time of his arraignment in 1956.

Again, leading the witness in the direction he needed to go, Eaman got Salmon to agree there were at least a couple of reasons this particular case was different from other homicides at the time.

Frank Eaman then asked if Salmon, as a politician who had to run for office, had a sense of mood in the community at the time.

Salmon asked Eaman, "About what?"

"About a homicide of an elderly farm couple by an escaped black convict," said Eaman.

When the former magistrate told Frank Eaman he wasn't aware of the mood of people around Stockbridge, Eaman countered with, "Are you telling me that you weren't aware that there were 50 to 100 people outside the jail the night before you accepted this plea?"

Salmon, calm and professional said, "I was not aware of any such situation."

Eggan stood, interjecting, "And I might add, Your Honor, that that is not, in fact, yet proven in evidence."

Frank Eaman, not giving up, pressed further, asking if it would have made any difference whether or not he would have accepted Buchanon's plea.

Judge Salmon told Eaman he might have done something differently, but he didn't know what that might be.

"Was Mr. Buchanon represented by a lawyer to argue his case before you?" asked Eaman.

Salmon said he wasn't.

Judge Carlson was getting tired of the same question being asked, and he reminded Frank Eaman that he had asked the same question "about 43 times," and everyone in the courtroom knew by now that Nealy Buchanon did not have the assistance of counsel.

Eaman moved on, asking the witness if it was unusual in 1956 for a black man to come before him without an attorney.

Salmon answered he had white men also appear without attorneys, and every case was handled the same in his court.

That was the answer Frank Eaman expected, and he continued his questioning, saying, "In your court. How about in your community in which you were elected?"

Salmon wasn't going down that path with Eaman.

"Let me ask you, did you know Malcolm X came from your community?" the attorney asked.

Carlson quickly interrupted saying, "I'm going to stop that line of questioning right now. It's absolutely irrelevant."

Eaman, not ready to give up, countered, saying, "But his allegation that everyone was treated alike in Lansing in 1956 is simply not a fact." He was referring to Salmon's previous answer.

Judge Marvin Salmon was quick to correct the attorney when he said, "I said in my court."

Frank Eaman was forced to change his line of questioning and asked if Judge Salmon testified earlier he had never used the word 'nigger' and had said it wasn't in his vocabulary.

Salmon reiterated his earlier testimony, saying, "It's not in my vocabulary, and I don't use such language."

Eaman wouldn't let go, asking, "Are you telling me that never in your life as a kid telling a joke, in any circumstances, that you've never used the word 'nigger?'"

Salmon said again, "I said I've never used the word 'nigger.'"

Eggan stood, objecting, telling the Court that Eaman was being argumentative. Carlson agreed, saying the question had already been answered. Salmon quickly chimed in, reminding Frank Eaman he was under oath.

"And Mr. Buchanon was under oath, and he was sitting there facing you, wasn't he?" Eaman said. He continued his editorial, saying, "Personally, I don't think there's a white person alive who's never used that word if they're living in this country."

Now more adamant than ever, Judge Marvin Salmon looked directly at Eaman and said, "Well, look at this one, and you'll see one."

Frank Eaman didn't believe the retired judge. In Eaman's mind, Salmon protested too much about the use of the derogatory word. Frank Eaman's job in representing his client was not to take Buchanon's word as gospel, but to try to verify what Nealy was telling him about the judge. In his preparation for the evidentiary hearing, Eaman had spoken with other attorneys who had appeared before Judge Salmon at one time or another, and they felt it was entirely possible the retired judge had two systems of justice depending on a person's color. For Judge Salmon to tell him the word was not in his vocabulary, and he had never used it before, made Eaman even more suspicious, but he knew there was no way he would ever get Salmon to admit it.

"Well, you're talking about 1956. That was before Martin Luther King, wasn't it?" Eaman continued.

Before Salmon could answer, Judge Carlson interjected again, telling Frank Eaman to simply ask the witness what he might know or what he might remember.

Eaman, now changing course, asked Salmon if there was any record taken during the in-chambers conference with Buchanon, and Salmon told him there wasn't.

"Just your word against Buchanon's, no other person was there, is that right?" Eaman asked.

Salmon answered the question, saying, "No other person was present; intentionally so."

"And you say the purpose of this meeting was to inquire into coercion, is that right?" Eaman continued.

Salmon told him that was right.

Frank Eaman asked the former judge about a court rule in effect in 1956 and whether or not the conference was solely to establish a factual basis for the plea, but Salmon couldn't remember specifically, although he knew the court rule Eaman was referring to.

Eaman continued pressing the witness, recounting his testimony about the in-chambers conference to inquire about coercion, then in open court asking Buchanon if there were any promises made to him, but not having asked him in chambers.

The retired judge said he thought he did.

Eaman continued, "So you're telling me it was your practice to ask on the record whether there were promises of leniency or anything, and then in chambers, whether there was coercion?"

Salmon was still polite and professional in his response, saying, "No, we didn't try to separate it. We weren't trying to trick anybody at all; we were trying to find out if anybody had abused him in any way, in good faith."

Eaman shot back, "Was it part of your good faith that you would accept a plea and sentence a man 36 hours after he was arrested? Was that part of the good faith?"

"I guess it was," Salmon replied.

"Did you find it at all unusual, given the practice of the day, that you would accept a plea to an open charge of murder when the accused was not represented by counsel?" Eaman continued.

Marvin Salmon said no.

Referring now to the arraignment transcript, Frank Eaman noted to the former judge that he had advised Buchanon he had the right to a lawyer.

Salmon thought he had said it to Buchanon during

the arraignment and didn't disagree with Eaman when he said Salmon's next question to Buchanon was, "How do you plead?"

The attorney continued, asking the witness, "Okay. Did you ever insert one other question in there once in a while: 'Now that you know your right to a lawyer, do you want one?' before you ask them to plead?"

Salmon said no.

"Did you feel it was part of your job in 1956 to inquire into the circumstances regarding a person's arrest, the making of a statement, and those circumstances which led to his being brought to your court and pleading guilty?" Eaman asked.

Again, "No."

The attorney continued, asking if Salmon thought it was part of his job to inquire about a person's educational background when they plead guilty.

The former judge said it would depend on the nature of the crime and what he had or had not done.

Judge Carlson interrupted again, letting counsel know he was becoming argumentative and telling him to simply ask the witness what he did.

Eaman rephrased his question, asking, "In this case, you did not ask Mr. Buchanon what his educational background was when he appeared without counsel, is that right?"

The former judge didn't think he had asked anything of Buchanon about that.

Asked whether he had a practice or procedure regarding a degree hearing in 1956, Judge Salmon told Eaman, "Simply as disclosed by the record, that's what our practice was."

Eaman, now nearing the end of his questioning, asked Salmon if he recalled Nealy Buchanon being present at the degree hearing.

When Salmon said he thought Buchanon was present, Eaman countered, "You think he was present...As to that, your memory has a good background, is that right?"

Carlson interjected, reminding counsel, yet again, of being argumentative. Frank Eaman withdrew his question, then asked Salmon what he based his thinking on regarding Buchanon being present at the hearing and if it was on the record somewhere.

Judge Salmon couldn't recall if it was on the record.

As Eaman began his next sentence, Judge Carlson stopped him, saying, "Counsel, I'm going to stop this one, too. The witness has said he doesn't have any independent recollection of whether or not Mr. Buchanon was present at that hearing; he thinks that he probably was or he thinks that he was. Now, that was the witness testimony. You can't get any more out of him."

Eaman continued, asking Salmon if it was his practice to allow defendants to participate in their degree hearing, and Salmon told him if a defendant wanted to, he would have permitted it.

Asked how he would know if the defendant wanted to participate, Salmon said he would ask.

"If he had a lawyer, the lawyer could ask, right?" Eaman said.

"Certainly," the former judge said.

Eaman, addressing Salmon, replied, "Well, I'm confused. I may be the only one confused, but if he's sitting there, did you ask him whether he wanted to participate, or did you require him to say something about asking questions?"

The retired judge couldn't recall and said he probably didn't ask Buchanon if he wanted to ask questions.

Frank Eaman tried to make his point by asking

Judge Salmon, "All right. So, based on your memory of practice and procedure in 1956, it wouldn't be unusual if a person sat there and was not afforded the opportunity to participate in degree hearings?"

Salmon responded, "When you say 'not afforded,' I wouldn't deny anybody the right to participate under those circumstances; certainly not."

"If they sat there and didn't say anything, would you advise them of their right to participate? Do you have a practice and procedure for that?"

"No, I didn't," said the former judge.

Eaman had nothing more, but the Court did. Judge Carlson asked Salmon if he recalled asking Buchanon specifics about the circumstances of the crime, and he said he did.

Carlson inquired whether or not he remembered asking Buchanon about statements either in Lansing or in Baltimore, but he couldn't remember if he had.

Carlson continued, asking the former judge if he recalled asking Buchanon about anything that happened in Baltimore, and, again, he couldn't recall asking the murderer about it.

Asked if he had, at any time, advised Nealy Buchanon to plead guilty, he said he didn't.

Judge Carlson had nothing more.

Frank Eaman still wanted to have the newspaper articles admitted as exhibits in the hearing, but Eggan protested, telling the Court they weren't "real" evidence, and they should be considered "absolute hearsay."

Eaman immediately asked to leave the court so he could call the reporters in to testify who had written the news articles. He said, "I have no reason to believe these reporters lied. He's telling me he's challenging the truthfulness of these written statements and quotes

A SLAYER WAITS

of the parties involved, and I'd like to leave to continue this hearing."

Eggan wasn't about to have that and addressed the Court again, saying, "Your Honor, I will certainly admit that this case caused great community interest, and I don't think there is any need to call these people; however, if Counsel does want to call these people and bring them in, I have no objection."

The former Judge Salmon still sat on the witness stand as the two attorneys bantered back and forth. Realizing he was still there, Judge Carlson told him he could step down, but Salmon wanted to make a statement for the record. Judge Carlson allowed him to address the Court:

> *"This may be—I think it's material, I'm sure it's interesting, at least: it was ten years ago, or thereabouts, someplace along this line, I was asked to go to Jackson Prison to make a speech to the people who had just come into the institution, about not more than 25 years of age, and went over one Sunday, Sunday afternoon, and a man came to the door after I was let in, and escorted me down the cellblock to a platform, and we had chairs lined up out front, and the men were let out of the lock-up, and came in, and sat down in the chairs, and we had a program, and I gave a talk and answered some questions, and there were some that preceded me, and about six months after that I was requested to come there again, and I was let in as usual, and we had the same set up pattern as*

> *to ceremony, and the men were let out,
> and they were about ready to start, and
> the man who was master of ceremonies
> says, 'You don't remember me, do you?'
> And I says, 'No, I don't,' and he says,
> 'I'm Nealy Buchanon. I'm the man you
> sentenced some years ago for double
> murder,' and we visited there that day
> and Nealy was very nice to me. That's all
> I have to add* [sic]."

Seizing the opportunity, Frank Eaman said he had a question with regard to the former Judge's statement. "Isn't it a fact that he also asked at that time if you would rescind the statement you made that he would never be let out of prison?" he asked.

Salmon said when he arrived back at his office on Monday, there was a petition from Buchanon to have his plea set aside.

Eaman asked the judge if he had understood his question and repeated it.

"No, he did not ask me that. We didn't talk about that at all," said Salmon.

Eaman wanted to recall Nealy Buchanon to counter Salmon's statement, just as Carlson excused the former judge.

Judge Carlson turned his attention to both attorneys, telling them he would allow the newspaper articles as evidence "for what they're worth." He said he thought the case would turn primarily "upon events as they were perceived by Mr. Buchanon." Carlson continued, "I don't know that any newspaper articles which indicated what was going on outside, being offered to prove, in fact, what was going on outside, are going to be that dispositive of the case. We have the Petitioner's

A SLAYER WAITS

testimony as to what he was aware of, and that really is all we're going to have to be worrying about." With that, Judge Carlson admitted the newspaper articles.

Frank Eaman assumed the attorney general would be filing opposing briefs in response to the brief he had already filed, so he asked the Court to set a timetable and to allow him a short period of time to file a reply, simply because he had the burden of proof.

Carlson asked if the attorneys wanted to wait for the transcripts of the proceeding to be filed first, and Eggan said no.

Judge Carlson told them both he would be filing a report and recommendation on the proceeding. He would be providing it to Judge DeMascio, telling both men there was an issue of credibility involved.

Eric Eggan renewed his motion before the Court to dismiss the matter, and he said he would wait for Carlson's report and recommendations before he would make a decision about filing briefs.

Eaman told the Court he would file a short brief, thinking he might have it done by September 11.

Eggan reserved the right to file his.

CHAPTER 14

The Briefs

On September 11, 1981, Frank Eaman filed his brief.[65] Highlighting the hearing, he noted:

> *"The testimony of the Petitioner consisted principally in regard to the atmosphere of coercion which surrounded his arrest and detention at the jail in Stockbridge, including the crowd outside the jail and to the efforts of the trial judge in chambers to get him to stick to his confession and guilty plea."*

He also noted Buchanon was advised of his right to a lawyer but wasn't afforded one, and at the time of his hearing to determine the degree of murder "of which he would stand convicted," he wasn't afforded the right to an attorney or an opportunity to participate in the hearing. He described Judge Salmon's testimony before the Court, saying there was no procedure in place to allow Buchanon's participation. Eaman then mentioned that the record of the degree hearing didn't disclose whether Nealy Buchanon was even present. In his further assessment of the previous legal proceeding, Eaman went on to describe Buchanon's arrest, interrogation, plea, and sentencing all occurring within 36 hours and then touched on what he described as a "collateral dispute" about whether Judge Salmon had used the word "nigger" during the in-chamber conference with Buchanon, while Buchanon insisted he had used the word and Judge Salmon saying he never used the word in his life.

The newspaper articles describing the atmosphere when Buchanon arrived in Mason were cited by Eaman also, including mention of extra guards being required because of the crowd of citizens.

Buchanon's attorney had not been allowed to pursue questioning at the hearing regarding the civil rights leader, Malcolm X, but in an effort to give an idea of what life was like for a black man in the Lansing area during the time period just prior to Judge Salmon becoming a judge, Frank Eaman cited "The Autobiography of Malcolm X" in his brief, using passages describing life in the Lansing area. After noting the passages from the book, Eaman wrote:

> *"The key question presented by this Writ of Habeas Corpus is whether the trial judge should have accepted the plea of a black man, without an attorney, pleading guilty to two (2) counts of murdering white people in 1955 in Ingham County, given the atmosphere of tension and the*

circumstances in which the Petitioner found himself before the Court on murder charges."

Noting the case of *Moore v. Michigan*, Eaman wrote that the similarities were enormous:

"A charge of murder raises the spector [sic] of degrees of murder, possible conviction on charges of manslaughter, and defenses of insanity. Any waiver of counsel under such circumstances should meet the test of VonMoltke, also cited in the Brief in Support of Amended Petition: 'A judge can make certain that an accused's professed waiver of counsel is understandingly and wisely made only from a penetrating and comprehensive examination of all the circumstances under which such a plea is tendered.'"

Frank Eaman continued his brief by citing four factors considered in setting aside Nealy Buchanon's 1956 guilty plea:

"…(1) The absence of counsel in any stage of the proceedings; (2) An atmosphere of physical or mental coercion; (3) The failure of the trial judge to establish on the record the complete circumstances of the plea and the absence of any coercion; and, (4) The inability of the defendant to receive advice on the consequences of the plea, the possible defenses available, or other legal matters.

A SLAYER WAITS

All these factors existed in the Petitioner's case."

Leading into the delay in bringing a petition before the Court, Eaman noted:

"A key circumstance in the length of delay is the complete absence of the advice of counsel as to the federal rights for more than twenty-three (23) years. 'Jailhouse lawyers' cannot be assumed to know the law or to readily advise people of their federal rights. There is no authority to that effect that Petitioner is aware of. In fact, it would be bitter irony if the Petitioner lost his claim in this Court because of ignorance of legal rights, when his claim is based on the fact that he was not afforded counsel at the time of his plea nor for any subsequent appellate proceedings."

Noting elementary rights of due process, Eaman wrote that they required notice, a hearing, and an opportunity to participate in the hearing. Testimony at the previous hearing showed Buchanon was never offered the right to participate in the hearing to determine the degree of murder. Eaman also noted, "To Nealy Buchanon, any killing was murder; he also thought he was facing the death penalty at one point and gave up on his case."

In closing the brief, Buchanon's attorney wrote:

"Since the Petitioner has been in prison in excess of twenty-four (24) years, he has

obviously suffered a great prejudice by his inability to participate in the Degree Hearing. The absence of counsel at a critical stage of the proceedings is never harmless error. The right to counsel, if absolute, absent any knowing and intelligent waiver...Petitioner's conviction, under the circumstances which existed at the time, without counsel, and without an opportunity to seek advice or counsel as to degrees of homicide, possible defenses, and his rights and circumstances, was a conviction without the most fundamental rights of due process and rights to counsel. Petitioner requests that his conviction be vacated."

On September 28, two-and-a-half weeks after Frank Eaman filed his brief following the evidentiary hearing, Assistant Attorney General Eric Eggan, working from his office at Plaza One in downtown Lansing, filed his own brief to dismiss the motion.[66]

Eggan noted Buchanon had testified "in support of his assertion that his conviction was obtained in violation of the Federal Sixth and Fourteenth Amendments," and noted Judge Marvin Salmon had also testified at the hearing.

Eggan cited four arguments to support his position. First, Eggan asserted that the Doctrine of Laches should bar the petition because the attorney general's office was unable to fully respond to it. By that, Eggan wrote it had been stipulated at the evidentiary hearing that there had been a twenty-five year period between Nealy Buchanon's conviction, and his writ of habeas corpus had erased the recollections of potential witnesses.

In arguing this point further, he said there was an understandable inability for some to recall the arrest of Buchanon, his plea, and his sentencing. Those factors, coupled with missing court files and prosecutor files, supported the State's inability to adequately respond to Buchanon's petition. Eggan continued, writing that Buchanon had stated prior to 1978 that he lacked the "knowledge requisite to bring the instant action." To counter his argument, Eggan contended in Buchanon's own testimony that he said he was literate when he was convicted, he had constant access to the prison law libraries, and he had the assistance of jailhouse lawyers. Had he used "reasonable diligence," the issues brought before the Court in this appeal could have been made long before this.

Eggan's second argument, The Presumption of Validity, was very detailed. He noted Buchanon had testified that his guilty pleas were the product of coercion resulting from threats by law enforcement in both Baltimore and Ingham County, by prosecutors who took his confession and by Judge Marvin Salmon. He also noted that Buchanon made the claim of racially-motivated and abusive language during the in-chambers conference with Judge Salmon and numerous threats of violence if he didn't confess. In writing further, Eggan noted:

> "Interestingly, however, despite Petitioner's ability to detail conversations and events supportive of his coercion argument, he was unable to recall the particulars of his in-chambers discussion with Judge Salmon."

Citing a previous court case in North Carolina, Eggan noted that the standard for determining the validity of a guilty plea under the Fourteenth Amendment was whether the plea represented a voluntary and intelligent choice among the alternative course of action. He argued the arraignment transcript, as well as the testimony of Judge Salmon, removed all doubt that Buchanon's plea was freely and voluntarily made.

Eggan moved to the in-chambers discussion between Judge Salmon and Nealy Buchanon. He noted that Judge Salmon testified the entire Ingham County Bench was participating in the practice to provide a more relaxed atmosphere, allowing a defendant to speak more freely outside the presence of police, prosecutors, and the victims' family. He also noted that the policy had been held to be constitutional by the Honorable Noel P. Fox, a judge for the Western District of Michigan in the case of *Winegar v. Department of Corrections*. He wrote that Judge Salmon "vehemently denied" any racial comments and any attempts at coercion. He also noted that Buchanon mentioned nothing about police or prosecutorial misconduct during his in-chambers conference with Salmon.

Eggan's entire second argument was summarized when he cited a United States Supreme Court decision which held, "State court findings of fact are entitled to a presumption of correctness," also noting, "the Court held that it is a habeas petitioner's burden to overcome this presumption with convincing evidence that the findings are erroneous."

In addition, Buchanon's argument that he didn't understand premeditation was an element of the crime he was pleading to lacked factual support. Eggan wrote in his brief that Prosecuting Attorney Chamberlain read an Information charging Buchanon under section 316, First Degree Murder. Buchanon said he recalled the Information read to him prior to his plea and read the elements (including premeditation) of the crime. He also noted that Buchanon knew his guilty plea would result in him being sent to prison for the rest of his life.

Moving to his third argument, Eggan wrote Judge Salmon had testified that hearings to determine the degree of guilt were 'non-adversary proceedings at which the defendant was always present.' He referenced the original arraignment transcript and a statement by the Court:

> *"THE COURT: It is the judgment of this court that the murder of Myra Herrick was murder in the first degree, and it is also the judgment of this court that the murder of Howard Herrick was murder in the first degree. Will you step up here, Mr. Buchanon? (Respondent standing before the bench)."*

It was the state's opinion that Nealy Buchanon was present at the time of his hearing.

The final argument in the brief asserted there was no violation of the Federal Sixth Amendment when Buchanon pled guilty to murdering Howard and Myra Herrick.

Once again, Eggan cited court transcripts from Buchanon's arraignment:

> *"THE COURT: Do you understand the charge Mr. Buchanon?*
> *THE RESPONDENT: Yes, Your Honor.*
> *THE COURT: The Court wishes to advise you that you are entitled to be represented by a lawyer, and if you are not finan-*

cially able to employ one and will so advise the Court, the Court will see that you have a lawyer. Do you understand that?
THE RESPONDENT: Yes, sir.
THE COURT: The Court also wishes to inform you that you are entitled to have a trial either before a jury or before the Court without a jury. Do you understand that?
THE RESPONDENT: Yes."

Noting the exchange from the transcript, Eggan wrote that Buchanon, who was no stranger to criminal proceedings, was advised of his right to a lawyer if he couldn't afford one and was told if he advised the court counsel, one would be appointed for him. It was now Buchanon's own position that the Court had not allowed him an opportunity to request a lawyer.

Eggan cited the Winegar case again because it was eerily similar to Buchanon's. Noting Judge Noel P. Fox's position regarding Winegar, the assistant attorney general included the Judge's written response to the case:

"The Court is well aware that the right to counsel does not depend upon a request and that waiver of counsel cannot be presumed from a silent record. Carnley v. Cochran, 369 US 506, 516 (1962). The record here, however, is not a silent one. The Court is also aware that 'waiver is ordinarily an intentional relinquishment or abandonment of a known right or privilege,' Johnson v. Zerbst, 304 US 458, 464 (1938), and that petitioner did not

say 'I waive counsel' in so many words. This definition of waiver, however, is followed by the following sentence:

'The determination of whether there has been an intelligent waiver of the right to counsel must depend, in each case, upon the particular facts and circumstances surrounding that case, including the background, experience, and conduct of the accused. 304 US at 464.'

This, then, is a case of an accused, who is no stranger to the judicial process, who is told that he has the right to appointed counsel if he cannot afford to hire one, and that if he will so advise the Court, the Court will appoint counsel for him. He is asked if he understands this, and he replies he does. He chooses not to do so. Under the circumstances, the Court finds that petitioner was fully advised of his right to appointed counsel, that he had ample opportunity to request counsel, that knowing and understanding his right, he chose not to have counsel, and that his choice was intentional, voluntary, and knowledgeable."

Summarizing his final argument, Eggan wrote similarly that Buchanon had ample opportunity to request counsel. Having testified at the evidentiary hearing, he had previously pled guilty to felonies on two occasions and was aware that the Court would inform him of his right to an attorney. He argued if Buchanon desired an attorney, he could have said so at the time of his arrest, at his preliminary examination, during his brief incarceration at the Ingham County Jail, or when he was informed of his right by the trial court. In addition, Eggan maintained he had an additional opportunity during his in-chambers conference with Judge Salmon. In his final sentence, Eggan wrote:

> "Respondent contends, therefore, that as in Winegar, supra, Petitioner in the case at bar was fully advised of his counsel right but voluntarily and intelligently waived said right."

Now it was a waiting game.

It was three weeks after Eric Eggan filed his brief regarding the evidentiary hearing when Judge Thomas Carlson issued his written opinion and recommendation.[67] The document, dated October 13, 1981, briefly outlined the testimony of Nealy Buchanon, in addition to his claims, and noted the testimony of Judge Marvin Salmon.

In the written recommendation, Judge Carlson noted Buchanon presented three challenges to the "validity of his plea-based conviction and sentence."

Beginning with Nealy's claim that he didn't knowingly, intelligently, and voluntarily waive his right to a lawyer, while relying on the case of *Moore v. Michigan*, the judge indicated Buchanon's own testimony made it clear he knew he had the right to court-appointed counsel, but he chose not to ask for a lawyer because he "simply did not think one would do him any good" and because he considered himself guilty of the murders. Based on that, the Judge wrote:

> "The undersigned finds, as a matter of fact, that his decision to waive counsel

A SLAYER WAITS

was made understandingly and intelligently."

With the similarities between Buchanon's case and the case of *Moore v. Michigan,*[68] Judge Carlson chose to compare the Moore case with Nealy's because he was relying so heavily on it.

Moore was a seventeen-year-old black youth with a seventh-grade education who, in 1938, had pled guilty to the murder of an elderly white woman without the benefit of a lawyer.

Like Buchanon, he had an in-chambers discussion with the presiding judge and a degree hearing he did not participate in. While there were similarities, there were also crucial differences. Moore was seventeen at the time, while Buchanon was thirty-two and had already served time in prison for two previous felony convictions. In the Moore case, the Supreme Court noted "reasonable" defenses could have been used, such as insanity. During his in-chambers conference, Moore had told the Judge he wanted to be examined, saying there was something wrong in his head and he had previous "queer sensations."

In Buchanon's case, Judge Carlson had written, despite counsel's claims, that there was no plausible basis for an insanity defense or irresistible impulse. In continuing his comparison of the two cases, Carlson noted in Moore's case that the sheriff specifically told Moore he might not be able to protect him because there were "some black people who might interfere with him and other people from Holland who might attempt something." In comparison, Buchanon said there might have been 50 to 100 people outside the jail, and there was a newspaper account saying extra guards were on duty, but there was nothing to indicate Buchanon's life was in danger. Carlson wrote, "The undersigned does not believe that Moore requires reversal of the conviction in this case."

Furthermore, from Nealy Buchanon's own testimony and the confession he gave to Sheriff Barnes, his statements were not coerced or the result of any threats. Carlson noted the only abuse Buchanon endured was at the hands of the Baltimore Police Department, who Buchanon claimed "roughed him up a little." Carlson said there was no abuse when he gave his statement to law enforcement after his arrival in Michigan.

Judge Carlson also didn't think Buchanon was a credible witness. He cited Buchanon's own affidavit, which Nealy said was truthful at the evidentiary hearing:

> *"During the trial, Judge Marvin J. Salmon stopped the proceedings and took me into his office. There he told me that if I wanted to protect my family and myself I had better go along with the program…I didn't do this, and I don't want to hang for it, and I want a lawyer. He then told me, 'We don't have the death penalty here in the state of Michigan.'"*

Buchanon's testimony at the evidentiary hearing was in direct conflict to his previous statements. He testified he never told Judge Salmon he wanted counsel, and he never told the judge he didn't commit the crime. Judge Carlson thought his reference to pleading guilty out of fear of the death penalty was suspect, as well, because of what he had written in his affidavit.

Other references made by Buchanon regarding fear or coercion were vague and unclear according to the appellate judge. He mentioned fear for his family, but they lived in Detroit, not in Ingham County. His fear of physical harm essentially boiled down to his fear of the "system" harming him.

In contrast to Carlson's opinion of Buchanon lacking any credibility, he found retired Judge Marvin Salmon to be credible and rejected any suggestion he had threatened or verbally abused Buchanon in any way.

Carlson found Buchanon's waiver of counsel was valid, and evidence presented at the evidentiary hearing didn't establish he was absent at the degree hearing. While neither Judge Salmon nor Nealy Buchanon could say whether or not Buchanon was actually present, the written court record indicated he was brought before the Court on the morning of October 19, 1956. After he entered his plea, and after the in-chambers conference, the prosecutor was ready to proceed. At the beginning of the hearing, Judge Salmon stated:

> *"I should like to have the record show that this is the Hearing on the Determination of the Degree of Guilt of the respondent, Nealy Joseph Buchanon, who is before the Court charged with the murder…"*

At the end of the hearing, the transcripts read:

> *"It is the judgment of this court that the*

> *murder of Myra Herrick was murder in the first degree, and it is also the judgment of this court that the murder of Howard Herrick was murder in the first degree. Will you step up here, Mr. Buchanon? The Court will sentence you."*

Carlson wrote that while the record wasn't absolutely clear, it strongly suggested Buchanon was present in the courtroom. Carlson couldn't find "as a matter of fact" that Buchanon wasn't, and even though he wasn't advised of his right to participate, Judge Salmon indicated he wouldn't have denied him that opportunity if he asked.

Judge Thomas Carlson concluded his opinions and recommendations, writing:

> *"For all the foregoing reasons then, the undersigned finds that Petitioner's guilty plea was entered knowingly, intelligently, and voluntarily, and accordingly, recommends that the instant Petition for Writ of Habeas Corpus be dismissed. While this 1956 plea may not comport with all the present-day requirements, the conviction remains sound and any relief to be accorded Petitioner must come from executive clemency for which he is eligible."*

A copy of Judge Carlson's recommendation was sent to Judge Robert DeMascio, Frank Eaman, and Eric Eggan. Both Eaman and Eggan were notified at the end of the recommendation that any objections would have to be filed with the Court within ten days of the copy being served.

Frank Eaman was disappointed at Magistrate Carlson's opinion, and he wasn't optimistic about Judge DeMascio, either. DeMascio wasn't known for his liberalism when it came to appellate cases.

On October 20, Frank Eaman filed his objections to Carlson's report. Citing case law in his objections, Eaman wrote that the factors considered by Carlson regarding Buchanon's "voluntary and intelligent" waiver were not the correct factors to be considered:

> "A waiver of a constitutional right must be a waiver which is the product of a clear and free mind, unclouded by mental incapacity, nervousness, confusion, or feelings of vulnerability; there can be no coercion, subtle or blatant, and the consent (or waiver) cannot have been the product of any illegal police conduct."

Eaman continued, citing eight circumstances accepted as factual by Judge Carlson during the evidentiary hearing, including information that Buchanon had never consulted with a lawyer regarding any legal rights he had. In addition, Frank Eaman noted that between his client's arrest and sentencing, he never spoke to or received advice from an attorney about his rights or possible defenses, and the time between his arraignment and his sentence was less than 36 hours. Continuing with his objections, Eaman wrote that Buchanon had been the victim of some physical abuse by the Baltimore Police, was incarcerated in a town jail in Michigan surrounded by a crowd of people who were allowed to look into his cell through a window, and a newspaper account indicated extra guards had to be posted to protect Buchanon.

Finishing his bulleted points, Eaman wrote that Buchanon was unaware of any defenses in his case, was never afforded, on record, the opportunity to participate in his degree hearing, and was not asked to waive counsel for purposes of the hearing.

Frank Eaman continued, saying Carlson had made an error in concluding that Buchanon's plea was voluntary. He said Nealy never entered his plea because of his prior coerced statement or fear of the death penalty. His state of mind at the time of the plea was entered into the record at the evidentiary hearing and was one of fear and resignation.

The similar cases of *Moore v. Michigan* and *Pennsylvania v. Claudy*[69] were cited again to show that the waiver of counsel was not voluntary and intelligent. *Moore v. Michigan* was cited a second time by Eaman because Carlson did not ask Buchanon about his arrest and speedy arraignment and wasn't aware of any "mob" around the jail while Buchanon was there.

Frank Eaman ended his objections to Judge Carlson's report and recommendations by writing:

> *"...That under the Constitution of the United States and in the twentieth century, pleas such as the instant plea cannot be allowed to stand; the protection of the Constitution and of the right to counsel must be extended to all people, regardless of personal feelings of guilt or innocence of the person who seeks protection of our Constitution."*

CHAPTER 15

Form Over Substance

It was the fall of 1981, and while the year had started with the end of President Jimmy Carter's administration, it began with the Reagan era. In January, as Ronald Reagan was being sworn in as America's newest president, Iran released fifty-two American hostages held since 1979 when the American Embassy was overrun in Tehran.

Just three months into his presidency, President Reagan was shot when a bullet ricocheted off his limousine and struck him in the chest, having been fired by a would-be assassin. The president's press secretary, a secret service agent, and a police officer were also wounded in the assassination attempt.

In May, Pope John Paul II was also wounded by a would-be assassin as he entered St. Peter's Square at the Vatican, and during the summer months, an estimated audience of over 700 million people watched the wedding of Prince Charles and Princess Diana, while MTV was launched as a twenty-four hour video music channel.

Twenty-five years had passed since Howard and Myra Herrick were bludgeoned to death in their barn, their bodies concealed under bales of hay, so their killer could escape. Like that autumn day in September, 1955, the trees had again started to slowly change and winter's chill would soon be everywhere.

Nealy, now much older and overweight with a barrel chest, had noticed a certain sense of urgency when using the bathroom, and while he wasn't too concerned, he still thought he should probably be checked by a doctor. During his physical exam, he mentioned he had noticed some occasional blood in his stool. Deciding to do a proctoscope exam, doctors discovered a lesion on the wall of Buchanon's colon, measuring about 7 centimeters by 12 centimeters.

Nealy had some decisions to make. Discussions with the doctors offered a couple of different options. The eventual outcome might involve a permanent colostomy, excision of his rectum, and possible impotence, but Nealy was optimistic. He had just had the evidentiary hearing and was confident there would be a ruling in his favor. He was certain it wouldn't be long until he was released. After his discussion with the doctors, he decided to have any procedures needed done "on the outside" and was sure it would be in the very near future.

It wasn't long before Buchanon noticed the amount of blood in his stool had increased. He decided he didn't want to wait, and on November 13, he was admitted under guard from the prison to W. A. Foote Hospital in Jackson for exploratory surgery. His surgery was on November 16, and doctors immediately noticed multiple areas of cancer had metastasized to his liver, varying from the size of a corn kernel to the size of a pea with both sides of his liver involved. It was obvious to the doctors they would not be able to save Buchanon. The only thing they could do at that point was give him a permanent colostomy, but it seemed redundant. The surgical incision was closed. It was now clear; Nealy Buchanon had terminal cancer.

The initial treatment offered was weekly chemotherapy, and the doctors felt it could be administered at the prison.

Nealy's attorney knew nothing of his sickness. Frank Eaman drove to the prison one afternoon to meet with him. Arriving at the front desk, he asked to see his client, and the corrections officer told him Nealy wasn't at the prison. Puzzled, Eaman asked where he was. The guard wasn't sure she could share the location, and Eaman told her he was there for an attorney/client meeting. A quick phone call was made, and she finally told him where his client was.

Eaman left the prison, driving directly to the hospital. When he saw Nealy, it was apparent how sick he was, and Buchanon broke the news to him.

Frank Eaman knew his client would never survive long enough to be released from prison, and he knew Nealy would likely die before his case progressed much further. As he gathered his thoughts, he realized there was still a chance to help out his client. He could file a motion in an attempt to have Nealy released on a bond.

Knowing his client was now suffering from terminal cancer, more than ever Frank Eaman wanted to get Nealy released. He knew the diagnosis, and he knew Judge DeMascio still hadn't issued an opinion from the evidentiary hearing.

On April 1, 1982, Eaman filed a Motion for Enlargement of Petitioner on Bond Pending Decision in the District Court.[70] In his motion, Eaman cited the fact that Buchanon had served twenty-six years in prison for charges he had "attacked" in court. Eaman described his client's medical diagnosis. He included the prognosis that his continued life would be short-term. His client was being "processed" by the Michigan Department of Corrections for recommendation to have his sentence commuted, based on his medical diagnosis, in addition to the time he had served in prison. Frank Eaman included his biggest fear in the motion; the commutation process wouldn't be done before Nealy Buchanon's death, and Eaman indicated in the motion he could provide proof of the diagnosis if needed. In his final point, Nealy's attorney told the Court that a friend of Buchanon's was prepared to let him stay at her home in Grand Rapids pending a disposition in the case, should he be released early.

Frank Eaman also filed a brief in support of his motion. In the brief, he cited the case of *Johnston v. Marsh*[71] which was similar to Buchanon's. The petitioner in that case, while incarcerated in prison, was an advanced diabetic and regressing toward total blindness. He had filed a motion on the condition that he stay in a private hospital, and the Court agreed.

Frank Eaman said Buchanon was simply asking for the opportunity to present his case. Because he was suffering from terminal cancer, if the Court agreed on terms of human decency, they might follow the ruling in *Johnston*. Even if the Court ruled against him, they could still release him if they felt it was appropriate, so Eaman requested a hearing.

Six months passed, and Frank Eaman still had no response regarding the release of his client. In October,

Eaman and Buchanon finally received at least some of the news they had waited for. Judge Robert DeMascio had reviewed all the documentation from the evidentiary hearing and had finally released his written opinion.[72]

In the document, Judge DeMascio began by noting Buchanon's application for a writ of habeas corpus, alleging that his plea to an "open" murder charge was not made intelligently and voluntarily because he was not represented by counsel, his plea was coerced by law enforcement, he was denied his right to counsel, and his absence at the degree hearing. He referenced the evidentiary hearing conducted the previous year and also referenced Judge Thomas Carlson's report about the hearing, saying that the magistrate reported Buchanon had knowingly and intelligently waived his right to counsel, had knowingly and intelligently entered a plea of guilty, had knowingly and intelligently waived his right to counsel at the degree hearing, and was present at the degree hearing. He also noted Judge Carlson's recommendation that Nealy Buchanon's petition be dismissed. Judge DeMascio agreed with everything in Carlson's report, except for his finding that Buchanon had waived his right to counsel at the degree hearing.

Judge DeMascio wrote Buchanon, as the petitioner, was relying on the previous court decision of *Conner v. Anderson*.[73] In that decision, Conner had a right to counsel at his degree hearing, and he should have been advised of it. DeMascio noted the case was unpublished, and it wasn't normally used as a precedent, unless it was believed the opinion might have value regarding a material issue and there were no other published opinions used. The Court couldn't find any other cases addressing the issue raised by Buchanon's attorney.

There were several Supreme Court decisions indicating Buchanon did, in fact, have a right to counsel at his degree hearing. Referring to *Moore v. Michigan*, DeMascio cited the Court's discussion regarding the right to counsel:

> *"Moreover, the proceedings to determine the degree of murder, the outcome of which determined the event of punishment, introduced their own complexities. With the aid of counsel, the petitioner, who we have said neither testified himself in the proceeding nor cross-examined the prosecution's witnesses, might have done much to establish a lesser degree of the substantive crime or to establish facts and make arguments which could have mitigated the sentence. The right to counsel is not a right confined to representation during the trial on the merits."*

Judge DeMascio also noted there were other recent Supreme Court decisions indicating a defendant had a right to counsel at each critical stage in a criminal proceeding. With the statement made by the Supreme Court in *Moore v. Michigan* and discussions in two other cases (*White and Hamilton*), the Court concluded that unless he knowingly and voluntarily waived his right, he did have the right to counsel at the degree hearing.

While Judge Carlson had concluded Buchanon waived his right to counsel at the degree hearing by earlier doing so at his arraignment, DeMascio wrote it was not a "permissable" [sic] conclusion to draw because the degree hearing involved a different query than the guilty plea.

During Buchanon's degree hearing, he said nothing and didn't offer any evidence on his own behalf. A waiver of counsel couldn't be implied simply because Buchanon remained silent.

The judge wrote:

> *"Additionally, we may not infer a waiver from the petitioner's conduct at the hearing unless it appears that the petitioner knew his rights and then acted in a manner inconsistent with the exercise of those rights. On the basis of the above cited cases, we find the reasoning in Conner persuasive and applicable here."*

Finally, Judge DeMascio wrote:

> *"Accordingly, the writ will issue, unless within a reasonable time, the state conducts a hearing with counsel afforded to the petitioner to determine the degree of the murder, or alternatively, amend petitioner's judgment of conviction to murder in the second degree.*

Judge DeMascio's memorandum and opinion was followed by a memorandum and order on December 7, 1982.[74] In the order, DeMascio wrote:

> *"In cases in which the Court has found that petitioner's state confinement is unlawful, the Court may release the prisoner or order the prisoner to be released at some future time pending a new trial. We*

did not, however, find that petitioner's confinement was unlawful. We held only that his conviction for first-degree murder could not stand. We did not order the petitioner's release at present or at some future time pending a new trial, only that the state afford him a new hearing with respect to the degree of murder committed. Moreover, the record amply demonstrates the brutality of the petitioner's crime. While the murders took place over twenty years ago, we believe the petitioner's release into society should be considered by individuals whose expertise in this area is far greater than ours. We, therefore, conclude that the decision to release the petitioner should be left to the state authorities."

Because DeMascio had returned Buchanon's case to the lower court, officials in Ingham County would now have to proceed with a new degree hearing and try to convict Nealy Buchanon of first-degree murder. Appropriately, the Court had assigned local attorney Lawrence Emery to represent Buchanon at his new hearing.

Eaman shared the news with his client, and Nealy was excited his case might be returning to court or that he might have the opportunity to plead to second-degree murder which would mean his release. Frank Eaman had also learned the state would not consider a second-degree murder plea for Buchanon and weren't going to consent to early release.

Eaman decided to appeal Judge DeMascio's ruling in the hope of getting Nealy's original plea set aside and beginning from square one.

On February 18, 1983, there was a brief hearing in front of Judge Thomas L. Brown in Ingham County Circuit Court regarding the scheduled degree hearing for Nealy Buchanon which had been set for February 22. Because of the pending appeals before the Sixth Circuit Court of Appeals, Judge Brown adjourned the new degree hearing for the killer pending the outcome of the appeal before the Sixth Circuit. His order regarding the adjournment was filed on March 3.[75]

Nealy Buchanon's case would now go forward to the United States Sixth District Court of Appeals in Cincinnati but likely wouldn't be held until the spring of 1983. If the case was rejected by the US District Court of Appeals, it would be returned to the Ingham County Circuit Court. Eric Eggan, still representing the case for the State of Michigan, said, "We feel the advice of Judge Salmon was sufficient and legal, although, perhaps two hours intervened between his arraignment and sentencing."

Ingham County Prosecuting Attorney Peter Houk felt Judge DeMascio was evaluating "form over substance." Houk said, "He was too concerned about procedure and not enough about the result—that a man had readily admitted and pleaded guilty to a heinous crime."

After DeMascio's decision, Houk's office began to receive several phone calls from people in and around Stockbridge offering to testify if needed.

"Some things we've uncovered after twenty-seven years are truly amazing. Some of the new information will be valuable if we eventually have to prove Nealy Buchanon was plotting first-degree murder," Houk said.[76]

In December, the State Journal newspaper in Lansing published a letter from Howard and Myra Herrick's daughter, Monnie Foreman.[77] She wrote:

> "Twenty-seven years ago (Sept 3, 1955), our parents were murdered in their barn by an escaped convict, Neally [sic] Buchanon. In October, over a year later, he was caught in Baltimore using our father's name and Social Security number. He was returned to Mason by airplane by Sheriff Barnes, Harry Doesburg, and two others. I can't recall their names. The next day he was brought into court in front of Judge Salmon. He waived his right for an attorney and a jury. He was taken out for an hour and then brought back. Judge Salmon said, 'I sentence you to prison for 99 years for the cold-blooded, premeditated murder of Myra Herrick and another 99 years for the cold-blooded, premeditated murder of Howard Herrick, to run concurrently. You are never to be let out on parole, ever.' We don't want him let out, no way. He is there to stay. Cancer? Well, we lost our oldest son with cancer 11 years ago. If he is let out, he can't get a job, so he'll go on welfare, and we will pay dearly for that. He will kill again. What's he got to lose? Why was he put in there (prison) in the first place? Have the records been checked in Detroit? Ask the people around Stockbridge if they want him out. When he was being hunted, they all carried guns and taught their families how to use

them. He hasn't paid his debt yet. A case
like this should have capital punishment."

It was clear that Monnie, acting on behalf of her entire family, was angry that the system would even consider releasing a man from prison who had brutally murdered her parents twenty-seven years earlier.

At each stage of the process in Buchanon's appeals, the Foreman family had been kept abreast of what was happening.

The Foremans had only heard about the possible release of their parents' killer a few days before Thanksgiving. When they read the news article, Monnie became so upset, in anger and tears, and threw the newspaper across the room. Fearing for their safety, she refused to let the reporter photograph her, thinking Buchanon might come back to kill her and her family, if he was eventually released.

On Christmas Day, The Detroit News published an article titled *She Has No Sympathy for Her Parents' Killer.* Monnie again described her son dying of cancer eleven years earlier. Referring to Buchanon, now 68, she said, "His punishment isn't done with." Contacted by the paper for a response, Frank Eaman said, "I'm just trying to get him out before he dies."

Monnie Foreman wasn't about to give up. She was a small woman with a heart of gold and was a very giving person. She spent much of her time selling Tupperware from her home on Georgia Street in Williamston. During the summer months, she would spend late nights sitting on her porch, while an occasional neighbor would stop by to chat until well after midnight. She knew everyone and everything going on in the neighborhood. But when it came to Buchanon and his appeals, she would not give up her own fight to keep him behind bars. On January 23, Frank Eaman received a handwritten letter penned by Monnie.[78] It read:

> Dear Sir:
> Do you know what it is like to lose some one [sic] you love by such means as Buchanon took our parents [sic] lives? Do you have Grandchildren [sic] and love them? Well our Grandchildren [sic] didn't have the privilege of knowing theirs. My children except 2 [sic] knew their Grandparents [sic] but my youngest brother didn't. Now you want to help him get out. Why? He hasn't paid his debt. Also he never was sentenced for escaping prison either. So you want to help? Help keep him in there. No one wants him out. His record goes way back. Have you considered that? There are real people need [sic] your help. Why not seek them out & [sic] dedicate the rest of your time to helping those that need it. Or maybe you want to pay more taxes to support him. Maybe he will turn on you or your family. That would be just what could happen. He has nothing to lose. With the record he has way back in the 1930's [sic] he should stay where he is. There are no jobs available now, that means welfare. We pay more taxes to support him who took 2 lives. No way. Our children all feel the same way. He killed 2 people for $45. He didn't have to he could [sic] have left the farm the next

morning & he wouldn't be there today.
  Monnie Herrick Foreman

It wasn't just the Herrick children who were out-
raged. The entire community was angered that
Buchanon might soon be a free man. While politicians
made visits to Monnie Foreman, in an article published
in the Lansing State Journal, Eaman said, "I don't think
the state should be requiring this sort of retribution for a
dying man."[79] While telling the paper that Buchanon
had terminal colon cancer, it still wasn't enough for the
state parole board to ask the governor to commute
Nealy's sentence.

Noting Buchanon's accusation about Sheriff Willard
Barnes, now dead, making the statement to the killer,
"A mob wants to hang your black ass, so you had better stick to your statement," Monnie laughed sarcas-
tically. Implying his arrest was somehow racially
motivated and it was why she wanted to keep him in
prison, she said, "I don't hate him because he's
black...I hate him because he murdered my mother
and father in cold blood. He has to pay his penalty."[80]

Knowing it would be an uphill battle, Peter Houk
told the paper he would proceed as if it were a twenty-
seven-year-old murder case, adding, "It's going to be
difficult to show premeditation." Eric Eggan was equal-
ly concerned, saying, "I'm not sure we could prove
first-degree murder again. Many of the witnesses have
died."[81]

Monnie's brother, Harold, the son who had found
his father bludgeoned to death in the family barn twenty-seven years earlier, was not going to take the Judge's
decision lying down. He, too, reached out through the
media. The State Journal in Lansing published an editorial titled *Only One Judge:*[82]

"This letter is addressed to the taxpayers of this state. In recent papers, you have prompted information concerning a convict now serving two natural life sentences for murder. His name is Nealy Buchanon; his victims: Howard and Myra Herrick. My mother and father. It is my belief he is trying to get his sentence reduced or complete freedom by some technicality at the time of his sentencing. I am no lawyer, judge, or student of law. It is my firm belief that the judge, Judge Salamon [sic] who handled this case, had sufficient experience in his work to do it properly and justifiably by law. The excuse to release him because he is dying of cancer is no more reasonable than him taking the lives of my folks for $45, a change of clothes, something to eat, and to help further his escape from prison. I am sure a lot of prisoners, life termers [sic], have died in prison. This is just an excuse to get people who don't understand the full situation to have sympathy for him and let him have his own way. There are thousands of people dying of cancer these days, and it doesn't matter if they are law-abiding people or criminals. Another thing about murder cases. The stories tell about the victim and the killer. Nothing is said about the trauma, fear, mental anguish, sickness and the true effect that the loved ones of the victim go through and endure for a period of a lifetime to them. Three of my four children

never knew their grandparents. We never told them the whole truth about their grandparents, but when they read the story in the State Journal, they called me and cried. I cried with them, because everything came back, and because I couldn't reach 25 to 50 miles over the phone lines to hug them and give them comfort. It is no fun to remember or think about this. After 25 years, we had it set aside and now it's all back, everything. I would rather use my tax money to support him in prison than on the outside from welfare and Medicaid. I'm sure it is cheaper support in prison. I was there when we found our parents. I saw my dad and uncovered his body. My wife and two sisters wanted to see. I immediately stopped them, held them back. I said, you don't want to see this, I've seen it in combat in Korea during the war, and you don't want to see him. I firmly believe if the law lets Buchanon out under the reasons he is claiming, then this state and nation may as well open the gates to all prisons, let out all the prisoners. Then we will have only one judge to answer to: God.

In order to proceed further after DeMascio's opinion, a transcript of the evidentiary hearing was needed. At the same time that Harold Herrick and Monnie

Foreman were speaking to the newspapers about the possibility of Buchanon's release, Eaman, on behalf of Buchanon, filed a motion in January, 1983 for the Court to provide a transcript of the evidentiary hearing, since he would be filing an appeal to Judge DeMascio's opinion. Buchanon was still considered an "in forma pauperis" defendant, and one of his rights was to secure a copy of the transcript. Eaman, citing Justice Black from the United States Supreme Court wrote:

> "There can be no equal justice where the kind of trial a man gets depends on the amount of money he has. Destitute defendants must be afforded as adequate appellate review as defendants who have money enough to buy transcripts."

Frank Eaman noted further if Buchanon weren't indigent, he would pay for a copy of the transcript which had already been typed and was waiting to be released to him upon an order by the Court. He also wrote that Buchanon was not pursuing a frivolous appeal. The United States District Court had already vacated his first-degree murder conviction, and the law allowed for the court reporter preparing the transcripts to be compensated.

The attorney general's office had already stipulated a transcript could be provided to Buchanon, but an order hadn't been issued after the stipulation.

In his brief to support his motion, Eaman was eloquent in his writing saying:

> "One of the basic and fundamental rights existing in the courts of this country is the right of an indigent defendant to obtain

transcripts and records, even though he cannot pay for the same. This right is the cornerstone of access to the courts by rich, and poor alike, and is one of the most sacred, basic, and fundamental rights protected by all Courts. Were it otherwise, only the rich could afford 'justice.'"[83]

Frank Eaman also filed an application for a certificate of probable cause to appeal DeMascio's decision in hopes he could take the case before the United States Court of Appeals. On February 11, Judge DeMascio granted Eaman's appeal.

The request for the hearing transcripts was denied by the Court on April 7, 1983.

Finding time to prepare for his client's case was becoming an issue because Nealy Buchanon's appeal was not the only case Frank Eaman was handling. As Buchanon's sole appellate attorney, and working with only one other law partner, he still had other cases to handle, including having to appear in four other trial courts for criminal cases, prepare for a pending jury trial in May, and file an 800-page index for another case. He also had to appear at a pretrial conference for a client facing charges of assault with intent to do great bodily harm and had to conduct a preliminary examination for another client charged with first-degree murder. With his plate full, Eaman filed a motion to file his appellate brief in Buchanon's case "out of time." He noted in his motion that in addition to being burdened with the brief preparation, he had been denied a request for the transcripts by the District Court Judge. He made certain the Court knew Buchanon, an "indigent prisoner," was in no way responsible for the delay in filing the motion. Prior to filing his motion, he spoke with Eric Eggan, and Eggan had no objections to Eaman filing it. Having been due in March, it was only three months late.

As the heat of the summer months settled in, Eggan filed additional motions too. In June, he filed a motion to file an appellate brief "out of time," just as Frank Eaman had done. In his motion, he wrote that while his had been due on July 6, he had to prepare for a separate five-day jury trial in the United States District Court Western Division and other pretrial discovery for two additional upcoming trials. Eggan asked the Court for a twenty-eight day extension.

As the appeals dragged on through the summer, Nealy Buchanon's condition was worsening. His weight loss had become noticeable, and his overall health had started to decline. It had been almost two years since his cancer diagnosis, and as the assistant attorney general was asking for an extension to file his motion, Frank Eaman was continuing his efforts to have Buchanon released early on bond. He told the Court, through his motion, of Buchanon's surgery in 1981 and how the malignant cancer had likely spread to his client's aorta. He wrote of the chemotherapy Buchanon had been undergoing and his short-term prognosis. In closing, he noted that if the Court contested anything in the motion, he would ask them for an evidentiary hearing to show the truthfulness of Nealy Buchanon's deteriorating health. In his brief to support the motion, he again cited the case of *Johnston vs. Marsh*, just as he had in 1982 after Buchanon's initial diagnosis. He also wrote that because part of Buchanon's appeal had been granted by the U.S. District Court, his motion for "enlargement" or bond could be treated as if it had been granted and, "...enlargement is therefore presumed unless otherwise ordered pursuant to [court rule] 23 (c)."

Also in support of his motion, Buchanon's attorney noted the Federal Court Rule 23 (b) and (c):

"(b) *Pending review of a decision failing or refusing to release a prisoner in such a proceeding, the prisoner may be detained in the custody from which release is sought, or in other appropriate custody, or may be enlarged upon as may appear fitting to the court or justice or judge rendering the decision, or to the court of appeals or to the Supreme Court, or to a judge or justice of the court.*

(c) Pending review of a decision ordering the release of a prisoner in such a proceeding, the prisoner shall be enlarged upon his recognizance, with or without surety, unless the court of justice or judge rendering the decision, or the court of appeals or the Supreme Court, or a judge or justice of either court shall otherwise order."[84]

By late July, Eric Eggan was informed he would be representing the State of Michigan in a complex trial involving the Department of Corrections beginning August 9. He knew the trial would take at least a week, and because the trial was so complex, any preparation for Buchanon's appeals would be consumed by preparation for the Department of Corrections trial. A second trial was waiting for Eggan when he completed the pending litigation for the Department of Corrections. Resources in the attorney general's office were dwindling, and Eggan's immediate future would be devoted to the two trials. It would be impossible for him to prepare for Buchanon's appeal, and on August 1, he filed a motion for a forty-day extension.

Fall had come again. It was now October, and after Judge DeMascio had found Nealy Buchanon's 1956 degree hearing unconstitutional, Eric Eggan, still working on behalf of the Herrick family, continued by appealing DeMascio's findings to the United States Court of Appeals, just as Eaman had, but by filing a cross appeal.

After hearing Eggan had filed the cross appeal, Frank Eaman was having second thoughts about having done the right thing when he appealed DeMascio's opinion, thinking if the case had been returned to the State court, maybe there would have been a new degree hearing or a second-degree murder conviction. He firmly believed Nealy's case was second-degree murder, and it could even be argued as a manslaughter case.

Eric Eggan had always anticipated he would be taking each appeal one step further. In his cross appeal to DeMascio's decision, Eggan began with a fact sheet answering four questions put forth by the U.S. Court of Appeals.

The first question posed in the "Statement of Facts" was whether Buchanon's conviction had been previously litigated in the U.S. courts, with Eggan answering it had. He wrote there had been a previous writ of certiorari which had been denied by the Michigan Supreme Court. The second part was to name the constitutional violation claims. The young assistant attorney general noted the Sixth Amendment: Right to

Counsel at a Guilty Plea, and the Fourteenth Amendment: Guilty Plea Obtained by Coercion.

Asking next if other remedies had been exhausted, Eggan noted they had.

The final question asked if there were factual disputes concerning Buchanon's claims, and Eggan wrote there were.

The next portion in Eggan's filing was the Counter-Statement of Questions Presented, asking whether the events surrounding Buchanon's guilty plea "offended" the Federal Constitution, whether Buchanon's claims regarding his waiver of counsel were barred by Court Rule 9(a), and whether the district court correctly concluded that he knowingly, intelligently, and voluntarily waived his right to counsel before pleading guilty. The last questions were whether Buchanon's claim of coercion was barred by Rule 9(a) and whether the district court correctly concluded his plea was not the product of coercion.

In his brief, Eric Eggan now asserted Nealy Buchanon's statement of the case was incomplete. Eggan noted each time Buchanon had petitioned the Court, beginning in 1966, when he filed a Delayed Motion for a New Trial with the Ingham County Circuit Court and the trial court appointed Hannibal Abood for him. Eggan was very detailed in chronicling each time Buchanon filed. He included Buchanon's Application for Leave to Appeal before the Michigan Supreme Court in 1968, noting it was also denied. He continued with Nealy's writ of certiorari and his petition for rehearing, both before the Michigan Supreme Court and their denials in 1969. The list went on, with two denials in 1973 and a denial in 1977, 1978, and 1979.

The course of proceedings finally reached the evidentiary hearing on September 3, 1981, and Judge

Carlson's report, which stated none of Buchanon's rights had been violated during his arraignment, plea-taking, or guilt-determination proceedings. Finally, Eggan noted that the United States District Court determined Buchanon had not voluntarily waived his right to counsel, and they had remanded Nealy's case back to the Ingham County Circuit Court for a rehearing of the degree determination phase.

Continuing on, Eric Eggan offered a 'Counter-Statement of Facts.' His first assertion was that Buchanon lacked objectivity, outlining the facts as seen by the State of Michigan, beginning with the murder of Howard and Myra Herrick on September 3, 1955 and Nealy Buchanon's capture in Baltimore, Maryland in October of 1956. His confession was outlined, including his understanding that any statements he made would be used against him. The document also outlined Buchanon acknowledging his statement was being given freely and voluntarily "without threat or promise." He referenced the transcript from Buchanon's arraignment in his counter-statement of facts, in addition to the transcript from the evidentiary hearing two years earlier, outlining each time Buchanon had said he understood his right to counsel and his feeling that an attorney would not have done him any good.

Finally, Eggan said in his brief that Judge Carlson was not "erroneous" in his report and any reversal would be inappropriate.

Eric Eggan moved on to address Buchanon's reliance on the case of *Moore v. Michigan*. He pointed out the difference in the cases, citing there was no supporting evidence other than Buchanon's unsupported testimony to indicate that his life or his safety were in danger.

Addressing the *Winegar* case, which had been a

A SLAYER WAITS

part of several previous appeals for Buchanon, Eggan pointed out that Nealy had "ample opportunity" to request counsel. Additionally, Eggan said, "If Petitioner had genuinely desired legal assistance, he could have so stated upon his arrest at his preliminary examination during his brief Ingham County incarceration prior to rendering his confession, or at a minimum, when he was informed of his right to counsel by the trial court."

After addressing those issues, the assistant attorney general moved into Nealy Buchanon's claims of coercion, telling the Court that Buchanon's argument about coercion was based solely on his own testimony and on an unspecific account in a local newspaper. Addressing the issue further, Eggan noted Buchanon couldn't produce any witnesses surrounding his arrest, confession, or pleas.

Eggan wrote:

> *"This effort and its result is well documented in the federal evidentiary hearing transcript. The absence of witnesses with independent recollection is understandable in light of the twenty-five-year lapse of time between guilty plea and evidentiary hearing. Respondent, therefore, contends that it has been prejudiced by the passage of time and that review of Petitioner's 'coercion' claim is barred by 28 U.S.C. foll. 2254."*

He continued, noting that Judge Carlson had not found Nealy Buchanon to be a credible witness at the evidentiary hearing.

Concerning his argument about Buchanon's claim of coercion, he addressed Judge Salmon's in-chambers conference with the killer just prior to his sentencing. He wrote that Judge Salmon had recalled having Buchanon in his chambers and "unequivocally and indignantly denied ever calling him or anyone else a 'nigger,' and everyone, black or white, was treated alike."

Moving on, Eric Eggan mentioned that Judge Salmon's factual findings were entitled to a presumption of correctness. The State's attorney, arguing against the coercion claim, wrote:

> "In light of the forgoing analysis and the absence of solid support for a coercion claim, Petitioner cannot demonstrate that his plea was the product result of 'ignorance, incomprehension, coercion, terror, inducement, or subtle or blatant threats."

In addition, Eric Eggan argued whether the Equitable Doctrine of Laches should bar any consideration of Buchanon's claims and whether a hearing to determine Nealy's degree of guilt was constitutionally infirm.

Essentially, Eggan was asking for a review of Judge DeMascio's decision to grant, in part, Buchanon's application for a federal writ of habeas corpus.

Citing the case of *McMann v. Richardson*,[85] he noted:

> "What is at stake in this phase of the case is not the integrity of the state convictions obtained on guilty pleas, but whether years later, defendants must be permitted to withdraw their pleas which were perfectly valid when made, and given another choice between admitting their guilt

and putting the state to its proof."

Eggan argued Buchanon was seeking a review of his plea-based conviction obtained twenty-seven years prior. He wrote that the conviction had been repeatedly affirmed by the trial court and "Michigan's appellate tribunals." Continuing, he said the span of time between the conviction and the killer's applications had "erased the memories of principal parties involved." He did indicate that Judge Marvin Salmon, a single principal in the case, could recall some of the things, but even his memory was limited. He also mentioned that critical records, ordinarily available, were lost, including all the files regarding Buchanon's initial motion to withdraw his plea, and any subsequent pleadings were gone. Those files and records were critical not only for their content, but for memory refreshment.

Moving on, Eggan wrote that the Court had created a two-prong test for review of delayed petitions:

> *"First, the state must appear to have been prejudiced in its ability to respond to Petitioner's claims. Second, the Petitioner must be given the opportunity to meet, or rebut, the apparent prejudice to the state or to show that whatever prejudice the state has suffered would not have been avoided had the petition been filed earlier."*

With that, Eric Eggan argued that the case required dismissal of Nealy Buchanon's claims because the State of Michigan had been prejudiced in its ability to respond to each of the claims made. Any effective response to Buchanon's claims, absent records, files, or witnesses with independent recollection, was impossible.

Continuing on in the written cross-appeal, Eggan noted the case of *Ford v. Superintendent,* in which the Court said the defendant's allegations appeared to change with the passage of time. Eggan wrote, "Therein it is noted that Petitioner, at various times, admits and then denies his presence at the hearing to ascertain degree of guilt."

Arguing the degree of guilt hearing was not unconstitutional, the assistant attorney general wrote that Judge Carlson determined Buchanon was present at the degree hearing, indicated no desire to participate, and knew of his right to counsel, but felt an attorney would be of no use to him. Eggan maintained that Judge Carlson had correctly analyzed Buchanon's claims, and the District Court had erred in remanding the case back to the Ingham County Circuit Court for a rehearing.

Continuing on, Eggan noted that Buchanon had only one hour earlier waived his right to counsel when he pled guilty. At the same time he pled guilty, he was informed that a degree hearing would be held, yet he made no comment regarding a desire for an attorney:

> *"Respondent contends that Petitioner's waiver was silent upon being informed of the degree hearing, and his comments at the federal evidentiary hearing that he felt no need for an attorney because he was guilty of murder support a view that Petitioner's statement at the guilty plea constituted a waiver for all proceedings."*

His final "circumstance of significance to a valid waiver" was Nealy Buchanon's detailed and voluntary confession. The confession contained all the elements of first-degree murder under Michigan law. Eggan maintained that the presence of an attorney wouldn't have prevented its entry and couldn't have minimized its effect.

Moving to the end of his cross-appeal, Eric Eggan noted the district court had concluded that the guilt determination phase of Buchanon's state trial was a critical stage, and he should have been afforded the right to counsel, but he argued Buchanon had already pled guilty to first-degree murder, when Prosecuting Attorney Chamberlain read the information to the Court charging Buchanon:

> *"Sec. 316. First Degree Murder—All murder which shall be perpetrated by means of poison, or lying in wait, or any other kind of willful, deliberate and premeditated killing, or which shall be committed in the perpetration, or attempt to perpetrate any arson, rape robbery or burglary, shall be murder in the first degree and shall be punished by solitary confinement at hard labor in the state prison for life."*

Buchanon had told Judge Salmon that he understood the charges against him and then pled guilty to the charges. Eggan maintained the subsequent degree hearing was simply a "factual basis" hearing designed to protect Nealy Buchanon from overcharging, and he contended that no additional waiver of counsel was required.

The assistant attorney general, after writing his brief, outlined his position for the Court in the footnotes. He said the district court had dismissed Buchanon's claims about not being present at his own degree hearing and his claim about his guilty plea being obtained as the result of coercion. Beyond that, the attorney went a step further saying Court Rule 9 should be used to dismiss Nealy Buchanon's other claims that he didn't waive counsel at his guilty plea and his degree hearing.

After Eggan had filed his brief, he received word that the transcript of Nealy Buchanon's waiver of the preliminary examination had been found. Eggan promptly provided a copy to Frank Eaman, and Eaman noted it when filing his own appeal to Eggan's brief.

In his supplemental statement of facts filed with his brief two months after Eggan's, Eaman noted he had a copy of the transcript. It left no doubt that Buchanon's waiver was done without the assistance of counsel and without a waiver of the right to counsel.

With those documents, Frank Eaman also pointed out that the exact timeline of his client's appeals was now known.

Buchanon's arraignment was on October 18, 1956 at 8:00 pm. On October 19, his guilty plea occurred thirteen hours after the arraignment, and the degree hearing and sentencing occurred at 11:10 am. Being more succinct, Eaman wrote that Buchanon was arraigned in district court, waived his preliminary examination, was arraigned in circuit court, pled guilty, had a degree hearing, and was sentenced to life in prison without parole in a period of less than twenty-four hours. All the proceedings occurred without the assistance of an attorney.

Eaman also wrote that in the twelve years of appeals, the state never complained of prejudice from any delay in Buchanon's filings. It seemed obvious to him this was something new.

Opposing the brief filed by Eggan, Buchanon's defense counsel argued that his client's claims were not barred by Rule 9(a). Judge DeMascio had ruled, at least partly, in favor of both Buchanon and the attorney general. Now, on behalf of his client, Eaman was appealing the two findings that DeMascio had ruled on which were adverse to his position, including "no valid waiver of counsel" and "no voluntary plea." Citing the existence of the transcript from the preliminary examination and the testimony of both Buchanon and Judge Salmon at the evidentiary hearing, Eaman argued that the State was in no way prejudiced by Buchanon's delay in filing his appeal, writing, "District court opinions have refused to apply Rule 9(a) to claims where the state has not been prejudiced because of the existence of a transcript and trial record." He also noted that DeMascio's opinion had demonstrated the state was not prejudiced in responding to the claim the petitioner did not waive his right to counsel at his plea.

When Eaman addressed the state's claim that the degree hearing was only to provide a factual basis for a plea, he described the statement as ludicrous, given that the Court's power to find a conviction could be entered for murder in the first degree or murder in the second degree. He was clear when he wrote that a degree hearing was a critical sentencing proceeding which could result in either a sentence for the defendant to a term of less than life, thus allowing him some eligibility for parole, or could result in mandatory life in prison. To bolster his argument, Eaman noted that the case of *Oliver v. Cowan* (487 F2d 895, 896), where the Court said, "We view sentencing as more than a mere ministerial ceremony in light of the possible steps available to the defendant in that proceeding." He wrote that since the trial judge could determine the degree of punishment at a degree hearing, the presence of counsel was even more critical.

In his final argument, he wrote that the Seventh Circuit had recognized if a defendant had validly waived counsel at the time of his plea, a subsequent sentencing proceeding wasn't valid if there was no counsel present at the sentencing and no separate waiver of counsel at the proceedings.

As the date of the hearing before the United States Court of Appeals approached, the Lansing State Journal newspaper ran an article about the hearing and Buchanon seeking an immediate reversal of his conviction. Eric Eggan spoke with a reporter, and when asked about the hearing, he said he felt confident the appeals court would confirm Nealy Buchanon's conviction, but the guilt stage was up in the air.

On January 26, 1984, both attorneys' arguments were heard before the United States Court of Appeals Sixth District in Cincinnati, Ohio.

Judge Anthony Celebreeze, the senior circuit judge, was appointed to the Court of Appeals in 1965. Having attended Fenn College and John Carroll University, he graduated from Ohio Northern University with his law degree in 1936. In 1950, he had been elected to the Ohio Senate and was twice voted as one of Ohio's top senators. He was elected five consecutive times as Cleveland's mayor. In 1962, he was appointed to a cabinet post under President Kennedy as Secretary of Health, Education and Welfare and was responsible for enacting the Medicare Act and the Civil Rights Act of 1964. In September of 1965, ten years after Howard and Myra Herrick were viciously murdered in their Stockbridge barn, Celebreeze was sworn in as Judge for the United States Circuit Court of Appeals.

Appointed by President Reagan, Judge Harry Wellford took his oath of office on August 20, 1982, having attended Washington and Lee University and Vanderbilt University Law School after serving in the United States Navy. Prior to serving the Sixth District, Judge Wellford had been appointed by President Richard Nixon to serve on the United States District Court for the Western District of Tennessee. In 1976, President Gerald Ford, having replaced Nixon after his resignation, nominated Wellford for a Sixth District position, but civil rights groups objected, and because it was so late in Ford's presidency, no vote was taken to affirm the nomination. It was only after Ronald Reagan's election when Wellford was finally appointed to the Sixth District.

Judge Leroy J. Contie, Jr was also appointed to the United States Sixth Circuit Court of Appeals in 1982 by President Reagan. He had previously served the United States District Court in the Northern District of Ohio after being nominated for the position by President Nixon. He had received his bachelor's degree from the University of Michigan and his juris doctorate from the University of Michigan Law School in 1948.

In their written opinion published on May 9, the three judges wrote separately.[86]

Judge Wellford began by describing Buchanon's case as, "...A kind of microcosm of the pro se actions taken by prisoners incarcerated for serious crimes in state prisons, who present frequent challenges to the basis of their convictions and sentences, and the responses made by trial and appellate courts, state and federal, to these post-conviction efforts."

Wellford acknowledged Buchanon's petition being filed twenty-three years after his confession and sentencing for the brutal murders of Howard and Myra Herrick and noted Buchanon's three assertions before the Court: He was being unconstitutionally detained, he had exhausted all remedies available through the state, and he hadn't made any previous applications to the Court. He also outlined the history of Buchanon's appeals through the years, beginning in the late 1960s and continuing through the late 1970s. The judge wrote of Buchanon's complaints, adding his assertion that he was forced into making a confession and didn't knowingly and intelligently waive his right to an attorney prior to submitting his guilty plea at the degree hearing and at sentencing after the Court had accepted his guilty plea. Finally, Buchanon's final assertion before the Court was that he wasn't even present at the degree hearing.

In opposition to Buchanon's position, Wellford wrote the State's defense to Nealy Buchanon's petition as Rule 9(a) of 28 U.S.C. Sec. 2254.2, that he, in fact, did make a knowingly and intelligent waiver of counsel at all material stages of the proceedings, and he was present at the degree hearing.

In specifically addressing the petition by Buchanon, Judge Wellford said the Advisory Committee to Rule 9(1) foresaw the problem in 1976 when they wrote:

> *"The assertion of stale claims is a problem which is not likely to decrease in frequency...The grounds most often troublesome to the courts are...plea of guilty unlawfully induced, use of a coerced confession...When they are asserted after the passage of many years, both*

the attorney for the defendant and the state have difficulty in ascertaining what the facts are."

The courts had developed a two-pronged test because they considered Court Rule 9(a) as invoking the Doctrine of Laches. "First, the state must appear to have been prejudiced in its ability to respond to petitioner's claims. Second, the petitioner must be given the opportunity to meet or rebut the apparent prejudice to the state or to show that whatever prejudice the state has suffered would not have been avoided had the petition been filed earlier," Judge Wellford wrote.

In considering Buchanon's petition, the judges considered three other cases, because they involved appeals made years after sentencing.

In the first case considered, the Court reviewed the case of *Ford v. Superintendent*, Kentucky State Penitentiary (687 F.2d 870 [6th Cir.1982]). In that case, a petition was denied because the prisoner had filed his appeals in the state court fourteen years after having pled guilty. Twenty-three years after he had been sentenced, the prisoner filed his petition in federal court saying he had been denied counsel at his plea and sentencing. The court records indicated the prisoner had been appointed counsel, and the attorney was present at his plea. Testimony taken later had shed some doubt on whether the appointed counsel was actually present at the time the plea was taken and at the time of sentencing. In that matter, the Court said the prisoner was afforded a hearing on the matter and was given the opportunity to establish his claim to show lack of prejudice, and he failed in both respects.

In the second case of *Phillips v. Black* (367 F.Supp.

774 [E.D.Ky.1973]), there was a challenge to a guilty plea in a 1955 case in which the prisoner alleged there was no attorney present at his sentencing. The prisoner's petition was granted because the record didn't indicate whether or not the attorney, who had represented the prisoner in previous proceedings, was present at the sentencing or not. When the petition was filed sixteen years after the sentencing, the attorney couldn't recall whether or not he was present.

The last case the Court considered in Nealy Buchanon's petition was *Arnold v. Marshall*, (657 F.2d 83 [6th Cir.1981]). The prisoner was convicted in 1953, never appealed, and was released in 1973, prior to being charged as a habitual offender in another case, and was subsequently sentenced in 1975 to life imprisonment. One of the four previous cases the Court considered in his life sentence for being a habitual offender was the 1953 conviction. This was the basis of his appeal twenty-seven years later after his unappealed conviction because he had not been advised of his right to appeal. The petition was denied because there was no written record of the case, witnesses were either missing or dead, and trial notes couldn't be located. The Court concluded the state was prejudiced in its ability to respond to the petition because of that.

After considering the other cases, Judge Wellford wrote:

> "We agree with the district court that the Rule 9(a) tests set out in Davis have been met on the issues pertaining to the allegedly-coerced confession, the circumstances of the guilty plea, and with respect to the alleged absence of Buchanon from the degree hearing. The

A SLAYER WAITS

state clearly has been prejudiced by the passage of some 25 years from the time of petitioner's guilty plea and sentencing to the time of the hearing on this habeas corpus writ."

The judges agreed the alleged coercion at the Ingham County Jail, the absence at the degree hearing, and the circumstances surrounding the guilty plea couldn't prevail. They cited the fact that the confession was taken before a court reporter and Buchanon had indicated he was making his statement freely and willingly. They also noted that he knew the authorities couldn't force him to make a statement, he knew it could be used against him, he wasn't the subject of any physical abuse to make him give a statement, and there weren't any promises made in exchange for his statement. At his plea hearing, he admitted he plead guilty because he felt he was guilty, and he had been advised he could have an attorney regardless of his financial ability.

The panel of three judges also sided with Judge DeMascio's opinion regarding any alleged abuse in Baltimore. Wellford wrote, "Buchanon failed to meet or rebut the prejudice which resulted from the passage of many years in this regard."

Moving to Buchanon's last point in his petition, the judge noted the degree hearing was critical and bore directly on Buchanon's punishment, noting, "The right to counsel was a matter of 'supreme importance' at this state of the proceeding."

Wellford continued:

"Courts indulge every reasonable presumption against waiver of fundamental

*constitutional rights, and we do not pre-
sume acquiesce in the loss of fundamental rights. The constitutional right of an
accused to be represented by counsel in-
vokes, of itself, the protection of a trial
court...this protecting duty imposes the
serious and weighty responsibility upon
the trial judge of determining whether
there is an intelligent and competent
waiver by the accused."*

Judge Wellford also agreed with Judge DeMascio
regarding the record of the evidentiary hearing. The
original trial court record didn't indicate whether
Buchanon was advised of his right to counsel at the degree hearing or at sentencing. Mere silence on the part
of the defendant didn't indicate a valid waiver. Based
on that, he agreed with DeMascio's opinion, writing,
"A writ of habeas corpus should be issued unless within a reasonable time the state conducts another degree
hearing and re-sentencing," with the opportunity for
Nealy Buchanon to have an attorney assist him.

Wellford closed his opinion by stating they disagreed with DeMascio's alternative order suggesting the
judgment of conviction should be amended to second-
degree murder in lieu of a new degree hearing and re-
sentencing.

Circuit Judge Leroy Contie agreed with Judge Wellford on two points. He agreed that Rule 9(a) didn't bar
Buchanon's claim that he didn't waive his right to
counsel at the degree hearing and at his sentencing.
Contie also agreed that Rule 9(a) did bar the claim that
his confession was coerced and he was not present at
the degree hearing and sentencing. But Judge Contie
disagreed with his colleague regarding Rule 9(a) being

applied to Nealy Buchanon's other claims. He noted that the state, if relying on Rule 9(a), had to show prejudice, and it couldn't be shown by the mere passage of time.

Contie wrote it was apparent that any resolution with regard to Nealy's claim of "lack of knowledge" when it came to waiving counsel and pleading guilty could only be resolved by the trial court transcript. He noted that the transcript of the plea had been preserved, and Judge Marvin Salmon had been able to recall the context of the in-chambers discussion prior to sentencing, so therefore, no additional proof was needed to disprove Buchanon's claim of "lack of knowledge" in waiving counsel and entering his plea. It was Contie's opinion that the State had failed to show any prejudice in its ability to respond to Buchanon's claims.

Finally, Judge Contie wrote that he agreed with Judge Wellford and the district court; Rule 9(a) barred consideration of Buchanon's claims that his confession was coerced and he was absent from the degree hearing and sentencing.

In summarizing his opinion, Judge Leroy Contie wrote:

> "I join Judge Wellford's opinion only insofar as it finds that Rule 9(a) bars relief for the claim of a coerced confession and the claim that Buchanon was not present at the degree and sentencing hearing and finds for Buchanon on the merits of his claim that he did not waive counsel at the degree and sentencing hearing."

Senior Circuit Court Judge Anthony Celebreeze disagreed with both of his colleagues. Celebreeze wrote it was his opinion that Rule 9(a) completely barred all claims in this "long, delayed petition." He concluded the State of Michigan had established that the twenty-three-year delay had adversely affected its ability to respond to Buchanon's claims. Celebreeze wrote:

> "Although courts cannot presume a waiver of counsel from a silent record, the silence in this instance is due primarily to petitioner's inexcusable delay; the record contains no legitimate explanation for the more than twenty-three-year delay which has affected clearly the memories of the only potential witnesses in this case."

While the case had been argued before the United States Circuit Court of Appeals in January, it was decided on May 9, 1984. Eric Eggan had only one choice. If the case wasn't appealed to the United States Supreme Court, it would be returned to the original trial court in Ingham County for a new degree hearing based on the opinion of the U.S. Court of Appeals. If the case was returned to Ingham County, the new hearing to determine the degree of guilt would be held in front of Circuit Judge Thomas Brown, who had replaced Judge Marvin Salmon after his retirement.

Michigan Attorney General Frank Kelly, for whom Eric Eggan was working, spoke to the media about the State's next move in the appeals process. Kelly told a reporter that he was, "...Repulsed at the possibility a convicted murderer could be roaming our streets." He continued, "There is no doubt regarding the guilt of Mr. Buchanon, but the facts are the convicted may be set free because of this antiquated law that permits this inmate, after almost thirty years, to file an appeal." Frank Kelly was quoted in a final sentence, saying, "It has long been my contention that criminals convicted of a felony should not have an unlimited time frame in which to appeal their conviction." Kelly maintained the loophole allowing inmates to do it should have been closed years earlier.[87]

Frank Kelly, Eric Eggan, and Frank Eaman all knew that if Nealy Buchanon's case wasn't appealed to the United States Supreme Court, he would be released. While Eggan was continuing the fight to keep the killer behind bars, and Eaman was fighting for his freedom, Buchanon's cancer had progressed, and his health was slowly slipping away.

Before appealing to the U.S. Supreme Court, Eric Eggan's next step had already been planned. On May 21, nine days after the U.S. Court of Appeals had made their decision, Eggan filed a petition for Rehearing and Suggestion for Rehearing En Banc,[88] essentially asking for the entire Court of Appeals to review the petition, rather than the panel of three judges. It was common for the attorney general's office to file the Suggestion for Rehearing En Banc if the state lost a case with the Court of Appeals. If the case continued to the United States Supreme Court, the motion for the rehearing was nice to have, even though it was very rare that a motion for a rehearing was ever granted. There was a required statement at the beginning of Eggan's appeal. It began:

> *"I express a belief, based on a reasoned and studied professional judgment, that the panel decision heretofore rendered in the instant cause is contrary to the follow-*

ing decisions of the United States Court of Appeals for the Sixth Circuit and the Supreme Court of the United States and that consideration by the full court is necessary to secure and maintain uniformity of decision in this court and in this circuit."

Eggan cited several cases from earlier testimony before the Court and indicated that this new appeal involved questions of exceptional importance, which were the same two issues in his previous argument before the three-judge panel.

On July 3, Eric Eggan's appeal for Suggestion of Rehearing En Banc was denied, but the order of the denial wasn't received by the attorney general's office until Friday, July 6, the delay likely due to the July 4 holiday. Because time was of the essence in any appeal process, upon receiving the order, Eggan quickly drafted a motion to stop the issuance of the order. The motion was mailed on July 9, and it wasn't received by the Court of Appeals until July 12. The "ordinary" time frame for a motion to be received was within seven days. Because the holiday likely delayed the mailing, the Court concluded on July 23 that it was in the interest of justice to have the order recalled.

Eric Eggan now filed a Petition for a Writ of Certiorari to the United States Court of Appeals for the Sixth District. It was filed with the United States Supreme Court. In it, he presented two questions:

1) *Is the Equitable Doctrine of Laches, embodied in 28 U.S.C. foll. 2254, Rule 9(a), applicable to a twenty-five-year-old plea-based conviction of first-degree*

murder where a state shows prejudice from the delay?

2) Whether a single waiver of counsel is constitutionally acceptable for purposes of a unitary proceeding to accept a guilty plea and ascertain degree of guilt under Michigan's open murder statute.[89]

As each step of Buchanon's appeals progressed further into the federal courts, the assistant attorney general had been conferring with the State's Solicitor General, Robert Derengoski. Derengoski was a senior assistant attorney general, having held the position since 1963 and worked in the Solicitor General Division. If the case was to be heard by the United States Supreme Court, the Solicitor General would be the attorney presenting oral arguments, and Eggan would be seated next to him.

In the meetings with Derengoski, Eric Eggan would discuss the case with him, and while he already knew the answer, at one meeting he asked Derengoski if he might be allowed to present oral arguments before the Supreme Court. Eggan knew that in very rare cases, the attorney who argued the case before the Court of Appeals would be allowed to argue it before the Supreme Court. Knowing only cases of great importance were heard by the United States Supreme Court, he was surprised when Derengoski didn't start laughing at him. The veteran attorney was very professional when he explained to the young assistant attorney general that he wasn't quite ready for that. In February of 1982, Derengoski retired, and the new Solicitor General for the State of Michigan became Louis Caruso. If the case progressed that far, Caruso would now be the attorney presenting oral arguments.

Eggan filed the sixteen-page document, citing four-teen legal cases referenced in the petition. He outlined all the appeals Nealy Buchanon had made since his 1956 plea-based sentencing for the murders of Howard and Myra Herrick. Eggan was quoted in the Lansing State Journal as saying, "This will give the Court the opportunity to rule that old, stale convictions cannot be brought up for review."

Knowing Buchanon's health was deteriorating, Frank Eaman opposed Eggan's appeal to the United States Supreme Court. There was no way Buchanon would survive the length of time it would take the Court to render a decision.

On October 20, Buchanon's attorney received notice from the Supreme Court of the United States indicating a writ of certiorari had been docketed on September 28.

Like Eggan had done, Frank Eaman submitted two questions to the United States Supreme Court for review on October 24, 1984:

> 1) Where the respondent presented to Federal Court a habeas corpus petition asking action of his 23-year-old conviction of murder in the first degree because he was not afforded the assistance of counsel at the time of his conviction, where full proceedings exist, where the trial judge and the respondent [sic] retained memory of the court proceedings, and where the State does not dispute that respondent was denied the assistance of counsel, does rule 9(a) of 28 U.S.C. foll. 2254 bar relief to the respondent?
> 2) Was a hearing held by the state

*court to determine whether the respond-
ent would be found guilty of murder in
the first degree or murder in the second
degree to determine their respondent's
punishment a separate, critical state of
the state court proceedings which required the court to afford the assistance
of counsel to respondent or secure a
waiver of counsel from respondent?*[90]

As Frank Eaman had so many times before, he outlined the statement of facts in the case he was opposing. It included outlining to the Court a full transcript of
all the state court proceedings including Buchanon's
arraignment, waiver of his preliminary examination in
the state district court, and his guilty plea in the state
circuit court, in addition to his degree hearing on the
open charge of murder. In his brief, he also pointed out
Buchanon's 'counselless' [sic] sentence to life in prison
without parole.

Nealy Buchanon's attorney outlined his first reason
for not granting the writ being filed by Eric Eggan:

*"The case, where it is undisputed that the
respondent has been imprisoned as a result of counselless [sic] proceedings,
where full transcripts exist of all state
court proceedings, and where the trial
judge and the respondent retained
memory of the proceedings and testified
in Federal District Court, is an inappropriate case to review the application of
laches or rules embodied in 28 U.S.C.
foll. 2254."*

Eaman continued by describing the earlier appeals and decisions by Judge DeMascio, and the U.S. Court of Appeals. Citing his second reason for not granting the pending writ, Eaman wrote:

> "*Respondent's counselless* [sic] *conviction of murder in the first degree was not a unitary proceeding; the degree hearing which followed the respondent's plea to open charge of murder was a critical stage of the proceedings at which witnesses testified and the outcome of which determined the difference in respondent's sentence; respondent should have been afforded counsel at that state of the proceedings or explicitly waived counsel.*"

Eaman also noted the U.S. Court of Appeals had already granted relief to his client and had recognized the significance of a degree hearing in Michigan. He also wrote that Judge Wellford had noted in the case of *Moore* the right to counsel was a matter of supreme importance.

Included with his brief was a Motion for Leave to Proceed in Forma Pauperis, asking if the Court granted the attorney general's petition to hear the case and that he be appointed to continue to represent Buchanon.

With his Brief in Opposition, Frank Eaman also attached a formal letter to the Clerk of the Court stating he was the appointed counsel for Nealy Buchanon in both the United States District Court and the United States Court of Appeals, and because his client was indigent, it was his responsibility to continue to represent him. Because Eaman was not a member of the Bar of the United States Supreme Court, he attached his Application for Admission to the Bar.

On October 24, 1984, the United States Supreme Court agreed to hear Nealy Buchanon's case by granting the Writ of Certiorari.

CHAPTER 16

1984

In the first gallery of 11 block at the prison, Nealy Buchanon was a shell of the man he had once been. He was gaunt and his voice was weak. He lay in his cell with the door slightly open—a privilege afforded to the few inmates suffering a terminal illness and who were close to death.

Perry Johnson, Director of the Michigan Department of Corrections, stood in the cell with Buchanon, who was lying on his cot. Johnson had known Nealy for nearly thirty years. In 1956, as a new counselor at the prison, Perry was assigned to inmates who had prison numbers with a six, and Nealy Buchanon was one of those. Johnson had done one of his first inmate evaluations on Buchanon when he arrived at the prison.

Johnson had worked his way up through corrections, eventually holding the title of Warden for the prison, and finally, moving to a position as the Director for the entire Michigan Department of Corrections.

This particular day, Buchanon had asked specifically for Perry, who happened to be at the prison for his last day. Johnson knew nothing of Buchanon's cancer.

As the director stood in Nealy's cell, they spoke of days gone by, but Johnson was curious why Buchanon had asked for him.

Nealy spoke quietly to Johnson, asking him if would speak with Frank Kelly, the Michigan Attorney General. He told Perry he had won his case before the Court of Appeals, and it would likely be heard before the Supreme Court. Nealy knew he would be dead long before it reached that point.

Perry Johnson knew why Nealy was in prison and knew of the appeal process he had been going through for years. He always felt the murders of Howard and Myra Herrick were out of character for Buchanon and, in a panic situation, he was simply desperate to get away. Over the years, after having come to know him, Johnson thought Buchanon was a reasonable man, and when they would cross paths, they were always straight with each other. Johnson always felt if Buchanon were ever released, there was no way he would ever be a threat to society.

He politely told Buchanon there was nothing he could do to change the attorney general's mind, while trying to explain why. Nealy quietly acknowledged Perry Johnson's position.

Years earlier, when Buchanon had been transferred to Marquette, Perry had been called up to the prison for a potential problem among the inmates. When he saw Buchanon in the law library, they spoke briefly, and it seemed Buchanon was planning ahead, years before he had ever developed cancer. He told Johnson he would file an appeal based on what inmates call "quick justice." He wasn't going to claim innocence, but ask for mercy when he was near the end. He told Perry Johnson, "After I have a lot of years in, I hope the Court will grant bond during the new trial, and I will be able to die peacefully outside the wall." It was all Nealy Buchanon really wanted, as he spoke with Perry Johnson; to die peacefully outside the wall.[91]

It was an unusual spring-like November. The temperature hovered in the mid-50s, and there was no sign of snow on the horizon. On November 7, Buchanon's condition had worsened to a point where the treatment required was more than the prison could provide. He was transferred from the prison to Ingham Medical Hospital in Lansing.

Thanksgiving had passed, and the Christmas shopping season was in full swing. To his credit, Frank Eaman had been admitted to the United States Supreme Court Bar during their October session. On Friday, November 30, he met with Nealy at the hospital in Lansing. Buchanon had to officially request that he be represented by Frank Eaman in the case now before the Supreme Court.

Frank couldn't help but notice how gaunt Buchanon looked as the two met. The maroon-colored eyes now sagged, almost sleepy-like. Nealy had lost considerable weight. While nothing was said between the two, both men knew time was not on their side now.

He told Nealy his case was going to be heard by the Supreme Court. In a weak voice, Nealy said, "That's great." But Frank Eaman knew otherwise. It wasn't great. Though they had won in the Sixth Circuit Court of Appeals, the Supreme Court could take it all away.

Knowing his client was dying, Eaman felt horrible

because he had once promised Buchanon he would walk him out of prison. More than ever he wanted to see Nealy reunited with his family. As he looked at his client, he knew Nealy was just an old man who had served a very long time in prison, never denying responsibility for what he had done. He had changed his life around in prison over the many years, even though prior to 1981, he had never once had an attorney represent him. To Frank Eaman, the Nealy Buchanon who was dying in front of him was not the same man who was in the Herrick barn in 1955.

Leaving his client at Ingham Medical Hospital, Eaman walked to his car after their meeting, and sitting behind the steering wheel, began sobbing. As the tears rolled down his face, he thought of his own father who had died of cancer years before.

Eaman prepared to file a motion with the Supreme Court to be appointed as counsel for his client. The following Thursday, he filed the motion indicating he was familiar with the entirety of the case; Buchanon was still considered indigent, and he had acted as counsel for Buchanon during his previous federal appeals.

Eaman didn't realize it, but between the time he had last spoken to Nealy and the day he filed his motion, his client's health had deteriorated even more. Frank Eaman's motion to represent his client before the Supreme Court was filed on December 7, the same day Nealy Buchanon died.

On December 10, Frank Eaman called Eric Eggan at his office to let him know Nealy Buchanon was dead. Both attorneys knew it wasn't the end of the matter completely. The Court would have to be notified of Buchanon's death by the state filing a Suggestion of Mootness.

Monnie Forman's phone rang on that December afternoon. The spring-like temperatures had turned cold, and as she answered, she heard an all-too-familiar voice on the other end of the line. It was Eric Eggan, and he was calling to tell her the man who had murdered her parents was dead. Eggan had kept in touch with her throughout the entire appeal process, and this was the phone call she had reluctantly waited for.

After the murder of her parents and throughout the rest of her life, Monnie had feared Buchanon's return, thinking he would come back to "finish the job" if he were ever released from prison. She was relieved to some degree that he was dead, and she would never have to worry about his release again, but she also had wished the case would continue to the Supreme Court for some sort of resolution.

Later that evening, family and friends gathered at the Foreman house on Georgia Street in Williamston to remember Howard and Myra and share some of their memories from the past.

No one claimed Nealy Buchanon's body. He was quietly buried in Cherry Hill Cemetery at Jackson Prison alongside numerous other unclaimed prison inmates who had died there.

A day after letting the Herrick children know Buchanon was dead, Eric Eggan filed the Suggestion of Mootness with the United States Supreme Court. Because of his death and the Supreme Court having previously issued the writ of certiorari on October 24, Eggan was "compelled to suggest" that the case be rendered as "moot." Frank Eaman agreed, however, he didn't agree with the disposition that Eric Eggan was asking for. Without filing the motion, any rulings by the lower courts would stand. Speaking with the media, Eggan explained, "A favorable ruling on the request to dismiss the appeals decisions would leave the whole thing not up in the air like it is now."

If the Supreme Court decided in favor of Eggan's recommendation, he suggested the previous judgments by the Court of Appeals and the United States District Court be vacated. In his closing, Eggan wrote:

> *"This Court has already recognized the significance of the issues in this case by granting certiorari, and under the circumstances, it would be unjust to permit the erroneous judgments of the Court of Appeals, and District Court to remain in effect."*[92]

Eggan had disagreed with the lower court decisions and had appealed to the Supreme Court. As a matter of procedure, because Buchanon was dead, he wanted the Court to dismiss those earlier decisions by the lower courts, so they wouldn't be used as precedent for future cases regarding the same issues.

On April 15, 1985, the United States Supreme Court dismissed the writ of certiorari it had granted the previous October. Contrary to Eric Eggan's motion, the decision of the Court of Appeals was left standing. United States Supreme Court Justice Warren Berger disagreed with the decision. Chief Justice Berger felt the Court should follow its previous rulings regarding suggestions of mootness and dismiss the writ of certiorari, then remand the case back to the Court of Appeals with directions to dismiss their previous decision. He cited the case of *McMann v. Ross*,[93] when he wrote:

> *"In McMann v. Ross, the only case to have presented the precise issue we have here, the court vacated the judgment of the Court of Appeals and remanded to the District Court with instructions to dismiss the respondent's petition for writ of habeas corpus as moot. I would, as petitioner urges, dispose of this case in the same way. This is the course we have chosen to pursue in every civil case that becomes moot, either pending a decision on certiorari or after we have granted a writ of certiorari, except Warden v. Palermo, which even if it were correct, is plainly distinguishable. Thirty-five years ago, the court noted that '[t]he established practice of the court in dealing with a civil case from a court in the federal system which has become moot while on its way here or pending our decision on the merits is to reverse or vacate the judgment below and remand with a direction to dismiss.'"*

The Herrick children seldom spoke of their parents' murders. Monnie Foreman literally had feared for her own safety and the safety of her family if Buchanon was ever released from prison. With his death, the long nightmare was over, and while she could rest easier, the void created thirty years earlier had not been erased. It was still there and always would be.

For Frank Eaman, who knew in his own heart that Nealy Buchanon was a changed man and who had cried when he learned of Buchanon's impending death, would never be able to argue his client's case before the Supreme Court. In the end, the decision by the country's highest court was Frank Eaman's one small victory. While Chief Justice Warren Berger had dissented, his was the only dissenting voice from the Supreme Court. The certiorari before the Court was dismissed but was not sent back to the Court of Appeals to have the lower court's opinion vacated. The decision by the United States Court of Appeals regarding Nealy Buchanon still stands.

For Eric Eggan, he had fought for the Herricks until the end and had kept in touch with the family throughout the years, learning there was more to legal proceedings than appeals and briefs. The victims and their family were real, and they mattered. Eric Eggan had made a lasting friendship with Monnie and the rest of the family. When Nealy Buchanon died, there was no joy. Eggan had expected a resolution from the highest court in the land, but he didn't get it.

For Howard and Myra Herrick, their silenced voices were heard. They were heard again and again for nearly thirty years, through the efforts of everyone who had fought to keep their slayer behind bars.

References

Barry Mitzes, Warden v. Nealy Buchanon
47 USC 154, 105 S. Ct. 2006, 85. L. Ed.2d 120
Buchanon v Mintzes, 734 F.2d 274
https://familysearch.org/ark:/61903/1:1:XQB9-K9C
Jackson: The Rise and Fall of the World's Largest Walled Prison, Johnson, Perry, 2015
24-Hour Vigil of Death, Master Detective, Brown, James P., September 1957
Annual Report 1955, Michigan Corrections Commission,
Memory Book of LBTS: An Informal History of the Lansing Boys Training School,
Graphic Communications, 1972
Stockbridge Area 175th Anniversary Souvenir Book, Stockbridge Area Genealogical Society and The Stockbridge Area Anniversary Committee, 2010
A Hanging in Detroit, Chardavoyne, David G., Wayne State University Press, 2003

Report of Survey Made for Michigan Boys Vocational School, Governor's Survey Commission, 1942

The Innocent Prisoner's Dilemma: Consequences of Failing to Admit Guilt at Parole Hearings, Medwed, Daniel S., 2008

Historical Sketch of the Indeterminate Sentence and Parole System, Lindsey, Edward, 1925, Journal of Criminal Law and Criminology, Vol 16, Issue 1

Death of Innocence: The Story of the Hate Crime That Changed America, Till-Mobley, Mamie & Benson, Christopher, The Random House Publishing Group, 2004

Soul on Ink, Texas Reporter, Elkind, Peter, October 1983

Peek Through Time: Jackson Officers Narrowly Escape With Their Lives in 1961 Kidnapping, http://www.mlive.com/news/jackson/index.ssf/2015/07/peek_through_time_jackson_offi.html

Michigan Court of Appeals, Filing Appeals and Original Actions, 2000, Clerks Office of the Michigan Court of Appeals

The Ann Arbor News, *Farm Couple Slain Near Stockbridge*, September 6, 1955

The Ann Arbor News, *Fingerprints Found In Killing*, September 7, 1955

The Ann Arbor News, *Buchanon [sic] Sought In Jackson Area*, September 9, 1955

The Ann Arbor News, *Stockbridge Slayings' Suspect Held*, October 17, 1956

The Ann Arbor News, *Slayings Bring Two Life Terms*, October 19, 1956

The Battle Creek Enquirer, *Couple Slain; Seek Fugitive*, September 6, 1955

The Battle Creek Enquirer, *Hunt Near Jackson For Murder Suspect*, September 9, 1955

The Battle Creek Enquirer, *Village Locks Its Doors In Fear,* September 23, 1955

The Battle Creek Enquirer, *$1,400 Reward Posted For Farm Pair Slayer,* October 31, 1955

The Battle Creek Enquirer, *Slain Couple's Neighbor Raises Reward Money*, December 15, 1955

The Battle Creek Enquirer, *Southern Michigan Prison Fertile Field For Movie Escape Thrillers,*
April 23, 1956

The Battle Creek Enquirer, *Seek Car Passenger Who Fled From Wreck*, May 25, 1956

The Battle Creek Enquirer, *Slayer of Couple Returned to State*, October 18, 1956

The Battle Creek Enquirer, *Recaptured Killer Sentenced to Life*, October 20, 1956

The Battle Creek Enquirer, *Family Fights Killer's Bid For Freedom*, December 29, 1982

The Battle Creek Enquirer, *Kelley Wants to Keep Killer in Prison,* September 28, 1984

The Bay City Times, *Fugitive Seek Killer of Two*, September 6, 1955

The Chicago Daily Tribune, *Hunt Convict in Slaying of Farm Couple,* September 7, 1955

The Muskegon Chronicle, *Victim's Daughter Has no Sympathy for Killer's Freedom Bid*, Dec. 22, 1982

The News-Palladium, Benton Harbor, *Hammer Slayer Hunted, September 6, 1955*

The News-Palladium, Benton Harbor, *Identity of Killer Fixed,* September 7, 1955

The News-Palladium, Benton Harbor, *Village Lives in*

Terror, September 22, 1955

The News-Palladium, Benton Harbor, *Fugitive Returned*, October 19, 1956

The News-Palladium, Benton Harbor, *Neighbors Will Give $3000 to Find Killer*, December 15, 1955

The News-Palladium, Benton Harbor, *Was Sheriff Nipping, Napping?*, October 10, 1959

The News-Palladium, Benton Harbor, *Trial Delay for Sheriff in Ingham*, October 21, 1959

The News-Palladium, Benton Harbor, *Sick, Says Sheriff of Ingham County*, December 29, 1959

The News-Palladium, Benton Harbor, *Arresting Policeman Seeks Ingham County Sheriff's Job*,
January 15, 1960

Record-Eagle, Traverse City, *Farm Couple Found Slain,* September 6, 1955

Record-Eagle, Traverse City, *Link Convict With Murders*, September 7, 1955

Record-Eagle, Traverse City, *Fugitive Charged With Two Murders,* September 10, 1955

Record-Eagle, Traverse City, *Sheriff Quits State Post*, October 19, 1959

Record-Eagle, Traverse City, *Delay Trial For Sheriff*, October 21, 1959

Holland Evening Sentinel, *Merchant Fed Up With Lag in Hunt For Suspect*, January 4, 1956

Ironwood Daily Globe, *Couple is Found Slain on Farm-Hunt Fugitive*, September 6, 1955

Ironwood Daily Globe, *Fear Blankets Scene of Slaying of Farm Couple*, September 22, 1955

Ironwood Daily Globe, *Escaped Convict Caught in East,* October 17, 1956

Ironwood Daily Globe, *Slayer Given Two Life Terms,* October 19, 1956

Ironwood Daily Globe, *Gathers Fund For a Reward*, December 15, 1955

Ironwood Daily Globe, *Ingham Sheriff Facing Charge*, October 10, 1959

Ironwood Daily Globe, *Barnes Back From Trip, No Plans on Resigning*, January 23, 1960

Ironwood Daily Globe, *Sheriff's Case is Dismissed,* December 22, 1960

Ludington Daily News, *Chicken Farmer-Wife Slain*, September 9, 1955

Ludington Daily News, *Police Capture Wanted Killer,* October 17, 1956

Ludington Daily News, *In Seclusion*, December 31, 1959

Toledo Blade, *Reward Up For Capture of Escapee,* October 27, 1955

Toledo Blade, *Judge Appointed,* December 30, 1973

Argus-Press, Owosso, *Kelley Asks High Court to Overturn Appellate Ruling*, September 28, 1984

Jackson Citizen Patriot, *Stockbridge Farm Couple Found Slain*, September 6, 1955

Jackson Citizen Patriot, *Escaper Seen Near Tragedy,* September 6, 1955

Jackson Citizen Patriot, *Fingerprints Spur Felon Hunt*, September 7, 1955

Jackson Citizen Patriot, *Buchanon Caught in Baltimore,* October 17, 1956

Jackson Citizen Patriot, *Store Man Plays Part in Case*, October 17, 1956

State Journal, *Babcock Carries Old Star Badge,* January 20, 1955

State Journal, *Ingham Sheriff Promotes Aides*, June 2, 1955

State Journal, Lansing, *Trusty Hunted in Killing, Elderly Couple Slain in Barn,* September 6, 1955

State Journal, Lansing, *Posse Hunt Seeks Out Prowler*, September 16, 1955

State Journal, *Posse Ends Hunt Near Stockbridge,* September 17, 1955

State Journal, *Stockbridge Has Air of Army Camp,* September 21, 1955

State Journal, *Policeman's Wife Spots Escaper,* September 21, 1955

State Journal, *FBI Joins Manhunt,* September 22, 1955

State Journal, *Prowler Reported Near Herrick Farm,* September 19, 1955

State Journal, *Reports Slayer is in Jackson*, November 30, 1955

State Journal, *Prints Link Trusty to Death Barn*, September 7, 1955

State Journal, *Stockbridge Couple Fall Before Hammer of Escaped Convict,* September 7, 1955

State Journal, *Search Widens for Suspect in Double Slaying,* September 7, 1955

State Journal, *Trusty, 31, Came Here*, September 8, 1955

State Journal, *Herrick Will Leaves Farm to Two Sons*, September 9, 1955

State Journal, *Seek Trace of Slayer,* September 9, 1955

State Journal, *No Trace of Suspect*, September 10, 1955

State Journal, *Officers Gain No Good Tips on Murderer*, September 9, 1955

State Journal, *Police Reach Dead End in Murder Hunt,* September 10, 1955

State Journal, *Caught,* October 17, 1956

State Journal, *Stockbridge Prayer Answered*, October 17, 1956

State Journal, *Nealy Buchanon Caught,* October 17, 1956

State Journal, *Early Court Action Set For Buchanon*, October 18, 1956

State Journal, *Suspect Will Return for Trial in Slaying of Stockbridge Couple*, October 17, 1956

State Journal, *Stockbridge Slayer Appeals For Trial*, July 7, 1966

State Journal, *Can Aged Files Prove Slayer Plotted Crime*, November 32, 1982

State Journal, *Early Court Action Set For Buchanon*, October 18, 1956

State Journal, *Buchanon Sentenced to Life Prison Term*, October 19, 1956

State Journal, *Stockbridge Man's Persistence Trapped Murderer,* October 28, 1956

State Journal, *Crime is Retold*, January, 1956

State Journal, *Hunt Continues*, April 26, 1956

Detroit Free Press, *Detroit Trusty Flees Prison*, September 3, 1955

Detroit Free Press, *Ignored Cries Give Slayer Head Start*, September 7, 1955

Detroit Free Press, *Prints Tie Detroiter to Farm Slayings*, September 7, 1955

Detroit Free Press, *Reader's Tip Traps Slayer,* October 17, 1956

Detroit Free Press, *Murderer of Pair Gets Life Term*, October 20, 1956

Detroit Free Press, *Tip Convict is On Train Proves Dud,* September 8, 1955

Detroit Free Press, *Reward of $500 is Offered For Crime Solution*, 1955

Detroit Free Press, *Crime Magazine Carried His Photo*, October 17, 1956

Detroit Free Press, *Murderer of Pair Gets Life Term,* October 20, 1956

Detroit Free Press, *Sentence to Get Review,* November 28, 1984

Detroit Free Press, *Kelley Appeals In Killer's Case*, September 29, 1984

Detroit Free Press, *State Appeal Moot*, December 13, 1984

Detroit News, *Convicted Killer May Win Freedom,* December 20, 1982

Detroit News, *Couple Slain; Hunt Convict,* September 6, 1955

Detroit News, *Hunt for Killer of 2 Turns to Detroit,* September 7, 1955

Ingham County News, *Slayer Took Name of Victim*, October 16, 1956

Ingham County News, *Buchanon Relates How He Killed Man and Wife,* October 18, 1956

Ingham County News, *In The Wake of Crime and Punishment,* 1956

Ingham County Democrat, *Convict Admits Double Slaying,* October 18, 1956

Lansing State Journal, *New Sheriff Learns Duties of His Trade at County Jail,* January 2, 1951

Lansing State Journal, *Trusty Hunted in Killing*, September 6, 1955

Lansing State Journal, *Prints Link Trusty to Death Barn,* September 7, 1955

Lansing State Journal, *Suspect in Murder May Be Hiding in Lansing*, September 8, 1955

Lansing State Journal, *FBI May Join Fugitive Search,* September 8, 1955

Lansing State Journal, *Seek Trace of Slayer,* September 9, 1955

Lansing State Journal, *Buchanan Trail Blank*, September 14, 1955

Lansing State Journal, *Herrick Will Leaves Farm to Two Sons*, September 15, 1955

Lansing State Journal, P*osse Hunt Seeks Out A Prowler*, September 16, 1955

Lansing State Journal, *Posse Ends Hunt Near Stockbridge*, September 17, 1955

Lansing State Journal, *Ghost of Suspect Slayer is Fading At Stockbridge*, September 26, 1955

Lansing State Journal, *Supervisors Post Reward in Stockbridge Slaying*, September 29, 1955

Lansing State Journal, *$1,400 Reward Up For Slayer*, October 27, 1955

Lansing State Journal, *Reports Suspect is in Jackson*, November 30, 1955

Lansing State Journal, *No Trace Found of Buchanan*, December 1, 1955

Lansing State Journal, *Stockbridge Man Keeps Case Alive*, July 1, 1956

Lansing State Journal, *Grounding of Airline Slows Trip*, October 18, 1956

Lansing State Journal, *Stick to Mother, Shun Rum is Nealy Buchanan Advice,* October 19, 1956

Lansing State Journal, *Nealy Back in Jackson,* October 20, 1956

Lansing State Journal, *Last Chapter*, October 25, 1956

Lansing State Journal, *Stockbridge Man Persistence Trapped Murderer*, October 28, 1956

Lansing State Journal, *Cash Paid For Reward,* November 14, 1956

Lansing State Journal, *Warrant Authorized for Sheriff*, October 9, 1959

Lansing State Journal, *Barnes Resigns as Sheriff,* January 23, 1960

Lansing State Journal, *Outgoing Sheriff to Buy Bar,*

March 22, 1960

Lansing State Journal, *Lechler Takes Over as Sheriff,* May 2, 1960

Lansing State Journal, *Ex-Sheriff Arrested*, October 5, 1960

Lansing State Journal, *Plea of Stockbridge Murderer Rejected,* January 17, 1969

Lansing State Journal, *Can Aged Files Prove Slayer Plotted Crime?*, November 23, 1982

Lansing State Journal, *Buchanon To Get Hearing*, December 3, 1982

Lansing State Journal, *Don't Free Him*, December 6, 1982

Lansing State Journal, *Only One Judge*, January 16, 1983

Lansing State Journal, *Talk of Freeing Killer Stirs Anger,* January 3, 1983

Lansing State Journal, *Supreme Court to Hear Buchanon Appeal,* November 27, 1984

Lansing State Journal, *Buchanon Decision Pondered*, January 29, 1984

Lansing State Journal, *Bludgeon Killer Gets Hearing*, May 16, 1984

Lansing State Journal, *Kelley Doesn't Want 'Murderer on Street'*, May 24, 1984

Lansing State Journal, *Over-Stretching Justice*, May 25, 1984

Lansing State Journal, *US Supreme Court Asked to Rule in Old Murder Case,* July 10, 1984

Lansing State Journal, *High Court to Get Killer's Case*, September 28, 1984

Lansing State Journal, *Supreme Court Receives Slayer Case*, September 28, 1984

Lansing State Journal, *Buchanan Dies of Cancer,* December 10, 1984

Lansing State Journal, *Buchanon Dead; Case Was Before US Supreme Court*, December 11, 1984

Lansing State Journal, *Judge Bell Not Only Makes History - He Writes It*, July 27, 1987

Detroit News, *She Has No Sympathy For Her Parent's Killer*, December 25, 1982

Detroit News, *Guard Killer of 2 In Jail At Mason*, October 19, 1956

Owosso Argus-Press, *Couple Slain; Hunt Convict,* September 6, 1955

Detroit Times, *Bludgeoned Pair Hidden in Barn*, September 6, 1955

Detroit Times, *Trail Felon in Two Murders*, September 6, 1955

Detroit Times, *Pals Doubt 'Mild' Felon Slew Couple*, September 6, 1955

Detroit Times, *Seize Suspect in 2 Slayings*, October 16, 1956

Flint Journal, *Farm Couple Slain; Escaped Convict Hunted,* September 6, 1955

Flint Journal, *Double Murder Suspect Held For Michigan*, October 17, 1956

Flint Journal, *Slayer of Farm Couple Sentenced*, October 18, 1956

Grand Rapids Press, *Farm Couple Found Slain*, September 6, 1955

Kalamazoo Gazette, *Police Seek Slayer of Farm Couple*, September 6, 1955

Kalamazoo Gazette, *Suspect in Killings Still At Large,* September 7, 1955

Kalamazoo Gazette, *Nab Suspect in Slaying of State Couple*, October 17, 1956

Escanaba Daily Press, *Farm Couple Found Murdered in Barn; Big Convict Hunted,* September 6, 1955

Escanaba Daily Press, *Crime Magazine Fan Helps Trap Michigan Killer,* October 17, 1956

Escanaba Daily Press, *Escapee Admits Slaying Couple,* October 19, 1956

Escanaba Daily Press, *Tip on Slayer Worth $2,000,* October 26, 1956

Escanaba Daily Press, *Sheriff Finds No Humor In Charge,* Oct 15, 1959

Escanaba Daily Press, *Lansing Sheriff Goes Into Hiding,* December 21, 1959

Escanaba Daily Press, *Police Officer Who Arrested Sheriff Now Seeks His Job,* January 15, 1960

New Castle News, *Escapee From Prison Suspect in Dual Murder,* September 6, 1955

The Lima News, *Prison Fugitive Major Suspect in Dual Slaying,* September 6, 1955

Logansport Pharos Tribune, *Chicken Farmer, Wife Slain,* September 9, 1955

Spokane Daily Chronicle, *Stark Fear Haunts Village Located Near Big Prison,* Sept. 22, 1955

The Spectator, *Court Orders Buchanon's Release, 1981*

The Sandusky Register Star-News, *Escapee Sought in Double Murder,* Sept. 6, 1955

Oshkosh Daily Northwestern, *Sought,* Sept. 8, 1955

Alexandria Times-Tribune, *Chicken Farmer, Wife Slain,* September 12, 1955

The Daily Reporter, Greenfield, IN, *Chicken Farmer, Wife Slain,* September 10, 1955

East Liverpool Review, *For Escape, Murder,* September 8, 1955

The Daily Telegram, Eau Claire WI, *Tiny Town in Michigan Looks Like Armed Camp,* September 22, 1955

Janesville Daily Gazette, Janesville, WI, Michigan Village Arms Itself After Murder of Pair, Sept 22, 1955

Miami Daily Record, Miami, OK, *Michigan Town Living in Fear*, September 22, 1955

The Bee, Danville, VA, *Town on Edge After Killing of Farm Couple*, September 22, 1955

The Daily Chronicle, Centralia, WA, *Town Fearful After Killings*, September 22, 1955

Santa Cruz Sentinel, Santa Cruz, CA, *Fear Blankets Michigan Town After Farm Couple Are Slain*, September 22, 1955

The Kane Republican, Kane, PA, *Chicken Farmer, Wife Slain*, September 9, 1955

The News-Review, Roseburg, OR, *One-Time Friendly Town Afraid After Prisoner Escaped*, September 29, 1955

Macon Chronicle-Hearld, Macon, MO, Chicken Farmer, Wife Slain, September 12, 1955

The Lethbridge Hearld, Lethbridge, Alberta, Canada, Lock and Gun Replace Open Door After Slayings, September 23, 1955

The Progress-Index, Petersburg, VA, Lock and Gun Replace Open Door in Mich. Town After Slayings, September 22, 1955

Abilene Reporter-News, Abilene, TX, *Fear Grips Murder Town*, September 22, 1955

The News Tribune, Fort Pierce, FL, *Lock and Gun Replace Open Door, Friendly Handshake,* September 22, 1955

The Daily Telegram, Adrian, MI, *Ingham Sheriff to Enter Bar Business*, March 23, 1960

The Times Herald, Port Huron, MI, *Seek Escaped Felon in Couple's Murder,* September 6 ,1955

The Times Herald, Port Huron, MI, *Slayer of Farm Couple Gets Double Life Terms*, October 21, 1956

The Times Herald, Port Huron, MI, *Sharp-Eyed Crime*

Mag Reader to get $2,000, October 25, 1956

The Times Herald, Port Huron, MI, *Killer Gets Little Sympathy*, December 17, 1982

The Times Herald, Port Huron, MI, *Kelley Fights Ruling*, September 28, 1984

The Times Herald, Port Huron, MI, *Court to Consider Sentence*, November 17, 1984

The Cincinnati Enquirer, *Court Backs Convict*, May 14, 1984

The Baltimore Sun, *Man Wanted in 2 Murders Seized Here*, October 17, 1956

A SLAYER WAITS

Endnotes

[1] *Report of Survey Made for Michigan Boys Vocational School, Governor's Survey Commission,* 1942

[2] A. Eaton, J. Knox, F. Sudia, M. Carduner, R. Doppelt, J. George, E. Leopold, C. Bright, *A History of Jackson Prison, 1920-1075,,* 1979, University of Michigan, Residential College

[3] A. Eaton, J. Knox, F. Sudia, M. Carduner, R. Doppelt, J. George, E. Leopold, C. Bright, *A History of Jackson Prison, 1920-1075,,* 1979, University of Michigan, Residential College

[4] Historical Sketch of the Indeterminate Sentence and Parole System, Lindsey, Edward, 1925, Journal of Criminal Law and Criminology, Vol 16, Issue 1

[5] Historical Sketch of the Indeterminate Sentence and Parole System, Lindsey, Edward, 1925, Journal of

[6] Stockbridge Has Air of Army Camp, State Journal, September 21, 1955

[7] Ignored Cries Give Slayer Head Start, Detroit Free Press, September 7, 1955

[8] Stockbridge Has Air of Army Camp, State Journal, September 21, 1955

[9] Trail Felon in Two Murders, Detroit Times, September 6, 1955

[10] Pals Doubt 'Mild' Felon Slew Couple, Detroit Times, September 6, 1955

[11] Search Widens as FBI Joins Convict Hunt, State Journal, September 22, 1955

[12] Stockbridge Has Air of Army Camp, State Journal, September 21, 1955

[13] Stockbridge Has Air of Army Camp, State Journal, September 21, 1955

[14] Stockbridge Has Air of Army Camp, State Journal, September 21, 1955

[15] Stockbridge Has Air of Army Camp, State Journal, September 21, 1955

[16] Stockbridge Has Air of Army Camp, State Journal, September 21, 1955

[17] Stockbridge Has Air of Army Camp, State Journal, September 21, 1955

[18] Stockbridge Has Air of Army Camp, State Journal, September 21, 1955

[19] Stockbridge Has Air of Army Camp, State Journal, September 21, 1955

[20] No Trace of Suspect, State Journal, September 10, 1955

[21] Stockbridge Has Air of Army Camp, State Journal, September 21, 1955

[22] Merchant Fed Up With Lag in Hunt For Suspect, Hol-

land Evening Sentinel, January 4, 1956

[23] Reward of $500 is Offered For Crime Solution, Detroit Free Press, September, 1955

[24] Supervisors Post Reward in Stockbridge Slaying, State Journal, September, 1955

[25] Is Your Name Listed In This Ad, Lansing State Journal, January, 1956

[26] Crime is Retold, State Journal, February, 1956

[27] Merchant Fed Up With Lag in Hunt For Suspect, Holland Evening Sentinel, January 4, 1956

[28] Buchanon Caught in Baltimore, Jackson Citizen Patriot, October 17, 1956

[29] Stockbridge Prayer Answered; Capture Ends Long Campaign, Lansing State Journal, October 17, 1956

[30] Nealy Buchanon Caught, The State Journal, October 17, 1956

[31] Nealy Buchanon Caught, The State Journal, October 17, 1956

[32] Nealy Buchanon Caught, The State Journal, October 17, 1956

[33] Store Man Plays Part in Case, Jackson Citizen Patriot, October 17, 1956

[34] Stockbridge Prayer Answered; Capture Ends Long Campaign, The State Journal, October 17, 1956

[35] Stockbridge Prayer Answered; Capture Ends Long Campaign, The State Journal, October 17, 1956

[36] Caught, Special to the State Journal, October 17, 1956

[37] Early Court Action Set For Buchanon, The State Journal, October 18, 1956

[38] Round Trip to Baltimore, Ingham County Democrat, October 18, 1956

[39] In The Wake of Crime and Punishment, Ingham County Democrat, October, 1956

[40] Transcript of confession made by Nealy Buchanon, October 18, 1956

[41] Transcript of the district court arraignment for Nealy Buchanon, October 18, 1956

[42] Transcript of circuit court arraignment for Newly Buchanon, October 19, 1956

[43] Transcript testimony of Captain Versile Babcock in Degree of Guilt Hearing, October 19, 1956

[44] Transcript testimony of Dr. Charles Black in Degree of Guilt Hearing, October 19, 1956

[45] Transcript testimony of Sheriff Willard P. Barnes in Degree of Guilt Hearing, October 19, 1956

[46] Transcript of sentencing for Nealy Buchanon, October 19, 1956

[47] Chardavoyne, David G. *A Hanging in Detroit*. Detroit; Wayne State University Press, 2003 (Jour. A, July 26, 1830, *NWJ*, September 22, 1830)

[48] Chardavoyne, David G. *A Hanging in Detroit*. Detroit; Wayne State University Press, 2003

[49] Chardavoyne, David G. *A Hanging in Detroit*. Detroit; Wayne State University Press, 2003

[50] People v. Winegar, 380 Mich 719 (1968)

[51] The American Presidency Project, Richard Nixon, 162-States About the Watergate Investigations, May 22, 1973, www.presidency.ucsb.edu

[52] Affidavit of Nealy J. Buchanon, January 12, 1977 *This affidavit appears exactly as it was written by the defendant.

[53] Order Denying Application For Leave To Appeal, 12396-12397, April 1, 1977

[54] People v. Olson, 396 Mich 30 (1976)

[55] Answer To Application For Leave To Appeal, People v. Nealy J. Buchanon, 12396-12397,

[56] People v. Bergin, 62 Mich App 526, 529;234 NW2d 463 (1976)
[57] Motion to Dismiss, Or, In the Alternative, Motion for Summary Judgment, United States District Court, Eastern District of Michigan, southern Division, Nealy J. Buchanon v. Charles E. Anderson, August 29, 1980
[58] Bute v. Illinois, 333 US at 671
[59] Rice v. Olson, 324 US 786
[60] Von Moltke v. Gillies, 332 U.S., 708, (1948)
[61] Gideon v. Wainwright, 372 U.S. 335 (1963)
[62] Till-Mobley, Mamie. *Death of Innocence.* The Random House Publishing Group, 2003
[63] Miranda V. Arizona, 384 U.S. 436
[64] *Barnes Resigns as Sheriff*, Lansing State Journal, January 23, 1960
[65] Petitioners Brief After Evidentiary Hearing, United States District Court For the Eastern District of Michigan, Southern Division, 79-73820, September 11, 1981
[66] Supplemental Brief In Support of Motion to Dismiss, or in the Alternative, Motion for Summary Judgment, United States District Court, Eastern District of Michigan, Southern Division, 79-73820, September 28, 1981
[67] Magistrate's Report and Recommendation, United States District Court, Eastern District of Michigan, Southern Division, 79-73820, October 13, 1981
[68] Moore v. Michigan, 355 US 155 (1957)
[69] Commonwealth ex rel. Wing v. Cloudy, 370 Pa. 366 (1952)
[70] Motion For Enlargement of Petitioner on Bond Pending Decision in The District Court, United States

District Court, Eastern District of Michigan, Southern Division, 79-73820, April 1, 1982

[71] Johnston v. Marsh, 227 F2d 528 (5th Cir. 1955)

[72] Memorandum Opinion, United States District Court, Eastern District of Michigan, Southern Division, October 21, 1982

[73] Conner v. Anderson, No. 80-1262 (6th Cir. Nov. 30, 1981)

[74] Memorandum and Order, United States District Court, Eastern District of Michigan, Southern Division, December 7, 1982

[75] Order of Adjournment, Ingham County Circuit Court, 56-12396-FY & 56-12397-FY, March 3, 1983

[76] *Buchanon to Get Hearing,* The State Journal, December 3, 1982

[77] *Don't Free Him,* The State Journal, December 6, 1982

[78] Handwritten letter to Frank Eaman, January 23, 1983

[79] Talk of Freeing Killer Stirs Anger, The Lansing State Journal, January 3, 1983

[80] Talk of Freeing Killer Stirs Anger, The Lansing State Journal, January 3, 1983

[81] Talk of Freeing Killer Stirs Anger, The Lansing State Journal, January 3, 1983

[82] Only One Judge, The Lansing State Journal, January 16, 1983

[83] Brief in Support of Motion of In Forma Pauperis Petitioner For Copy of Transcript of district Court Proceedings, United States District Court, Eastern District of Michigan, Southern Division, January 19, 1983

[84] Motion For Enlargement of Petitioner on Bond Pending Decision on Appeal, United States Court of Ap-

A SLAYER WAITS

peals For The Sixth District, 83-1252, July 5, 1983

[85] McMann v. Richardson, 297 US 759, 773, 90 S Ct 1441, 25 L Ed 2d 763 (1970)

[86] Nealy J. Buchanon v. Barry Mintzes, 83-2352, 83-2353, United States Court of Appeals for the Sixth District, May 9 1984

[87] Kelly Doesn't Want 'Murderer on Street', Lansing State Journal, May 24, 1984

[88] Petition For Rehearing And Suggestion For Rehearing En Banc, Habeas Corpus Appeal from the District Court of the United States for the Eastern District of Michigan, Southern Division, 83-1252, 83-2353,

[89] Motion For Stay o Mandate Pending Application for Certiorari, 83-1252/83-1253, United States Court of Appeals for the Sixth District, July 9, 1984

[90] Brief in Opposition to Petition for Write of Certiorari, United States Court of Appeals for the Sixth District, Supreme Court of the United States, 84-501, October 24, 1984

[91] Johnson, Perry M. *Jackson: The Rise and Fall of the World's Largest Walled Prison*. Perry M. Johnson, 2014

[92] Suggestion of Mootness, Supreme Court of the United States, 84-501, December 11, 1984

[93] McMann v. Ross, 396 U.S. 118, 90 S.Ct. 395, 24 L.Ed.2d 303 (1969)

CPSIA information can be obtained
at www.ICGtesting.com
Printed in the USA
LVHW021125110322
713034LV00004B/281

9 781478 790365